FREE Study Skills DVD Of

Dear Customer,

Thank you for your purchase from Mometrix! We consider it an honor and a privilege that you have purchased our product and we want to ensure your satisfaction.

As a way of showing our appreciation and to help us better serve you, we have developed a Study Skills DVD that we would like to give you for <u>FREE</u>. This DVD covers our *best practices* for getting ready for your exam, from how to use our study materials to how to best prepare for the day of the test.

All that we ask is that you email us with feedback that would describe your experience so far with our product. Good, bad, or indifferent, we want to know what you think!

To get your FREE Study Skills DVD, email <u>freedvd@mometrix.com</u> with *FREE STUDY SKILLS DVD* in the subject line and the following information in the body of the email:

- The name of the product you purchased.
- Your product rating on a scale of 1-5, with 5 being the highest rating.
- Your feedback. It can be long, short, or anything in between. We just want to know your impressions and experience so far with our product. (Good feedback might include how our study material met your needs and ways we might be able to make it even better. You could highlight features that you found helpful or features that you think we should add.)
- Your full name and shipping address where you would like us to send your free DVD.

If you have any questions or concerns, please don't hesitate to contact me directly.

Thanks again!

Sincerely,

Jay Willis
Vice President
<u>jay.willis@mometrix.com</u>
1-800-673-8175

GMAT Test Prep

GMAT®

SECRETS

Study Guide
Your Key to Exam Success

Complete Review, Practice Tests, Video Tutorials for the
Graduate Management Admission Test®

Published by
Mometrix Test Preparation
Mometrix Business School Admissions Test Team

Written and edited by the Mometrix Business School Admissions Test Team

Printed in the United States of America

This paper meets the requirements of ANSI/NISO Z39.48-1992 (Permanence of Paper).

Mometrix offers volume discount pricing to institutions. For more information or a price quote, please contact our sales department at sales@mometrix.com or 888-248-1219.

Mometrix Media LLC is not affiliated with or endorsed by any official testing organization. All organizational and test names are trademarks of their respective owners.

Paperback
ISBN 13: 978-1-5167-0228-2
ISBN 10: 1-5167-0228-X

Ebook
ISBN 13: 978-1-5167-0764-5
ISBN 10: 1-5167-0764-8

Hardback
ISBN 13: 978-1-5167-0528-3
ISBN 10: 1-5167-0528-9

Dear Future Exam Success Story:

First of all, **THANK YOU** for purchasing Mometrix study materials!

Second, congratulations! You are one of the few determined test-takers who are committed to doing whatever it takes to excel on your exam. **You have come to the right place.** We developed these study materials with one goal in mind: to deliver you the information you need in a format that's concise and easy to use.

In addition to optimizing your guide for the content of the test, we've outlined our recommended steps for breaking down the preparation process into small, attainable goals so you can make sure you stay on track.

We've also analyzed the entire test-taking process, identifying the most common pitfalls and showing how you can overcome them and be ready for any curveball the test throws you.

Standardized testing is one of the biggest obstacles on your road to success, which only increases the importance of doing well in the high-pressure, high-stakes environment of test day. Your results on this test could have a significant impact on your future, and this guide provides the information and practical advice to help you achieve your full potential on test day.

Your success is our success

We would love to hear from you! If you would like to share the story of your exam success or if you have any questions or comments in regard to our products, please contact us at **800-673-8175** or **support@mometrix.com**.

Thanks again for your business and we wish you continued success!

Sincerely,
The Mometrix Test Preparation Team

Need more help? Check out our flashcards at: http://MometrixFlashcards.com/GMAT

TABLE OF CONTENTS

Introduction

Thank you for purchasing this resource! You have made the choice to prepare yourself for a test that could have a huge impact on your future, and this guide is designed to help you be fully ready for test day. Obviously, it's important to have a solid understanding of the test material, but you also need to be prepared for the unique environment and stressors of the test, so that you can perform to the best of your abilities.

For this purpose, the first section that appears in this guide is the **Secret Keys**. We've devoted countless hours to meticulously researching what works and what doesn't, and we've boiled down our findings to the five most impactful steps you can take to improve your performance on the test. We start at the beginning with study planning and move through the preparation process, all the way to the testing strategies that will help you get the most out of what you know when you're finally sitting in front of the test.

We recommend that you start preparing for your test as far in advance as possible. However, if you've bought this guide as a last-minute study resource and only have a few days before your test, we recommend that you skip over the first two Secret Keys since they address a long-term study plan.

If you struggle with **test anxiety**, we strongly encourage you to check out our recommendations for how you can overcome it. Test anxiety is a formidable foe, but it can be beaten, and we want to make sure you have the tools you need to defeat it.

Secret Key #1 – Plan Big, Study Small

There's a lot riding on your performance. If you want to ace this test, you're going to need to keep your skills sharp and the material fresh in your mind. You need a plan that lets you review everything you need to know while still fitting in your schedule. We'll break this strategy down into three categories.

Information Organization

Start with the information you already have: the official test outline. From this, you can make a complete list of all the concepts you need to cover before the test. Organize these concepts into groups that can be studied together, and create a list of any related vocabulary you need to learn so you can brush up on any difficult terms. You'll want to keep this vocabulary list handy once you actually start studying since you may need to add to it along the way.

Time Management

Once you have your set of study concepts, decide how to spread them out over the time you have left before the test. Break your study plan into small, clear goals so you have a manageable task for each day and know exactly what you're doing. Then just focus on one small step at a time. When you manage your time this way, you don't need to spend hours at a time studying. Studying a small block of content for a short period each day helps you retain information better and avoid stressing over how much you have left to do. You can relax knowing that you have a plan to cover everything in time. In order for this strategy to be effective though, you have to start studying early and stick to your schedule. Avoid the exhaustion and futility that comes from last-minute cramming!

Study Environment

The environment you study in has a big impact on your learning. Studying in a coffee shop, while probably more enjoyable, is not likely to be as fruitful as studying in a quiet room. It's important to keep distractions to a minimum. You're only planning to study for a short block of time, so make the most of it. Don't pause to check your phone or get up to find a snack. It's also important to **avoid multitasking**. Research has consistently shown that multitasking will make your studying dramatically less effective. Your study area should also be comfortable and well-lit so you don't have the distraction of straining your eyes or sitting on an uncomfortable chair.

The time of day you study is also important. You want to be rested and alert. Don't wait until just before bedtime. Study when you'll be most likely to comprehend and remember. Even better, if you know what time of day your test will be, set that time aside for study. That way your brain will be used to working on that subject at that specific time and you'll have a better chance of recalling information.

Finally, it can be helpful to team up with others who are studying for the same test. Your actual studying should be done in as isolated an environment as possible, but the work of organizing the information and setting up the study plan can be divided up. In between study sessions, you can discuss with your teammates the concepts that you're all studying and quiz each other on the details. Just be sure that your teammates are as serious about the test as you are. If you find that your study time is being replaced with social time, you might need to find a new team.

Secret Key #2 – Make Your Studying Count

You're devoting a lot of time and effort to preparing for this test, so you want to be absolutely certain it will pay off. This means doing more than just reading the content and hoping you can remember it on test day. It's important to make every minute of study count. There are two main areas you can focus on to make your studying count:

Retention

It doesn't matter how much time you study if you can't remember the material. You need to make sure you are retaining the concepts. To check your retention of the information you're learning, try recalling it at later times with minimal prompting. Try carrying around flashcards and glance at one or two from time to time or ask a friend who's also studying for the test to quiz you.

To enhance your retention, look for ways to put the information into practice so that you can apply it rather than simply recalling it. If you're using the information in practical ways, it will be much easier to remember. Similarly, it helps to solidify a concept in your mind if you're not only reading it to yourself but also explaining it to someone else. Ask a friend to let you teach them about a concept you're a little shaky on (or speak aloud to an imaginary audience if necessary). As you try to summarize, define, give examples, and answer your friend's questions, you'll understand the concepts better and they will stay with you longer. Finally, step back for a big picture view and ask yourself how each piece of information fits with the whole subject. When you link the different concepts together and see them working together as a whole, it's easier to remember the individual components.

Finally, practice showing your work on any multi-step problems, even if you're just studying. Writing out each step you take to solve a problem will help solidify the process in your mind, and you'll be more likely to remember it during the test.

Modality

Modality simply refers to the means or method by which you study. Choosing a study modality that fits your own individual learning style is crucial. No two people learn best in exactly the same way, so it's important to know your strengths and use them to your advantage.

For example, if you learn best by visualization, focus on visualizing a concept in your mind and draw an image or a diagram. Try color-coding your notes, illustrating them, or creating symbols that will trigger your mind to recall a learned concept. If you learn best by hearing or discussing information, find a study partner who learns the same way or read aloud to yourself. Think about how to put the information in your own words. Imagine that you are giving a lecture on the topic and record yourself so you can listen to it later.

For any learning style, flashcards can be helpful. Organize the information so you can take advantage of spare moments to review. Underline key words or phrases. Use different colors for different categories. Mnemonic devices (such as creating a short list in which every item starts with the same letter) can also help with retention. Find what works best for you and use it to store the information in your mind most effectively and easily.

Secret Key #3 – Practice the Right Way

Your success on test day depends not only on how many hours you put into preparing, but also on whether you prepared the right way. It's good to check along the way to see if your studying is paying off. One of the most effective ways to do this is by taking practice tests to evaluate your progress. Practice tests are useful because they show exactly where you need to improve. Every time you take a practice test, pay special attention to these three groups of questions:

- The questions you got wrong
- The questions you had to guess on, even if you guessed right
- The questions you found difficult or slow to work through

This will show you exactly what your weak areas are, and where you need to devote more study time. Ask yourself why each of these questions gave you trouble. Was it because you didn't understand the material? Was it because you didn't remember the vocabulary? Do you need more repetitions on this type of question to build speed and confidence? Dig into those questions and figure out how you can strengthen your weak areas as you go back to review the material.

Additionally, many practice tests have a section explaining the answer choices. It can be tempting to read the explanation and think that you now have a good understanding of the concept. However, an explanation likely only covers part of the question's broader context. Even if the explanation makes sense, **go back and investigate** every concept related to the question until you're positive you have a thorough understanding.

As you go along, keep in mind that the practice test is just that: practice. Memorizing these questions and answers will not be very helpful on the actual test because it is unlikely to have any of the same exact questions. If you only know the right answers to the sample questions, you won't be prepared for the real thing. **Study the concepts** until you understand them fully, and then you'll be able to answer any question that shows up on the test.

It's important to wait on the practice tests until you're ready. If you take a test on your first day of study, you may be overwhelmed by the amount of material covered and how much you need to learn. Work up to it gradually.

On test day, you'll need to be prepared for answering questions, managing your time, and using the test-taking strategies you've learned. It's a lot to balance, like a mental marathon that will have a big impact on your future. Like training for a marathon, you'll need to start slowly and work your way up. When test day arrives, you'll be ready.

Start with the strategies you've read in the first two Secret Keys—plan your course and study in the way that works best for you. If you have time, consider using multiple study resources to get different approaches to the same concepts. It can be helpful to see difficult concepts from more than one angle. Then find a good source for practice tests. Many times, the test website will suggest potential study resources or provide sample tests.

Practice Test Strategy

When you're ready to start taking practice tests, follow this strategy:

Untimed and Open-Book Practice

Take the first test with no time constraints and with your notes and study guide handy. Take your time and focus on applying the strategies you've learned.

Timed and Open-Book Practice

Take the second practice test open-book as well, but set a timer and practice pacing yourself to finish in time.

Timed and Closed-Book Practice

Take any other practice tests as if it were test day. Set a timer and put away your study materials. Sit at a table or desk in a quiet room, imagine yourself at the testing center, and answer questions as quickly and accurately as possible.

Keep repeating timed and closed-book tests on a regular basis until you run out of practice tests or it's time for the actual test. Your mind will be ready for the schedule and stress of test day, and you'll be able to focus on recalling the material you've learned.

Secret Key #4 – Pace Yourself

Once you're fully prepared for the material on the test, your biggest challenge on test day will be managing your time. Just knowing that the clock is ticking can make you panic even if you have plenty of time left. Work on pacing yourself so you can build confidence against the time constraints of the exam. Pacing is a difficult skill to master, especially in a high-pressure environment, so **practice is vital**.

Set time expectations for your pace based on how much time is available. For example, if a section has 60 questions and the time limit is 30 minutes, you know you have to average 30 seconds or less per question in order to answer them all. Although 30 seconds is the hard limit, set 25 seconds per question as your goal, so you reserve extra time to spend on harder questions. When you budget extra time for the harder questions, you no longer have any reason to stress when those questions take longer to answer.

Don't let this time expectation distract you from working through the test at a calm, steady pace, but keep it in mind so you don't spend too much time on any one question. Recognize that taking extra time on one question you don't understand may keep you from answering two that you do understand later in the test. If your time limit for a question is up and you're still not sure of the answer, mark it and move on, and come back to it later if the time and the test format allow. If the testing format doesn't allow you to return to earlier questions, just make an educated guess; then put it out of your mind and move on.

On the easier questions, be careful not to rush. It may seem wise to hurry through them so you have more time for the challenging ones, but it's not worth missing one if you know the concept and just didn't take the time to read the question fully. Work efficiently but make sure you understand the question and have looked at all of the answer choices, since more than one may seem right at first.

Even if you're paying attention to the time, you may find yourself a little behind at some point. You should speed up to get back on track, but do so wisely. Don't panic; just take a few seconds less on each question until you're caught up. Don't guess without thinking, but do look through the answer choices and eliminate any you know are wrong. If you can get down to two choices, it is often worthwhile to guess from those. Once you've chosen an answer, move on and don't dwell on any that you skipped or had to hurry through. If a question was taking too long, chances are it was one of the harder ones, so you weren't as likely to get it right anyway.

On the other hand, if you find yourself getting ahead of schedule, it may be beneficial to slow down a little. The more quickly you work, the more likely you are to make a careless mistake that will affect your score. You've budgeted time for each question, so don't be afraid to spend that time. Practice an efficient but careful pace to get the most out of the time you have.

Secret Key #5 – Have a Plan for Guessing

When you're taking the test, you may find yourself stuck on a question. Some of the answer choices seem better than others, but you don't see the one answer choice that is obviously correct. What do you do?

The scenario described above is very common, yet most test takers have not effectively prepared for it. Developing and practicing a plan for guessing may be one of the single most effective uses of your time as you get ready for the exam.

In developing your plan for guessing, there are three questions to address:

- When should you start the guessing process?
- How should you narrow down the choices?
- Which answer should you choose?

When to Start the Guessing Process

Unless your plan for guessing is to select C every time (which, despite its merits, is not what we recommend), you need to leave yourself enough time to apply your answer elimination strategies. Since you have a limited amount of time for each question, that means that if you're going to give yourself the best shot at guessing correctly, you have to decide quickly whether or not you will guess.

Of course, the best-case scenario is that you don't have to guess at all, so first, see if you can answer the question based on your knowledge of the subject and basic reasoning skills. Focus on the key words in the question and try to jog your memory of related topics. Give yourself a chance to bring the knowledge to mind, but once you realize that you don't have (or you can't access) the knowledge you need to answer the question, it's time to start the guessing process.

It's almost always better to start the guessing process too early than too late. It only takes a few seconds to remember something and answer the question from knowledge. Carefully eliminating wrong answer choices takes longer. Plus, going through the process of eliminating answer choices can actually help jog your memory.

Summary: Start the guessing process as soon as you decide that you can't answer the question based on your knowledge.

How to Narrow Down the Choices

The next chapter in this book (**Test-Taking Strategies**) includes a wide range of strategies for how to approach questions and how to look for answer choices to eliminate. You will definitely want to read those carefully, practice them, and figure out which ones work best for you. Here though, we're going to address a mindset rather than a particular strategy.

Your chances of guessing an answer correctly depend on how many options you are choosing from.

How many choices you have	How likely you are to guess correctly
5	20%
4	25%
3	33%
2	50%
1	100%

You can see from this chart just how valuable it is to be able to eliminate incorrect answers and make an educated guess, but there are two things that many test takers do that cause them to miss out on the benefits of guessing:

- Accidentally eliminating the correct answer
- Selecting an answer based on an impression

We'll look at the first one here, and the second one in the next section.

To avoid accidentally eliminating the correct answer, we recommend a thought exercise called **the $5 challenge**. In this challenge, you only eliminate an answer choice from contention if you are willing to bet $5 on it being wrong. Why $5? Five dollars is a small but not insignificant amount of money. It's an amount you could afford to lose but wouldn't want to throw away. And while losing $5 once might not hurt too much, doing it twenty times will set you back $100. In the same way, each small decision you make—eliminating a choice here, guessing on a question there—won't by itself impact your score very much, but when you put them all together, they can make a big difference. By holding each answer choice elimination decision to a higher standard, you can reduce the risk of accidentally eliminating the correct answer.

The $5 challenge can also be applied in a positive sense: If you are willing to bet $5 that an answer choice *is* correct, go ahead and mark it as correct.

Summary: Only eliminate an answer choice if you are willing to bet $5 that it is wrong.

Which Answer to Choose

You're taking the test. You've run into a hard question and decided you'll have to guess. You've eliminated all the answer choices you're willing to bet $5 on. Now you have to pick an answer. Why do we even need to talk about this? Why can't you just pick whichever one you feel like when the time comes?

The answer to these questions is that if you don't come into the test with a plan, you'll rely on your impression to select an answer choice, and if you do that, you risk falling into a trap. The test writers know that everyone who takes their test will be guessing on some of the questions, so they intentionally write wrong answer choices to seem plausible. You still have to pick an answer though, and if the wrong answer choices are designed to look right, how can you ever be sure that you're not falling for their trap? The best solution we've found to this dilemma is to take the decision out of your hands entirely. Here is the process we recommend:

Once you've eliminated any choices that you are confident (willing to bet $5) are wrong, select the first remaining choice as your answer.

Whether you choose to select the first remaining choice, the second, or the last, the important thing is that you use some preselected standard. Using this approach guarantees that you will not be enticed into selecting an answer choice that looks right, because you are not basing your decision on how the answer choices look.

This is not meant to make you question your knowledge. Instead, it is to help you recognize the difference between your knowledge and your impressions. There's a huge difference between thinking an answer is right because of what you know, and thinking an answer is right because it looks or sounds like it should be right.

Summary: To ensure that your selection is appropriately random, make a predetermined selection from among all answer choices you have not eliminated.

Test-Taking Strategies

This section contains a list of test-taking strategies that you may find helpful as you work through the test. By taking what you know and applying logical thought, you can maximize your chances of answering any question correctly!

It is very important to realize that every question is different and every person is different: no single strategy will work on every question, and no single strategy will work for every person. That's why we've included all of them here, so you can try them out and determine which ones work best for different types of questions and which ones work best for you.

Question Strategies

Read Carefully

Read the question and answer choices carefully. Don't miss the question because you misread the terms. You have plenty of time to read each question thoroughly and make sure you understand what is being asked. Yet a happy medium must be attained, so don't waste too much time. You must read carefully, but efficiently.

Contextual Clues

Look for contextual clues. If the question includes a word you are not familiar with, look at the immediate context for some indication of what the word might mean. Contextual clues can often give you all the information you need to decipher the meaning of an unfamiliar word. Even if you can't determine the meaning, you may be able to narrow down the possibilities enough to make a solid guess at the answer to the question.

Prefixes

If you're having trouble with a word in the question or answer choices, try dissecting it. Take advantage of every clue that the word might include. Prefixes and suffixes can be a huge help. Usually they allow you to determine a basic meaning. Pre- means before, post- means after, pro - is positive, de- is negative. From prefixes and suffixes, you can get an idea of the general meaning of the word and try to put it into context.

Hedge Words

Watch out for critical hedge words, such as *likely, may, can, sometimes, often, almost, mostly, usually, generally, rarely,* and *sometimes.* Question writers insert these hedge phrases to cover every possibility. Often an answer choice will be wrong simply because it leaves no room for exception. Be on guard for answer choices that have definitive words such as *exactly* and *always.*

Switchback Words

Stay alert for *switchbacks.* These are the words and phrases frequently used to alert you to shifts in thought. The most common switchback words are *but, although,* and *however.* Others include *nevertheless, on the other hand, even though, while, in spite of, despite, regardless of.* Switchback words are important to catch because they can change the direction of the question or an answer choice.

Face Value

When in doubt, use common sense. Accept the situation in the problem at face value. Don't read too much into it. These problems will not require you to make wild assumptions. If you have to go beyond creativity and warp time or space in order to have an answer choice fit the question, then you should move on and consider the other answer choices. These are normal problems rooted in reality. The applicable relationship or explanation may not be readily apparent, but it is there for you to figure out. Use your common sense to interpret anything that isn't clear.

Answer Choice Strategies

Answer Selection

The most thorough way to pick an answer choice is to identify and eliminate wrong answers until only one is left, then confirm it is the correct answer. Sometimes an answer choice may immediately seem right, but be careful. The test writers will usually put more than one reasonable answer choice on each question, so take a second to read all of them and make sure that the other choices are not equally obvious. As long as you have time left, it is better to read every answer choice than to pick the first one that looks right without checking the others.

Answer Choice Families

An answer choice family consists of two (in rare cases, three) answer choices that are very similar in construction and cannot all be true at the same time. If you see two answer choices that are direct opposites or parallels, one of them is usually the correct answer. For instance, if one answer choice says that quantity x increases and another either says that quantity x decreases (opposite) or says that quantity y increases (parallel), then those answer choices would fall into the same family. An answer choice that doesn't match the construction of the answer choice family is more likely to be incorrect. Most questions will not have answer choice families, but when they do appear, you should be prepared to recognize them.

Eliminate Answers

Eliminate answer choices as soon as you realize they are wrong, but make sure you consider all possibilities. If you are eliminating answer choices and realize that the last one you are left with is also wrong, don't panic. Start over and consider each choice again. There may be something you missed the first time that you will realize on the second pass.

Avoid Fact Traps

Don't be distracted by an answer choice that is factually true but doesn't answer the question. You are looking for the choice that answers the question. Stay focused on what the question is asking for so you don't accidentally pick an answer that is true but incorrect. Always go back to the question and make sure the answer choice you've selected actually answers the question and is not merely a true statement.

Extreme Statements

In general, you should avoid answers that put forth extreme actions as standard practice or proclaim controversial ideas as established fact. An answer choice that states the "process should be used in certain situations, if…" is much more likely to be correct than one that states the "process should be discontinued completely." The first is a calm rational statement and doesn't even make a definitive, uncompromising stance, using a hedge word *if* to provide wiggle room, whereas the second choice is a radical idea and far more extreme.

Benchmark

As you read through the answer choices and you come across one that seems to answer the question well, mentally select that answer choice. This is not your final answer, but it's the one that will help you evaluate the other answer choices. The one that you selected is your benchmark or standard for judging each of the other answer choices. Every other answer choice must be compared to your benchmark. That choice is correct until proven otherwise by another answer choice beating it. If you find a better answer, then that one becomes your new benchmark. Once you've decided that no other choice answers the question as well as your benchmark, you have your final answer.

Predict the Answer

Before you even start looking at the answer choices, it is often best to try to predict the answer. When you come up with the answer on your own, it is easier to avoid distractions and traps because you will know exactly what to look for. The right answer choice is unlikely to be word-for-word what you came up with, but it should be a close match. Even if you are confident that you have the right answer, you should still take the time to read each option before moving on.

General Strategies

Tough Questions

If you are stumped on a problem or it appears too hard or too difficult, don't waste time. Move on! Remember though, if you can quickly check for obviously incorrect answer choices, your chances of guessing correctly are greatly improved. Before you completely give up, at least try to knock out a couple of possible answers. Eliminate what you can and then guess at the remaining answer choices before moving on.

Check Your Work

Since you will probably not know every term listed and the answer to every question, it is important that you get credit for the ones that you do know. Don't miss any questions through careless mistakes. If at all possible, try to take a second to look back over your answer selection and make sure you've selected the correct answer choice and haven't made a costly careless mistake (such as marking an answer choice that you didn't mean to mark). This quick double check should more than pay for itself in caught mistakes for the time it costs.

Pace Yourself

It's easy to be overwhelmed when you're looking at a page full of questions; your mind is confused and full of random thoughts, and the clock is ticking down faster than you would like. Calm down and maintain the pace that you have set for yourself. Especially as you get down to the last few minutes of the test, don't let the small numbers on the clock make you panic. As long as you are on track by monitoring your pace, you are guaranteed to have time for each question.

Don't Rush

It is very easy to make errors when you are in a hurry. Maintaining a fast pace in answering questions is pointless if it makes you miss questions that you would have gotten right otherwise. Test writers like to include distracting information and wrong answers that seem right. Taking a little extra time to avoid careless mistakes can make all the difference in your test score. Find a pace that allows you to be confident in the answers that you select.

Keep Moving

Panicking will not help you pass the test, so do your best to stay calm and keep moving. Taking deep breaths and going through the answer elimination steps you practiced can help to break through a stress barrier and keep your pace.

Final Notes

The combination of a solid foundation of content knowledge and the confidence that comes from practicing your plan for applying that knowledge is the key to maximizing your performance on test day. As your foundation of content knowledge is built up and strengthened, you'll find that the strategies included in this chapter become more and more effective in helping you quickly sift through the distractions and traps of the test to isolate the correct answer.

Now it's time to move on to the test content chapters of this book, but be sure to keep your goal in mind. As you read, think about how you will be able to apply this information on the test. If you've already seen sample questions for the test and you have an idea of the question format and style, try to come up with questions of your own that you can answer based on what you're reading. This will give you valuable practice applying your knowledge in the same ways you can expect to on test day.

Good luck and good studying!

Analytical Writing Assessment

Preparing to Write

Writing is a skill that continues to need development throughout a person's life. For some people, writing seems to be a natural gift. They rarely struggle with writer's block. When you read their papers, they have persuasive ideas. For others, writing is an intimidating task that they endure. As you practice, you can improve your skills and be better prepared for writing a time-sensitive essay.

A traditional and reliable way to prepare for the writing section is to read. When you read newspapers, magazines, and books, you learn about new ideas. You can read newspapers and magazines to become informed about issues that affect many people. As you think about those issues and ideas, you can take a position and form opinions. Try to develop these ideas and your opinions by sharing them with friends. After you develop your opinions, try writing them down as if you were going to spread your ideas beyond your friends.

Remember that you are practicing for more than an exam. Two of the most valuable things in the workplace are the abilities to read critically and to write clearly. When you work on evaluating the arguments of a passage and explain your thoughts well, you are developing skills that you will use for a lifetime. In the following pages, you will find strategies and tools that will prepare you to write better essays.

Understanding Your Writing Assignment

For your exam, you will be given a prompt (i.e., a writing assignment) that needs your response within the time limit. However you feel about the prompt, you need to give an answer that addresses the entire prompt. Your response needs to be creative and informed. In other words, you need to keep the attention and interest of your audience. Most importantly, you need to show your readers that you know what you are talking about in your essay. As you consider the prompt, you may want to ask these questions to understand the assignment:

- What specifically is the assignment asking you to do?
- What information or knowledge is necessary to fulfill the assignment?
- Are there other requirements for the assignment?
- What is the purpose of the assignment?
- Who is the intended audience?
- What is the length of the assignment?

Brainstorming

Brainstorming is a technique that is used to find a creative approach to a subject. You can accomplish this by simple free-association with a topic. For example, with paper and pen, you write every thought that you have about the topic in a word or phrase. This is done without critical thinking. Everything that comes to your mind about the topic, you should put on your scratch paper. Then, you need to read the list over a few times. Next, you look for patterns, repetitions, and clusters of ideas. This allows a variety of fresh ideas to come as you think about the topic.

Freewriting

Free writing is a form of brainstorming, but the method occurs in a structured way. The method involves a limited amount of time (e.g., 2 to 3 minutes) and writing everything that comes to mind about the topic in complete sentences. When time expires, you need to review everything that has been written down. Many of your sentences may make little or no sense, but the insights and observations that can come from free writing make this method a valuable approach. Usually, free writing results in a fuller expression of ideas than brainstorming because thoughts and associations are written in complete sentences. However, both techniques can be used to complement the other.

Questioning

Depending on the topic, you may ask and answer questions to provide a structured approach of investigating a subject. Several types of questions may be used to illuminate an issue:

- Questions to describe a topic: *What is it?*; *What caused it?*; *What is it like or unlike?*; *What is it a part of?*; *What do people say about it?* These questions can help to explore a topic in a step-by-step approach.
- Questions to explain a topic: Who, how, and what is it?; Where does it end and begin?; What is at issue?; How is it done?
- Questions to persuade: What claims can be made about it?; What evidence supports the claims?; Can the claims be challenged?; What assumptions support the claims?

Purpose

Before you begin writing your essay, you need to ask: *What is the main purpose of the proposed piece?* This may be focused or unclear. You should be clear about the purpose of your writing. Generally, purposes may be divided into three groups:

- To educate or inform
- To entertain
- To persuade or convince

For your essay, you will be asked to persuade or inform; however, an assignment could ask for both. When you identify the major purpose of your prompt, you should consider if there are any secondary purposes. For example, the major purpose of a prompt may be to persuade your audience, and the secondary purpose would be to educate your audience.

> **Review Video: Purpose of an Author**
> Visit mometrix.com/academy and enter code: 497555

Formal Writing

The relationship between writer and reader is important in choosing a level of formality. Most writing requires some degree of formality. Formal writing is for addressing a superior in a school or work environment. Business letters, textbooks, and newspapers use a moderate to high level of formality in their work. Informal writing is appropriate for private letters, personal e-mails, and business correspondence between close associates. For your exam, you will want to maintain a high level of formality. As you write your essay, you need to be consistent with your level of formality. Shifts in levels of formality or point of view can confuse readers and discount the message of your essay. For example, unless you are using a personal example, you should avoid referring to yourself (e.g., "*I* think that *my* point is very clear.") in your essay. Also, try to avoid mentioning your audience directly in your essay (e.g., "Readers, *like you*, will understand this argument.").

Tone

Tone is the writer's attitude toward the topic and the audience. In other words, tone is the language used in your writing. If the language is unclear, then the tone becomes very difficult to understand. The tone of a passage should be appropriate to the topic and to the intended audience. While slang and jargon are welcome for some types of writing, you need to avoid them in your essay.

Tone can range from humorous to serious and all levels in between.

> **Review Video: Style, Tone, and Mood**
> Visit mometrix.com/academy and enter code: 416961

Introduction

An introduction announces the main point of the passage. Normally, the introduction ranges from 50 to 70 words (i.e., 3 or 4 sentences). The purpose of the introduction is to gain the reader's attention and conclude with the essay's main point. An introduction can begin with an interesting quote, question, or strong opinion that grabs the reader's attention. Your introduction should include a restatement of the prompt, a summary of the main points of your essay, and your position on the prompt (i.e., the thesis sentence/statement). Depending on the amount of available time, you may want to give more or less information on the main points of your essay. The important thing is to impress the audience with your thesis statement (i.e., your reason for writing the essay).

> **Review Video: Introduction**
> Visit mometrix.com/academy and enter code: 961328

Thesis

A thesis gives the main idea of the essay. A temporary thesis should be established early in the writing process because it will serve to keep the writer focused as ideas develop. This temporary thesis is subject to change as you continue to write.

The temporary thesis has two parts: a topic (i.e., the focus of your paper based on the prompt) and a comment. The comment makes an important point about the topic. A temporary thesis should be interesting and specific. Also, you need to limit the topic to a manageable scope. These three criteria are useful tools to measure the effectiveness of any temporary thesis:

- Does the focus of my essay have enough interest to hold an audience?
- Is the focus of my essay specific enough to generate interest?
- Is the focus of my essay manageable for the time limit? Too broad? Too narrow?

The thesis should be a generalization rather than a fact because the thesis prepares readers for facts and details that support the thesis. The process of bringing the thesis into sharp focus may help in outlining major sections of the work. Once the thesis and introduction are complete, you can address the body of the work.

Throughout your essay, the thesis should be explained clearly and supported adequately by additional arguments. The thesis sentence needs to contain a clear statement of the purpose of your essay and a comment about the thesis. With the thesis statement, you have an opportunity to state what is noteworthy of this particular treatment of the prompt. Each sentence and paragraph should build on and support the thesis.

When you respond to the prompt, use parts of the passage to support your argument or defend your position. With supporting evidence from the passage, you strengthen your argument because readers can see your attention to the entire passage and your response to the details and facts within the passage. You can use facts, details, statistics, and direct quotations from the passage to uphold your position. Be sure to point out which information comes from the original passage and base your argument around that evidence.

Review Video: Thesis Statements
Visit mometrix.com/academy and enter code: 691033

Paragraphs

Following the introduction, you will begin with body paragraphs. A paragraph should be unified around a main point. Normally, a good topic sentence summarizes the paragraph's main point. A topic sentence is a general sentence that gives an introduction to the paragraph. The sentences that follow are a support to the topic sentence. You may use the topic sentence as the final sentence to the paragraph if the earlier sentences give a clear explanation of the topic sentence. Overall, you need to stay true to the main point. This means that you need to remove unnecessary sentences that do not advance the main point.

The main point of a paragraph requires adequate development (i.e., a substantial paragraph that covers the main point). A paragraph of two or three sentences does not cover a main point. This is true when the main point of the paragraph gives strong support to the argument of the thesis. An occasional short paragraph is fine as a transitional device. However, you should aim to have six to seven sentences for each paragraph.

A common method of development in your essay can be done with **examples**. These examples are the supporting details to the main idea of a paragraph or passage. When you write about something that your audience may not understand, you can provide an example to show your point. When you write about something that is not easily accepted, you can give examples to prove your point.

Review Video: Drafting Body Paragraphs
Visit mometrix.com/academy and enter code: 724590

Illustrations are extended examples that require several sentences. Well selected illustrations can be a great way to develop a point that may not be familiar to your audience. With a time limit, you may have enough time to use one illustration. So, be sure that you use one that connects well with your main argument.

Analogies make comparisons between items that appear to have nothing in common. Analogies are employed by writers to provoke fresh thoughts about a subject. They may be used to explain the unfamiliar, to clarify an abstract point, or to argue a point. Although analogies are effective literary devices, they should be used carefully in arguments. Two things may be alike in some respects but completely different in others.

Cause and effect is an excellent device used when the cause and effect are accepted as true. One way of using cause and effect is to state the effect in the topic sentence of a paragraph and add the causes in the body of the paragraph. With this method, your paragraphs can have structure which always strengthens writing.

> **Review Video: Cause and Effect**
> Visit mometrix.com/academy and enter code: 428037

A **paragraph of narration** tells a story or a part of a story. Normally, the sentences are arranged in chronological order (i.e., the order that the events happened). However, you can include flashbacks (i.e., beginning the story at an earlier time).

> **Review Video: Rhetorical Strategy of Narration**
> Visit mometrix.com/academy and enter code: 827871

A **descriptive paragraph** makes a verbal portrait of a person, place, or thing. When you use specific details that appeal to one or more of the senses (i.e., sight, sound, smell, taste, and touch), you give your readers a sense of being present in the moment.

> **Review Video: Rhetorical Strategy of Description**
> Visit mometrix.com/academy and enter code: 639813

A **process paragraph** is related to time order (i.e., First, you open the bottle. Second, you pour the liquid, etc.). Usually, this describes a process or teaches readers how to perform a process.

Comparing two things draws attention to their similarities and indicates a number of differences. When you contrast, you focus only on differences. Both comparisons and contrasts may be used point-by-point or in following paragraphs.

> **Review Video: Rhetorical Strategy of Comparing and Contrasting**
> Visit mometrix.com/academy and enter code: 587299

Reasons for starting a new paragraph include:

1. To mark off the introduction and concluding paragraphs
2. To signal a shift to a new idea or topic
3. To indicate an important shift in time or place
4. To explain a point in additional detail
5. To highlight a comparison, contrast, or cause and effect relationship

Conclusion

A good conclusion should leave readers satisfied and provide a sense of completeness. Many conclusions state the thesis in different words and give a summary of the ideas in the body paragraphs. Some writers find ways to conclude in a dramatic fashion. They may conclude with a vivid image or a warning and remind readers of the main point. The conclusion can be a few sentences because the body of the text has made the case for the thesis. A conclusion can summarize the main points and offer advice or ask a question. You should never introduce new ideas or arguments in a conclusion. Also, you need to avoid vague and aimless endings. Instead, close with a clear and specific paragraph.

Review Video: Drafting Conclusions
Visit mometrix.com/academy and enter code: 209408

Argumentative and Persuasive Writing

Argumentative and persuasive writing takes a stand on a debatable issue, seeks to explore all sides of the issue, and finds the best possible solution. Argumentative and persuasive writing should not be combative or abusive. The word *argument* may remind you of two or more people shouting at each other and walking away in anger. However, an argumentative or persuasive essay should be a calm and reasonable presentation on your ideas for others to consider. When you write reasonable arguments, your goal is not to win or have the last word. Instead, you want to reveal current understanding of the question and suggest a solution to a problem. The purpose of argument and persuasion in a free society is to reach the best solution.

The introduction of an essay that argues for or against an issue should end with a thesis sentence that gives a position (i.e., the side that you want to defend or oppose) on the prompt. The thesis should be supported by strong arguments that back up your position. The main points of your argument should have a growing effect which convinces readers that the thesis has merit. In your introduction, you should list the main points of your argument which will outline the entire argumentative essay.

Evidence needs to be provided that supports the thesis and additional arguments. Most arguments must be supported by facts or statistics. Facts are something that is known with certainty and have been verified by several independent individuals. Examples and illustrations add an emotional component to arguments. With this component, you persuade readers in ways that facts and statistics cannot. The emotional component is effective when used with objective information that can be confirmed.

When you show both sides to the argument, you build trust with readers. The graders of your essay will be undecided or neutral. If you present only your side to the argument, your readers will be concerned at best. Showing the other side of the argument can take place anywhere in the essay, but one of the best places is after the thesis statement.

Building common ground with neutral or opposed readers can be appealing to skeptical readers. Sharing values with undecided readers can allow people to switch positions without giving up what they feel is important. For people who may oppose a position, they need to feel that they can change their minds without betraying who they are as a person. This appeal to having an open-mind can be a powerful tool in arguing a position without antagonizing other views. Objections can be countered on a point-by-point basis or in a summary paragraph. Be careful in how you point out flaws in counter arguments. If you are unfair to the other side of the argument, then you can lose trust with your audience.

Review Video: Persuasive Essay
Visit mometrix.com/academy and enter code: 621428

Coherence

A smooth flow of sentences and paragraphs without gaps or shifts is what is meant by coherent writing. When your writing is coherent, you give information in a way that helps your readers understand the connection between sentences or paragraphs. The ties between old and new information can be completed by several strategies.

Tips for Coherent Writing

Linking ideas clearly from the topic sentence to the body of the paragraph is essential for a smooth transition. The topic sentence states the main point, and this should be followed by specific details, examples, and illustrations that support the topic sentence.

The **repetition of key words** adds coherence to a paragraph. You can avoid overuse of a keyword by using synonyms of the key word.

Changing verb tenses in a paragraph can be confusing for your readers. Try to minimize shifting sentences from one verb tense to another. These shifts affect the smooth flows of words and can disrupt the coherence of the paragraph.

> **Review Video: Methods to Obtain Coherence in Writing**
> Visit mometrix.com/academy and enter code: 831344

Transitions

Transitions are bridges between what has been read and what is about to be read. Transitions smooth the reader's path between sentences and inform readers of connections to new ideas in the essay. When you think about the appropriate phrase for a transition, you need to consider the previous and upcoming sentences or paragraphs. Thus, transitional phrases should be used with care. Tone should be considered when you want to use a transitional phrase. For example, *in summary* would be preferable to the informal *in short*.

Consider these transitions:

- Restatement: He wanted to walk the trails at the park, *namely* Yosemite National Park.
- Contrast: This could be the best option. *On the other hand*, this option may lead to more damage.

> **Review Video: Transitions in Writing**
> Visit mometrix.com/academy and enter code: 233246

Cliches

Clichés are phrases that have been overused to the point that the phrase has no importance or has lost the original meaning. The phrases have no originality and add very little to your writing. Therefore, you should try to avoid the use of clichés. The best revision for clichés is to delete them. If this does not seem possible, then a cliché can be changed so that it is not predictable and empty of meaning.

Examples:

- When life gives you lemons, make lemonade.
- Every cloud has a silver lining.

Euphemisms

Euphemisms are acceptable words which replace language that seems too harsh or ugly. Normally, people use a euphemism when they speak about subjects such as death and bodily functions. These acceptable words can be unclear or misunderstood. If you are trying to decide between using a euphemism or avoiding a euphemism, then you should choose to avoid talking about the subject altogether. You want the graders of your work to understand your entire essay.

Examples:

- My grandmother passed away this weekend.
- He had to go to the mens' room.

Jargon

Jargon is a specialized vocabulary that is used among members of a trade or profession. Since jargon is understood by a small audience, you should not use such vocabulary in your essay. Jargon includes exaggerated language that tries to impress rather than inform. Sentences filled with jargon are not precise and difficult to understand.

Examples:

- "He is going to toenail these frames for us." (Toenail is construction jargon for nailing at an angle.)
- "They brought in a kip of material today." (Kip refers to 1000 pounds in architecture and engineering.)

Slang

Slang is an informal and sometimes private language that is understood by some individuals. Slang has some usefulness, but the language can have a small audience. Again, you should avoid this in your writing. While the grader of your exam may be aware of the word, he or she may not understand the use of the word as you do.

Examples:

- "Yes, the event was a blast!" (In this sentence, blast means that the event was a great experience.)
- "That attempt was an epic fail." (By epic fail, the speaker means that his or her attempt was not a success.)

Replacing General Nouns with Specific Nouns

A writer's choice of words is a signature of their style. Careful thought about the use of words can improve a piece of writing. When you pay attention to the use of specific nouns rather than general ones, you can make your essay an exciting piece to read.

Example:

- General: His kindness will never be forgotten.
- Specific: His thoughtful gifts and bear hugs will never be forgotten.

Replacing Passive Verbs with Active Verbs

Think about the kind of verbs that you use in your sentences. Active verbs (e.g., run, swim) should be about an action. Whenever possible, trade a linking verb for an active verb to provide clear examples for your arguments and to strengthen your essay overall.

Example:

- Passive: The winners were called to the stage by the judges.
- Active: The judges called the winners to the stage.

Revising and Editing Sentences

Revising sentences is done to make writing more effective. Editing sentences is done to correct any errors. Sentences are the building blocks of writing, and they can be changed by paying attention to sentence length, sentence structure, and sentence openings. You should add variety to sentence length, structure, and openings so that the essay does not seem boring or repetitive. A careful analysis of a piece of writing will expose these stylistic problems, and they can be corrected before you finish your essay. Changing up your sentence structure and sentence length can make your essay more inviting and appealing to readers.

> **Review Video: Revising and Editing**
> Visit mometrix.com/academy and enter code: 674181

Recursive Writing Process

The recursive writing process is not as difficult as the phrase appears to you. Simply put, the recursive writing process means that the steps in the writing process occur in no particular order. For example, planning, drafting, and revising (all a part of the writing process) take place at about the same time and you may not notice that all three happen so close together. Truly, the writing process is a series of moving back and forth between planning, drafting, and revising. Then, more planning, more drafting, and more revising until your essay is complete.

> **Review Video: Recursive Writing Process**
> Visit mometrix.com/academy and enter code: 951611

Evaluating the Draft of Your Essay

If there is available time and you have finished your essay, then you should do an evaluation of your work. In a classroom setting, you would want to review all of your work (i.e., from brainstorming for ideas to your final draft) with a critical eye. However, with a limited amount of time in your exam, you will want to do a quick review of your essay. There is no single checklist that guarantees a complete and effective evaluation, but there are some things that can be considered:

- Purpose - Does the draft accomplish everything that was contained in the prompt? Is the material and tone appropriate for the intended audience?
- Focus - Does the introduction and the conclusion focus on the main point? Are all supporting arguments focused on the thesis?
- Organization and Paragraphing - Are there enough transitions and appropriate paragraph breaks to guide the reader? Are any paragraphs too long or too short?

- Content - Is the supporting material persuasive? Are all ideas fully developed? Is there any material that needs to be removed?
- Point of view - Is the draft free of distracting shifts in point of view? Is the point of view appropriate for the subject and intended audience?

> **Review Video:** <u>Evaluation and Critique of One's Own Writing</u>
> Visit mometrix.com/academy and enter code: 255921

Integrated Reasoning

Logical Organization

There are six major types of logical organization that are frequently used:

1. Illustrations may be used to support the thesis. Examples are the most common form of this organization.
2. A series of definitions identifying what something is or is not is another way of organization. What are the characteristics of the topic?
3. Dividing or classifying information into separate items according to their similarities is a common and effective organizing method.
4. Comparing, focusing on the similarities of things, and contrasting, highlighting the differences between things, together form an excellent tool to use with certain kinds of information.
5. Cause and effect is a simple tool to logically understand relationships between things. A phenomenon may be traced to its causes for organizing a subject logically.
6. Problem and solution is a simple and effective manner of logically organizing material. It is very commonly used and lucidly presents information.

> **Review Video: Organization in a Paper**
> Visit mometrix.com/academy and enter code: 479120

Producing Clear and Coherent Writing Appropriate to the Task, Purpose, and Audience

Each genre of writing requires its own traits, but to attain clear and coherent writing it is necessary to plan what you will be writing. First, decide on your goal, or whether you are trying to inform, persuade, or entertain. With your goal in mind, you need to organize your material if you are writing a nonfiction piece. You need to have a clear idea of your main ideas and supporting details. If you are planning to write a narrative, you need to pay attention to developing your story in a clear and flowing manner. Then, create characters through skillful use of description, dialogue, and action. In addition in all types of writing you need to establish a tone. You also need to make sure your writing is free of grammatical or spelling errors. Close rereading and editing is part of the writing process, as well.

Analysis of Relationships between Similar Ideas and Ideas in Opposition

Many texts follow the **compare-and-contrast** model in which the similarities and differences between two ideas or things are explored. Analysis of the similarities between ideas is called comparison. In an ideal comparison, the author places ideas or things in an equivalent structure (i.e., the author presents the ideas in the same way). If an author wants to show the similarities between cricket and baseball, then he or she may do so by summarizing the equipment and rules for each game. Be mindful of the similarities as they appear in the passage and take note of any differences that are mentioned. Often, these small differences will only reinforce the more general similarity.

Thinking critically about ideas and conclusions can seem like a daunting task. One way to ease this task is to understand the basic elements of ideas and writing techniques. Looking at the way different ideas relate to each other can be a good way for readers to begin their analysis. For instance, sometimes authors will write about two ideas that are in opposition to each other. Or one author will provide his or her ideas on a topic, and another author may respond in opposition. The analysis of these opposing ideas is known as **contrast**. Contrast is often marred by the author's obvious partiality to one of the ideas. A discerning reader will be put off by an author who does not engage in a fair fight.

In an analysis of opposing ideas, both ideas should be presented in clear and reasonable terms. If the author does prefer a side, you need to read carefully to determine the areas where the author shows or avoids this preference. In an analysis of opposing ideas, you should proceed through the passage by marking the major differences point by point with an eye that is looking for an explanation of each side's view. For instance, in an analysis of capitalism and communism, there is an importance in outlining each side's view on labor, markets, prices, personal responsibility, etc. Additionally, as you read through the passages, you should note whether the opposing views present each side in a similar manner.

> **Review Video: Compare and Contrast**
> Visit mometrix.com/academy and enter code: 798319

Tables and Graphs

Tables present information that has been observed in a field of study and has been collected into a visual format for ease of reading and understanding. At the top of the table, there will be a title which consists of a short phrase indicating the information that the table or graph intends to convey. The title of a table could be something like *Average Income for Various Education Levels* or *Price of Milk Compared to Demand*. A table is composed of information laid out in vertical columns and horizontal rows. Typically, each column will have a label. If *Average Income for Various Education Levels* was placed in a table format, then the two columns could be labeled *Education Level* and *Average Income*. Each location on the table is called a cell. Cells are defined by their column and row (e.g., second column, fifth row). The obtained information for a table is placed within these cells.

> **Review Video: Tables**
> Visit mometrix.com/academy and enter code: 769453

Bar Graph and Line Graph

Readers need to consider the intention and the structure of a graph format. For instance, a **bar graph** is appropriate for displaying distinct quantities on a scale and showing the variation among those quantities. If one wanted to display the amount of money spent on groceries during the months of a year, then a bar graph would be appropriate. The vertical axis would represent values of money, and the horizontal axis would identify the bar representing each month. On the other hand, if the grocery expenses were plotted on a line graph instead of a bar graph, there would be an emphasis on whether the amount of spending rose or fell over the course of the year.

> **Review Video: Bar Graph**
> Visit mometrix.com/academy and enter code: 226729

Whereas a bar graph is good for showing the relationships between the different values plotted, the **line graph** is good for showing whether the values tend to increase, decrease, or remain stable. Generally, the bar graph is preferable to the line graph since there has to be some built-in relationship between the data points because the graph implies a relationship (e.g., the amount of different apples at a store or the speed of popular rollercoasters at an amusement park). The line graph is superior in particular situations (e.g., intervals of time or development) because the line graph shows the rate of change between period of times in a visual format (e.g., observing a stock on the Dow Jones rise and fall over the course of a month or tracking the height of a child over a period of years).

> **Review Video:** Line Graphs
> Visit mometrix.com/academy and enter code: 480147

Pie Chart

A **pie chart**, also known as a circle graph, is useful for depicting how a single unit or category is divided. The standard pie chart is a circle with designated wedges. Each wedge is proportional in size to a part of the whole. For instance, consider a pie chart representing a student's budget. If the student spends half of his or her money on rent, then the pie chart will represent that amount with a line through the center of the pie. If she spends a quarter of her money on food, there will be a line extending from the edge of the circle to the center at a right angle to the line depicting rent. This illustration would make it clear that the student spends twice the amount of money on rent as she does on food. A pie chart is effective at showing how a single entity is divided into parts. They are not effective at demonstrating the relationships between parts of different wholes. For example, an unhelpful use of a pie chart would be to compare the respective amounts of state and federal spending devoted to infrastructure since these values are only meaningful in the context of the entire budget.

> **Review Video:** Pie Chart
> Visit mometrix.com/academy and enter code: 895285

Effective Graphic Representation

A graph should strip the author's message down to the essentials with a clear title and should be in the appropriate format. Authors may elect to use tables, line or bar graphs, or pie charts to illustrate their message. Each of these formats is correct for different types of data. For instance, if the text is about the differences between federal spending on the military and on the space program, a pie chart or a bar graph would be the most effective choice. The pie chart could show each type of spending as a portion of total federal spending while the bar graph would be better for directly comparing the amounts of money spent on these two programs.

Interpretation of Information Presented in Graphs, Tables, Charts, and Diagrams

In most cases, the work of interpreting information presented in graphs, tables, charts, and diagrams is done for the reader. Usually, the author will make explicit his or her reasons for presenting a certain set of data in a certain way. However, an effective reader will avoid taking the author's claims for granted. Before considering the information presented in the graph, the reader should consider whether the author has chosen the correct format for presentation, whether the author has omitted variables or other information that might undermine his or her case. Interpreting the graphic itself is essentially an exercise in spotting trends. On a graph, for instance, the reader should be alert for how one variable responds to a change in the other. For example, if education level increases, does income increase as well? The same can be done for a table. Readers should be alert for values that break or exaggerate a trend; these may be meaningless outliers or indicators of a change in conditions.

Drawing Conclusions Based on the Information Presented in Graphics

When readers are required to draw conclusions from the information presented in graphs, tables, charts, or diagrams, they need to know the importance of limiting these conclusions to the terms of the graph. In other words, the reader should avoid inferring unknown values from known values in the data to make claims that are not supportable. As an example, consider a graph that compares the price of eggs to the demand. If the price and demand rise and fall together, a reader would be justified in saying that the demand for eggs and the price are tied together. However, this simple graph does not indicate which of these variables causes the other, so the reader would not be justified in concluding that the price of eggs raises or lowers the demand. In fact, demand could be tied to all sorts of other factors not included in such a chart.

Synthesizing Information Presented in Graphics

Graphs make information visual rather than only numerical or numerical and verbal. This enables you to see differences and similarities at a glance instead of having to compare or contrast numbers, e.g. those that go up and down over time. For example, a line graph clearly depicts overall patterns of amounts increasing or decreasing across designated time intervals. Bar graphs can also compare or contrast amounts occurring at the same time. Charts and tables can be used to summarize multiple, various numbers; however, looking at these generally requires more cognitive processing than looking at visual graphs. Synthesis involves combining information from multiple sources, including new information with prior knowledge. You can use existing knowledge to understand graphics, and combine new graphic sources with new verbal text for more complete understanding of a topic. As an example, if a text article reports that several business schools have recently lowered tuitions and redesigned curricula, and a graph shows new enrollment increases following these changes, it would be logical to connect these events.

Synthesizing Information from a Text with Existing Knowledge

Readers often merge new information they encounter in text with their own existing knowledge; this merger results in the reader's ability to generate new insights, concepts, opinions, perspectives, trains of thought and other ideas. Through synthesis, they also boost their reading comprehension via cognitive processes of rephrasing new information in their own words and connecting it with what they already know. This improved understanding increases the likelihood that they will retain the new information and be able to transfer it to other contexts and generalize it across applicable situations. Retention, transfer, and generalization additionally reinforce the new information further. The process of synthesizing while reading by good readers includes pausing to gather their thoughts; identifying a text's main idea; rephrasing information in their own terms and responding; and combining reading with what they previously knew and responding to the results. Students may make notes of questions they have as they read, review the notes to see whether they have found answers in text, and look for any unanswered questions as they continue and finish reading.

Graphic Organizers

A simple graphic organizer for comparing and contrasting two concepts, events, processes, or objects is a T-chart. The two sides of the top enable headings, with two vertical columns of characteristics. For example, with alligators and crocodiles as categories, one difference is identified under Alligators that bottom teeth are covered, and under Crocodiles that bottom teeth are exposed. T-charts can be expanded to include multiple columns for comparing more than two categories.

A Venn diagram uses overlapping circles to compare and contrast: commonalities shared by 2-3 categories appear in overlaps, differences separately in each circle.

A sequence of events chain connects boxes with arrows to depict chronological order in history or fiction. If arranged in a circle, connected end-to-end, they can display life cycles of organisms or other cyclical or recursive processes. Timelines are similar, but also clarify time durations between events.

Idea webs facilitate brainstorming. Students write a main idea or topic in a central circle with lines radiating out, ending in circles for secondary related ideas, optionally with additional lines drawn out to evidence supporting these ideas.

> **Review Video: Graphic Organizers**
> Visit mometrix.com/academy and enter code: 665513

Interrelating Multiple Problems

Problems encountered in many human activities are as complex as the humans and activities involved, in large part because they are interrelated and interact. One example of this from the medical field is dual diagnosis of a psychiatric disorder and a substance abuse disorder. The patient not only suffers the impacts of two separate conditions; these also interact. This interaction can cause some symptoms to mask others or symptoms to overlap, complicating diagnosis and treatment. Also, disorders can exacerbate each other, and each promotes relapse in the other. Substance abuse can trigger psychiatric symptoms and disorders, while people experiencing psychiatric problems often abuse substances to self-medicate. Substance abuse withdrawal symptoms may mimic psychiatric disorder symptoms. Similarly, either or both of these types of disorders can lead to other problems, also interrelated with one another, such as social withdrawal or isolation, relationship or family problems, financial difficulties, school or work problems, and legal problems.

Combining and Manipulating Information from Multiple Sources

In order to solve a problem, we must first determine what information is needed to solve it, and then we must set about gathering that information. We must synthesize this information, combining what we find from multiple, varied sources and organize it toward our problem solution. This entails several steps: First, carefully examine each information source. Second, keep your purpose in mind as you read the information in each source. Next, identify which specific details in each source will facilitate your solving the identified problem. Finally, assemble these details from all sources: combine them to inform a solution to the problem. If the problem requires you to draft an essay response, here are some additional steps to follow: Take notes about the details to help yourself see how they are related, how you can combine them, and how they contribute to solving the problem. Organize these notes by making an outline, putting them into a graphic organizer, making lists, etc. Finally, write an explanation of the solution based on the facts and details you researched.

Quantitative

Basic Mathematical Operations

There are four basic mathematical operations:

- *Addition* increases the value of one quantity by the value of another quantity. Example: 2 + 4 = 6; 8 + 9 = 17. The result is called the *sum*. With addition, the order does not matter. 4 + 2 = 2 + 4.
- *Subtraction* is the opposite operation of addition; it decreases the value of one quantity by the value of another quantity. Example: 6 – 4 = 2; 17 – 8 = 9. The result is called the *difference*. Note that with subtraction, the order *does* matter. 6 – 4 ≠ 4 – 6.
- *Multiplication* can be thought of as repeated addition. One number tells how many times to add the other number to itself. Example: 3 × 2 (three times two) = 2 + 2 + 2 = 6. With multiplication, the order does not matter. 2 × 3 (or 3 + 3) = 3 × 2 (or 2 + 2 + 2).
- *Division* is the opposite operation of multiplication; one number tells us how many parts to divide the other number into. Example: 20 ÷ 4 = 5; if 20 is split into 4 equal parts, each part is 5. With division, the order of the numbers *does* matter. 20 ÷ 4 ≠ 4 ÷ 20.

> **Review Video: Addition, Subtraction, Multiplication, and Division**
> Visit mometrix.com/academy and enter code: 208095

Common Arithmetic Terms Specific to Numbers

Numbers are the basic building blocks of mathematics. Specific features of numbers are identified by the following terms:

- *Integers* – The set of positive and negative numbers, including zero. Integers do not include fractions ($\frac{1}{3}$), decimals (0.56), or mixed numbers ($7\frac{3}{4}$).

> **Review Video: Integers, Decimals, and Fractions**
> Visit mometrix.com/academy and enter code: 688110

- *Prime number* – A whole number greater than 1 that has only two factors, itself and 1; that is, a number that can be divided evenly only by 1 and itself.

> **Review Video: Prime Numbers**
> Visit mometrix.com/academy and enter code: 737990

- *Composite number* – A whole number greater than 1 that has more than two different factors; in other words, any whole number that is not a prime number. For example: The composite number 8 has the factors of 1, 2, 4, and 8.
- *Even number* – Any integer that can be divided by 2 without leaving a remainder. For example: 2, 4, 6, 8, and so on.
- *Odd number* – Any integer that cannot be divided evenly by 2. For example: 3, 5, 7, 9, and so on.

Rational, Irrational, and Real Numbers

Rational, irrational, and real numbers can be described as follows:

- *Rational numbers* include all integers, decimals, and fractions. Any terminating or repeating decimal number is a rational number.

> **Review Video: Rational Numbers**
> Visit mometrix.com/academy and enter code: 280645

- *Irrational numbers* cannot be written as fractions or decimals because the number of decimal places is infinite and there is no recurring pattern of digits within the number. For example, pi (π) begins with 3.141592 and continues without terminating or repeating, so pi is an irrational number.
- *Real numbers* are the set of all rational and irrational numbers.

> **Review Video: Negative and Positive Number Line**
> Visit mometrix.com/academy and enter code: 816439

Factors

Factors are numbers that are multiplied together to obtain a *product*. For example, in the equation $2 \times 3 = 6$, the numbers 2 and 3 are factors. A prime number has only two factors (1 and itself), but other numbers can have many factors.

A *common factor* is a number that divides exactly into two or more other numbers. For example, the factors of 12 are 1, 2, 3, 4, 6, and 12, while the factors of 15 are 1, 3, 5, and 15. The common factors of 12 and 15 are 1 and 3.

A *prime factor* is also a prime number. Therefore, the prime factors of 12 are 2 and 3. For 15, the prime factors are 3 and 5.

> **Review Video: Factors**
> Visit mometrix.com/academy and enter code: 920086

Greatest Common Factor (GCF) and Least Common Multiple (LCM)

The *greatest common factor* (GCF) is the largest number that is a factor of two or more numbers. For example, the factors of 15 are 1, 3, 5, and 15; the factors of 35 are 1, 5, 7, and 35. Therefore, the greatest common factor of 15 and 35 is 5.

> **Review Video: Greatest Common Factor (GCF)**
> Visit mometrix.com/academy and enter code: 838699

The *least common multiple* (LCM) is the smallest number that is a multiple of two or more numbers. For example, the multiples of 3 include 3, 6, 9, 12, 15, etc.; the multiples of 5 include 5, 10, 15, 20, etc. Therefore, the least common multiple of 3 and 5 is 15.

> **Review Video: Least Common Multiple**
> Visit mometrix.com/academy and enter code: 946579

Finding the Greatest Common Factor of a Group of Algebraic Expressions

The greatest common factor of a group of algebraic expressions may be a *monomial* or a *polynomial*. Begin by factoring all the algebraic expressions until each expression is represented as a group of factors consisting of monomials and prime polynomials. To find the greatest common factor, take each monomial or polynomial that appear as a factor in every algebraic expression and multiply. This will give you a polynomial with the largest numerical coefficient and largest degree that is a factor of the given algebraic expressions.

Scientific Notation

Scientific notation is a way of writing large numbers in a shorter form. The form a × 10^n is used in scientific notation, where a is greater than or equal to 1, but less than 10, and n is the number of places the decimal must move to get from the original number to a.

Example: The number 230,400,000 is cumbersome to write. To write the value in scientific notation, place a decimal point between the first and second numbers, and include all digits through the last non-zero digit (a = 2.304). To find the appropriate power of 10, count the number of places the decimal point had to move (n = 8). The number is positive if the decimal moved to the left, and negative if it moved to the right. We can then write 230,400,000 as 2.304 × 10^8.

If we look instead at the number 0.00002304, we have the same value for a, but this time the decimal moved 5 places to the right (n = -5). Thus, 0.00002304 can be written as 2.304 × 10^{-5}. Using this notation makes it simple to compare very large or very small numbers. By comparing exponents, it is easy to see that 3.28 × 10^4 is smaller than 1.51 × 10^5, because 4 is less than 5.

> **Review Video: Scientific Notation**
> Visit mometrix.com/academy and enter code: 976454

Laws of Exponents

The laws of exponents are as follows:

1. Any number to the power of 1 is equal to itself: $a^1 = a$.
2. The number 1 raised to any power is equal to 1: $1^n = 1$.
3. Any number raised to the power of 0 is equal to 1: $a^0 = 1$.
4. Add exponents to multiply powers of the same base number: $a^n \times a^m = a^{n+m}$.
5. Subtract exponents to divide powers of the same number: $a^n \div a^m = a^{n-m}$.
6. Multiply exponents to raise a power to a power: $(a^n)^m = a^{n \times m}$.
7. If multiplied or divided numbers inside parentheses are collectively raised to a power, this is the same as each individual term being raised to that power: $(a \times b)^n = a^n \times b^n$; $(a \div b)^n = a^n \div b^n$.

Note: Exponents do not have to be integers. Fractional or decimal exponents follow all the rules above as well. Example: $5^{\frac{1}{4}} \times 5^{\frac{3}{4}} = 5^{\frac{1}{4}+\frac{3}{4}} = 5^1 = 5$.

> **Review Video: Laws of Exponents**
> Visit mometrix.com/academy and enter code: 532558

Decimal System

The decimal, or base 10, system is a number system that uses ten different digits (0, 1, 2, 3, 4, 5, 6, 7, 8, 9). An example of a number system that uses something other than ten digits is the binary, or base 2, number system, used by computers, which uses only the numbers 0 and 1. It is thought that the decimal system originated because people had only their 10 fingers for counting.

- *Decimal* – a number that uses a decimal point to show the part of the number that is less than one. Example: 1.234.
- *Decimal point* – a symbol used to separate the ones place from the tenths place in decimals or dollars from cents in currency.
- *Decimal place* – the position of a number to the right of the decimal point. In the decimal 0.123, the 1 is in the first place to the right of the decimal point, indicating tenths; the 2 is in the second place, indicating hundredths; and the 3 is in the third place, indicating thousandths.

> **Review Video: Decimals**
> Visit mometrix.com/academy and enter code: 837268

Standard Units in the Metric System Compared to the U.S. Customary System

Metric System
Length: meter

Mass or weight: gram

Volume: liter

Temperature: degrees Celsius

U.S. Customary System
Length: inch, foot, yard, mile

Capacity or volume: pint, quart, gallon

Mass or weight: ounce, pound, ton

Temperature: degrees Fahrenheit

Common Conversions for Length in the U.S. Customary System

1 foot = 12 inches

1 yard = 3 feet

1 mile = 5,280 feet

Common Prefixes Used in the Metric System

Milli – one one-thousandth, or .001

Centi – one one-hundredth, or .01

Kilo – one thousand, or 1,000

Common Conversions for Liquid Capacity in the U.S. Customary System

1 cup = 8 fluid ounces

1 pint = 2 cups

1 quart = 2 pints

1 gallon = 4 quarts

Common Conversions for Weight in the U.S. Customary System

1 pound = 16 ounces

1 ton = 2,000 pounds

Fractions, Numerators, and Denominators

A *fraction* is a number that is expressed as one integer written above another integer, with a dividing line between them $\left(\frac{x}{y}\right)$. It represents the quotient of the two numbers "x divided by y." It can also be thought of as *x* out of *y* equal parts.

The top number of a fraction is called the *numerator*, and it represents the number of parts under consideration. The 1 in $\frac{1}{4}$ means that 1 part out of the whole is being considered in the calculation. The bottom number of a fraction is called the *denominator*, and it represents the total number of equal parts. The 4 in $\frac{1}{4}$ means that the whole consists of 4 equal parts.

A fraction cannot have a denominator of zero; this is referred to as "undefined."

Review Video: <u>Fractions</u>
Visit mometrix.com/academy and enter code: 262335

Manipulating Fractions

Fractions can be manipulated by multiplying or dividing (but not adding or subtracting) both the numerator and denominator by the same number, without changing the value of the fraction. If you divide both numbers by a common factor, you are reducing or simplifying the fraction. Two fractions that have the same value, but are expressed differently are known as *equivalent fractions*. For example, $\frac{2}{10}, \frac{3}{15}, \frac{4}{20}$, and $\frac{5}{25}$ are all equivalent fractions. They can also all be reduced or simplified to $\frac{1}{5}$.

Review Video: <u>Dividing Fractions</u>
Visit mometrix.com/academy and enter code: 300874

When two fractions are manipulated so that they have the same denominator, this is known as finding a *common denominator*. The number chosen to be that common denominator should be the least common multiple of the two original denominators. Example: $\frac{3}{4}$ and $\frac{5}{6}$; the least common multiple of 4 and 6 is 12. Manipulating to achieve the common denominator: $\frac{3}{4} = \frac{9}{12}$; $\frac{5}{6} = \frac{10}{12}$.

Improper Fractions and Mixed Numbers

A fraction whose denominator is greater than its numerator is known as a *proper fraction*, while a fraction whose numerator is greater than its denominator is known as an *improper fraction*. Proper fractions have values less than one while improper fractions have values greater than one.

A *mixed number* is a number that contains both an integer and a fraction. Any improper fraction can be rewritten as a mixed number. Example: $\frac{8}{3} = \frac{6}{3} + \frac{2}{3} = 2 + \frac{2}{3} = 2\frac{2}{3}$. Similarly, any mixed number can be rewritten as an improper fraction. Example: $1\frac{3}{5} = 1 + \frac{3}{5} = \frac{5}{5} + \frac{3}{5} = \frac{8}{5}$.

> **Review Video:** **Improper Fractions and Mixed Numbers**
> Visit mometrix.com/academy and enter code: 731507

Adding, Subtracting, Multiplying, and Dividing Fractions

If two fractions have a common denominator, they can be added or subtracted simply by adding or subtracting the two numerators and retaining the same denominator. Example: $\frac{1}{2} + \frac{1}{4} = \frac{2}{4} + \frac{1}{4} = \frac{3}{4}$. If the two fractions do not already have the same denominator, one or both of them must be manipulated to achieve a common denominator before they can be added or subtracted.

> **Review Video:** **Adding and Subtracting Fractions**
> Visit mometrix.com/academy and enter code: 378080

Two fractions can be multiplied by multiplying the two numerators to find the new numerator and the two denominators to find the new denominator. Example: $\frac{1}{3} \times \frac{2}{3} = \frac{1 \times 2}{3 \times 3} = \frac{2}{9}$.

Two fractions can be divided flipping the numerator and denominator of the second fraction and then proceeding as though it were a multiplication. Example: $\frac{2}{3} \div \frac{3}{4} = \frac{2}{3} \times \frac{4}{3} = \frac{8}{9}$.

> **Review Video:** **Multiplying and Dividing Fractions**
> Visit mometrix.com/academy and enter code: 473632

Complex Fractions

Complex fraction: A fraction that contains a fraction in its numerator, denominator, or both. These can be solved in a number of ways, with the simplest being by following the order of operations.

For example, $\left(\frac{4}{7}\right) \Big/ \left(\frac{5}{8}\right) = 0.571 \big/ 0.625 = 0.914$.

Another way to solve this problem is to multiply the fraction in the numerator by the reciprical of the fraction in the denominator. For example, $\left(\frac{4}{7}\right) \Big/ \left(\frac{5}{8}\right) = \frac{4}{7} \times \frac{8}{5} = \frac{32}{35} = 0.914$.

Percentages, Fractions, and Decimals

Percentages can be thought of as fractions that are based on a whole of 100; that is, one whole is equal to 100%. The word percent means *per hundred*. Fractions can be expressed as percents by finding equivalent fractions with a denomination of 100. Example: $\frac{7}{10} = \frac{70}{100} = 70\%$; $\frac{1}{4} = \frac{25}{100} = 25\%$.

To express a percentage as a fraction, divide the percentage number by 100 and reduce the fraction to its simplest possible terms. Example: $60\% = \frac{60}{100} = \frac{3}{5}$; $96\% = \frac{96}{100} = \frac{24}{25}$.

Converting decimals to percentages and percentages to decimals is as simple as moving the decimal point. To convert from a decimal to a percent, move the decimal point two places to the right. To convert from a percent to a decimal, move it two places to the left. Example: 0.23 = 23%; 5.34 = 534%; 0.007 = 0.7%; 700% = 7.00; 86% = 0.86; 0.15% = 0.0015.

It may be helpful to remember that the percentage number will always be larger than the equivalent decimal number.

> **Review Video: Converting Decimals to Fractions and Percentages**
> Visit mometrix.com/academy and enter code: 986765

Percentage Problems

A percentage problem can be presented three main ways:

- Find what percentage of some number another number is. Example: What percentage of 40 is 8?
- Find what number is some percentage of a given number. Example: What number is 20% of 40?
- Find what number another number is a given percentage of. Example: What number is 8 20% of?

The three components in all of these cases are the same: a *whole* (W), a *part* (P), and a *percentage* (%). These are related by the equation:

- $P = W \times \%$. This is the form of the equation you would use to solve problems of type (2). To solve types (1) and (3), you would use these two forms: % = P/W and W = P/%.

The thing that frequently makes percentage problems difficult is that they are often also word problems, so a large part of solving them is figuring out which quantities are what. Example: In a school cafeteria, 7 students choose pizza, 9 choose hamburgers, and 4 choose tacos. Find the percentage that chooses tacos. To find the whole, you must first add all of the parts: 7 + 9 + 4 = 20. The percentage can then be found by dividing the part by the whole (% = P/W): $\frac{4}{20} = \frac{20}{100} = 20\%$

Ratio and Proportion

A *ratio* is a comparison of two quantities in a particular order. Example: if there are 14 computers in a lab, and the class has 20 students, there is a student to computer ratio of 20 to 14, commonly written as 20:14.

A proportion is a relationship between two quantities that dictates how one changes when the other changes. A *direct proportion* describes a relationship in which a quantity increases by a set amount for every increase in the other quantity, or decreases by that same amount for every decrease in the other quantity. Example: For every 1 sheet cake, 18 people can be served cake. The number of sheet cakes, and the number of people that can be served from them is directly proportional.

Inverse proportion is a relationship in which an increase in one quantity is accompanied by a decrease in the other, or vice versa. Example: the time required for a car trip decreases as the speed increases, and increases as the speed decreases, so the time required is inversely proportional to the speed of the car.

> **Review Video: Ratios, Rates, and Proportions**
> Visit mometrix.com/academy and enter code: 653882

Distance, Rate, and Time

Distance is achieved by moving at a given rate for a given length of time. The formulas that relate the three are

- $d = rt$, $r = \frac{d}{t}$, and $t = \frac{d}{r}$, where d is the distance, r is the rate of change over time, and t is total time.

In these formulas, the units used to express the rate must be the same units used to express the distance and the time.

Exponents and Parentheses

An *exponent* is a superscript number placed next to another number at the top right. It indicates how many times the base number is to be multiplied by itself. Exponents provide a shorthand way to write what would be a longer mathematical expression. Example: $a^2 = a \times a$; $2^4 = 2 \times 2 \times 2 \times 2$. A number with an exponent of 2 is said to be "squared," while a number with an exponent of 3 is said to be "cubed." The value of a number raised to an exponent is called its *power*. So, 8^4 is read as "8 to the 4th power," or "8 raised to the power of 4." A *negative exponent* is the same as the reciprocal of a positive exponent. Example: $a^{-2} = 1/a^2$.

> **Review Video: Exponents**
> Visit mometrix.com/academy and enter code: 600998

Parentheses are used to designate which operations should be done first when there are multiple operations. Example: $4 - (2 + 1) = 1$; the parentheses tell us that we must add 2 and 1, and then subtract the sum from 4, rather than subtracting 2 from 4 and then adding 1 (this would give us an answer of 3).

> **Review Video: Parentheses**
> Visit mometrix.com/academy and enter code: 947743

Rational Expressions

Rational expression: A fraction with polynomials in both the numerator and the denominator; the value of the polynomial in the denominator cannot be equal to zero.

To add or subtract rational expressions, first find the common denominator, then rewrite each fraction as an equivalent fraction with the common denominator. Finally, add or subtract the numerators to get the numerator of the answer, and keep the common denominator as the denominator of the answer.

When multiplying rational expressions, factor each polynomial and cancel like factors (a factor which appears in both the numerator and the denominator). Then, multiply all remaining factors in the numerator to get the numerator of the product, and multiply the remaining factors in the denominator to get the denominator of the product. Remember – cancel entire factors, not individual terms.

To divide rational expressions, take the reciprocal of the divisor (the rational expression you are dividing by) and multiply by the dividend.

Order of Operations and PEMDAS

Order of Operations is a set of rules that dictates the order in which we must perform each operation in an expression so that we will evaluate it accurately. If we have an expression that includes multiple different operations, Order of Operations tells us which operations to do first. The most common mnemonic for Order of Operations is *PEMDAS*, or *Please Excuse My Dear Aunt Sally*. PEMDAS stands for *Parentheses, Exponents, Multiplication, Division, Addition, Subtraction*. It is important to understand that multiplication and division have equal precedence, as do addition and subtraction, so those pairs of operations are simply worked from left to right in order.

Example: Evaluate the expression $5 + 20 \div 4 \times (2 + 3)^2 - 6$ using the correct order of operations.

P: Perform the operations inside the parentheses, $(2 + 3) = 5$.

E: Simplify the exponents, $(5)^2 = 25$.

The equation now looks like this: $5 + 20 \div 4 \times 25 - 6$.

MD: Perform multiplication and division from left to right, $20 \div 4 = 5$; then $5 \times 25 = 125$.

The equation now looks like this: $5 + 125 - 6$.

AS: Perform addition and subtraction from left to right, $5 + 125 = 130$; then $130 - 6 = 124$.

Review Video: Order of Operations
Visit mometrix.com/academy and enter code: 259675

Systems of Equations

System of equations: A set of simultaneous equations that all use the same variables. A solution to a system of equations must be true for each equation in the system.

Consistent system: A system of equations that has at least one solution.

Inconsistent System: A system of equations that has no solution.

Systems of equations may be solved using one of four methods: substitution, elimination, transformation of the augmented matrix and using the trace feature on a graphing calculator.

Equations

Equation: States that two mathematical expressions are equal.

One Variable Linear Equation: An equation written in the form $ax + b = 0$, where $a \neq 0$.

Root: A solution to a one-variable equation; a number that makes the equation true when it is substituted for the variable.

Solution Set: The set of all solutions of an equation.

Empty Set: A situation in which an equation has no true solution.

Equivalent Equations: Equations with identical solution sets.

Solving One-Variable Linear Equations

Multiply all terms by the lowest common denominator to eliminate any fractions. Look for addition or subtraction to undo so you can isolate the variable on one side of the equal sign. Divide both sides by the coefficient of the variable. When you have a value for the variable, substitute this value into the original equation to make sure you have a true equation.

Different Forms of Linear Equations

Linear equations can be written in three different forms, each used for a different purpose. The standard form of linear equations is $Ax + By = C$, where A, B and C are integers and A is a positive number. Any equation can be written in this form. This is helpful in solving and graphing systems of equations, where you must compare two or more equations. You can graph an equation in standard form by finding the intercepts. Determine the x-intercept by substituting zero in for y and vice versa. Next, the slope-intercept form of an equation is $y = mx + b$, where m is equal to the slope and b is equal to the y-intercept. You can graph an equation in this form by first plotting the y-intercept. If b is -2, you know that the y-intercept is equal to $(0, -2)$. From this point you can use the slope to create an additional point. If the slope is 4, or $\frac{4}{1}$, you would rise, or move up 4 units and run, or move over 1 unit from the y-intercept. Finally, the point-slope form of an equation is useful when you know the slope and a point on the line. It is written as $y - y_1 = m(x - x_1)$, where m is equal to the slope and (x_1, y_1) is a point on the line. You can graph an equation in point-slope form by plotting the given point and using the slope to plot additional points on the line.

Quadratic Formula

The *quadratic formula* is used to solve quadratic equations when other methods are more difficult. To use the quadratic formula to solve a quadratic equation, begin by rewriting the equation in standard form $ax^2 + bx + c = 0$, where a, b, and c are coefficients. Once you have identified the values of the coefficients, substitute those values into the quadratic formula $= \frac{-b \pm \sqrt{b^2 - 4ac}}{2a}$.
Evaluate the equation and simplify the expression. Again, check each root by substituting into the original equation. In the quadratic formula, the portion of the formula under the radical $(b^2 - 4ac)$ is called the *discriminant*. If the discriminant is zero, there is only one root: zero. If the discriminant is positive, there are two different real roots. If the discriminant is negative, there are no real roots.

One-Variable Quadratic Equations

One-Variable Quadratic Equation: An equation that can be written in the form $x^2 + bx + c = 0$, where a, b, and c are the coefficients. This is also known as the standard form of an equation.

The solutions of quadratic equations are called *roots*. A quadratic equation may have one real root, two different real roots, or no real roots. The roots can be found using one of three methods: factoring, completing the square, or using the quadratic formula.

Any time you are solving a quadratic equation, never divide both sides by the variable or any expression containing the variable. You are at risk of dividing by zero if you do, thus getting an extraneous, or invalid, root.

Solving Quadratic Equations by Factoring

Begin by rewriting the equation in standard form, if necessary. Factor the side with the variable. Set each of the factors equal to zero and solve the resulting linear equations. Check your answers by substituting the roots you found into the original equation.

If, when writing the equation in standard form, you have an equation in the form $x^2 + c = 0$ or $x^2 - c = 0$, set $x^2 = -c$ or $x^2 = c$ and take the square root of c. If $c = 0$, the only real root is zero. If c is positive, there are two real roots—the positive and negative square root values. If c is negative, there are no real roots because you cannot take the square root of a negative number.

Completing the Square to Solve a Quadratic Equation

To complete the square, rewrite the equation so that all terms containing the variable are on the left side of the equal sign, and all the constants are on the right side of the equal sign. Make sure the coefficient of the squared term is 1. If there is a coefficient with the squared term, divide each term on both sides of the equal side by that number. Next, work with the coefficient of the single-variable term. Square half of this coefficient, and add that value to both sides. Now you can factor the left side (the side containing the variable) as the square of a binomial. $x^2 + 2ax + a^2 = C \Rightarrow (x + a)^2 = C$, where x is the variable, and a and C are constants. Take the square root of both sides and solve for the variable. Substitute the value of the variable in the original problem to check your work.

> **Review Video: Polynomials**
> Visit mometrix.com/academy and enter code: 305005

Solving Systems of Two Linear Equations by Substitution

To solve a system of linear equations by substitution, start with the easier equation and solve for one of the variables. Express this variable in terms of the other variable. Substitute this expression into the other equation, and solve for the other variable. The solution should be expressed in the form (x, y). Substitute the values into both of the original equations to check your answer.

> **Review Video: The Substitution Method**
> Visit mometrix.com/academy and enter code: 565151

<u>Example</u>

Solve the following system using substitution:

$$x + 6y = 15$$
$$3x - 12y = 18$$

Solve the first equation for x:

$$x = 15 - 6y$$

Substitute this value in place of x in the second equation, and solve for y:

$$3(15 - 6y) - 12y = 18$$
$$45 - 18y - 12y = 18$$
$$30y = 27$$
$$y = \frac{27}{30} = \frac{9}{10} = 0.9$$

Plug this value for y back into the first equation to solve for x:

$$x = 15 - 6(0.9) = 15 - 5.4 = 9.6$$

Solving Systems of Two Linear Equations by Elimination

To solve a system of equations using elimination, begin by rewriting both equations in standard form $Ax + By = C$. Check to see if the coefficients of one pair of like variables adds to zero. If not, multiply one or both of the equations by a non-zero number to make one set of like variables add to zero. Add the two equations to solve for one of the variables. Substitute back into either original equation to solve for the other variable. Check your work by substituting into the other equation.

> **Review Video: The Elimination Method**
> Visit mometrix.com/academy and enter code: 449121

<u>Example</u>
Solve the system using elimination:

$$x + 6y = 15$$

$$3x - 12y = 18$$

If we multiply the first equation by 2, we can eliminate the y terms:

$$2x + 12y = 30$$

$$3x - 12y = 18$$

Add the equations together and solve for x:

$$5x = 48$$

$$x = \frac{48}{5} = 9.6$$

Plug value for x back into either of the original equations and solve for y:

$$9.6 + 6y = 15$$

$$y = \frac{15 - 9.6}{6} = 0.9$$

Monomials and Polynomials

Monomial: A single constant, variable, or product of constants and variables, such as 2, x, $2x$, or $\frac{2}{x}$. There will never be addition or subtraction symbols in a monomial. Like monomials have like variables, but they may have different coefficients.

Polynomial: An algebraic expression which uses addition and subtraction to combine two or more monomials. Two terms make a binomial; three terms make a trinomial.

> **Review Video: Polynomials**
> Visit mometrix.com/academy and enter code: 305005

Degree of a Monomial: The sum of the exponents of the variables.

Degree of a Polynomial: The highest degree of any individual term.

Dividing Polynomials

Set up a long division problem, dividing a polynomial by either a monomial or another polynomial of equal or lesser degree. When dividing by a monomial, divide each term of the polynomial by the monomial. When dividing a polynomial by a polynomial, begin by arranging the terms of each polynomial in order of one variable. You may arrange in ascending or descending order, but be consistent with both polynomials. To get the first term of the quotient, divide the first term of the dividend by the first term of the divisor. Multiply the first term of the quotient by the entire divisor and subtract that product from the dividend. Repeat for the second and successive terms until you either get a remainder of zero or a remainder whose degree is less than the degree of the divisor. If the quotient has a remainder, write the answer as a mixed expression in the form quotient + $\frac{\text{remainder}}{\text{divisor}}$.

Factoring a Polynomial

First, check for a common monomial factor. When the greatest common monomial factor has been factored out, look for patterns of special products: differences of two squares, the sum or difference of two cubes for binomial factors, or perfect trinomial squares for trinomial factors. If the factor is a trinomial but not a perfect trinomial square, look for a factorable form, such as

$$x^2 + (a + b)x + ab = (x + a)(x + b) \text{ or}$$

$$(ac)x^2 + (ad + bc)x + bd = (ax + b)(cx + d).$$

For factors with four terms, look for groups to factor. Once you have found the factors, write the original polynomial as the product of all the factors. Make sure all of the polynomial factors are prime. Monomial factors may be prime or composite. Check your work by multiplying the factors to make sure you get the original polynomial.

Mean and Weighted Mean

Mean: The same thing as the arithmetic average. Use the formula

$$\text{mean} = \frac{\text{sum of all numbers in the set}}{\text{quantity of numbers in the set}}$$

> **Review Video: Mean, Median, and Mode**
> Visit mometrix.com/academy and enter code: 286207

Weighted mean: Weighted values, such as $w_1, w_2, w_3, \ldots$ are assigned to each member of the set $x_1, x_2, x_3, \ldots$. Use the formula

$$\text{weighted mean} = \frac{w_1 x_1 + w_2 x_2 + w_3 x_3 + \cdots + w_n x_n}{w_1 + w_2 + w_3 + \cdots + w_n}$$

Make sure there is one weighted value for each member of the set.

Perfect Trinomial Squares, the Difference between Two Squares, the Sum and Difference of Two Cubes, and Perfect Cubes

Perfect trinomial squares: $x^2 + 2xy + y^2 = (x + y)^2$ or $x^2 - 2xy + y^2 = (x - y)^2$

Difference between two squares: $x^2 - y^2 = (x + y)(x - y)$

Sum of two cubes: $x^3 + y^3 = (x + y)(x^2 - xy + y^2)$

Note: the second factor is **not** the same as a perfect trinomial square, so do not try to factor it further.

Difference between two cubes: $x^3 - y^3 = (x - y)(x^2 + xy + y^2)$ Again, the second factor is **not** the same as a perfect trinomial square.

Perfect cubes: $x^3 + 3x^2y + 3xy^2 + y^3 = (x + y)^3$ and

$$x^3 - 3x^2y + 3xy^2 - y^3 = (x - y)^3$$

Multiplying Two Binomials

F = **F**irst: Multiply the first term of each binomial
O = **O**uter: Multiply the outer terms of the binomials
I = **I**nner: Multiply the inner terms of the binomials
L = **L**ast: Multiply the last term of each binomial

$$(Ax + By)(Cx + Dy) = ACx^2 + ADxy + BCxy + BDy^2$$

Slope, Horizontal, Vertical, Parallel, Perpendicular

Slope: A ratio of the change in height to the change in horizontal distance. On a graph with two points (x_1, y_1) and (x_2, y_2), the slope is represented by the formula $m = \frac{y_2 - y_1}{x_2 - x_1}$; $x_1 \neq x_2$. If the value of the slope is positive, the line slopes upward from left to right. If the value of the slope is negative, the line slopes downward from left to right. If the y-coordinates are the same for both points, the slope is 0 and the line is a horizontal line. If the x-coordinates are the same for both points, there is no slope and the line is a vertical line.

Horizontal: Having a slope of zero. On a graph, a line that is the same distance from the x-axis at all points.

Vertical: Having no slope. On a graph, a line that is the same distance from the y-axis at all points.

Parallel: Lines that have equal slopes.

Perpendicular: Lines that have slopes that are negative reciprocals of each other: $\frac{a}{b}$ and $\frac{-b}{a}$.

Statistics

Statistics may be descriptive or inferential, in nature. Descriptive statistics does not involve inferences and includes measures of center and spread, frequencies, and percentages. Inferential statistics involves the process of making inferences about large populations based on the characteristics of random samples from the population. This field of statistics is useful because, for large populations, it may be impractical or impossible to measure the characteristics of each element of the population

- 44 -

and determine the distributions of various properties exactly. By applying statistical methods, it's possible to make reasonable inferences about the distributions of a variable, or variables, throughout large populations by only examining a relatively small part of it. Of course, it's important that this be a "representative sample", that is, one in which the distribution of the variables of interest is similar to its distribution in the entire population. For this reason, it's desirable to create random samples, rather than choosing a set of similar samples.

Conditional Probability

Given two events A and B, the *conditional probability* $P(A|B)$ is the probability that event B will occur, *given that event A has occurred*. For instance, suppose you have a jar containing two red marbles and two blue marbles, and you draw two marbles at random. Note. The first drawn marble is not replaced. Consider event A being the event that the first marble drawn is red, and event B being the event that the *second* marble drawn is blue. With no conditions set, both $P(A)$ and $P(B)$ are equal to $\frac{1}{2}$. However, if we know that the first marble drawn was red—that is, that event A occurred—then that leaves one red marble and two blue marbles in the jar. In that case, the probability that the second marble is blue *given that the first marble was red*—that is, $P(A|B)$—is equal to $\frac{2}{3}$.

Calculating the Conditional Probability $P(A|B)$ in Terms of the Probabilities of Events A and B and their Union and/or Intersection

The conditional probability $P(A|B)$ is the probability that event B will occur given that event A occurs. This cannot be calculated simply from $P(A)$ and $P(B)$; these probabilities alone do not give sufficient information to determine the conditional probability. It can, however, be determined given also $P(A \cap B)$, the probability that events A and B both occur. Specifically, $P(A|B) = \frac{P(A \cap B)}{P(B)}$.

For instance, suppose you have a jar containing two red marbles and two blue marbles, and you draw two marbles at random. Consider event A being the event that the first marble drawn is red, and event B being the event that the *second* marble drawn is blue. $P(A)$ is $\frac{1}{2}$, and $P(A \cap B)$ is $\frac{1}{3}$. (The latter may not be obvious, but may be determined by finding the product of $\frac{1}{2}$ and $\frac{2}{3}$.) Therefore $P(A|B) = \frac{1/3}{1/2} = \frac{2}{3}$.

Verbal

Expository Passage

An **expository** passage aims to inform and enlighten readers. The passage is nonfiction and usually centers around a simple, easily defined topic. Since the goal of exposition is to teach, such a passage should be as clear as possible. Often, an expository passage contains helpful organizing words, like *first*, *next*, *for example*, and *therefore*. These words keep the reader oriented in the text. Although expository passages do not need to feature colorful language and artful writing, they are often more effective with these features. For a reader, the challenge of expository passages is to maintain steady attention. Expository passages are not always about subjects that will naturally interest a reader, and the writer is often more concerned with clarity and comprehensibility than with engaging the reader. By reading actively, you will ensure a good habit of focus when reading an expository passage.

> **Review Video: Expository Passages**
> Visit mometrix.com/academy and enter code: 256515

Technical Passage

A **technical** passage is written to describe a complex object or process. Technical writing is common in medical and technological fields, in which complex ideas of mathematics, science, and engineering need to be explained simply and clearly. To ease comprehension, a technical passage usually proceeds in a very logical order. Technical passages often have clear headings and subheadings, which are used to keep the reader oriented in the text. Additionally, you will find that these passages divide sections up with numbers or letters. Many technical passages look more like an outline than a piece of prose. The amount of jargon or difficult vocabulary will vary in a technical passage depending on the intended audience. As much as possible, technical passages try to avoid language that the reader will have to research in order to understand the message, yet readers will find that jargon cannot always be avoided.

> **Review Video: A Technical Passage**
> Visit mometrix.com/academy and enter code: 198064

Informative Text

An **informative text** is written to educate and enlighten readers. Informative texts are almost always nonfiction and are rarely structured as a story. The intention of an informative text is to deliver information in the most comprehensible way. So, look for the structure of the text to be very clear.

In an informative text, the thesis statement (i.e., a stance or assertion on the topic of a text that is supported by evidence) is one or two sentences that normally appears at end of the first paragraph. The author may use some colorful language, but he or she is likely to put more emphasis on clarity and precision. Informative essays do not typically appeal to the emotions. They often contain facts and figures and rarely include the opinion of the author; however, readers should remain aware of the possibility for a bias as those facts are presented. Sometimes a persuasive essay can resemble an informative essay, especially if the author maintains an even tone and presents his or her views as if they were established fact.

Descriptive Text

In a sense, almost all writing is descriptive, insofar as an author seeks to describe events, ideas, or people to the reader. Some texts, however, are primarily concerned with **description**. A descriptive text focuses on a particular subject and attempts to depict the subject in a way that will be clear to readers. Descriptive texts contain many adjectives and adverbs (i.e., words that give shades of meaning and create a more detailed mental picture for the reader). A descriptive text fails when it is unclear to the reader. A descriptive text will certainly be informative, and the passage may be persuasive and entertaining as well.

Identifying an Author's Purpose

Usually, identifying the **purpose** of an author is easier than identifying his or her position. In most cases, the author has no interest in hiding his or her purpose. A text that is meant to entertain, for instance, should be written to please the reader. Most narratives, or stories, are written to entertain, though they may also inform or persuade. Informative texts are easy to identify, while the most difficult purpose of a text to identify is persuasion because the author has an interest in making this purpose hard to detect. When a reader discovers that the author is trying to persuade, he or she should be skeptical of the argument. For this reason persuasive texts often try to establish an entertaining tone and hope to amuse the reader into agreement. On the other hand, an informative tone may be implemented to create an appearance of authority and objectivity.

An author's purpose is evident often in the organization of the text (e.g., section headings in bold font points to an informative text). However, you may not have such organization available to you in your exam. Instead, if the author makes his or her main idea clear from the beginning, then the likely purpose of the text is to inform. If the author begins by making a claim and provides various arguments to support that claim, then the purpose is probably to persuade. If the author tells a story or seems to want the attention of the reader more than to push a particular point or deliver information, then his or her purpose is most likely to entertain. As a reader, you must judge authors on how well they accomplish their purpose. In other words, you need to consider the type of passage (e.g., technical, persuasive, etc.) that the author has written and whether the author has followed the requirements of the passage type.

Comparing and Contrasting

Authors will use different stylistic and writing devices to make their meaning clear for readers. One of those devices is comparison and contrast. As mentioned previously, when an author describes the ways in which two things are alike, he or she is **comparing** them. When the author describes the ways in which two things are different, he or she is **contrasting** them. The "compare and contrast" essay is one of the most common forms in nonfiction. These passages are often signaled with certain words: a comparison may have indicating terms such as *both, same, like, too,* and *as well*; while a contrast may have terms like *but, however, on the other hand, instead,* and *yet*. Of course, comparisons and contrasts may be implicit without using any such signaling language. A single sentence may both compare and contrast. Consider the sentence *Brian and Sheila love ice cream, but Brian prefers vanilla and Sheila prefers strawberry*. In one sentence, the author has described both a similarity (love of ice cream) and a difference (favorite flavor).

Review Video: <u>Rhetorical Strategy of Comparing and Contrasting</u>
Visit mometrix.com/academy and enter code: 587299

Cause and Effect

One of the most common text structures is **cause and effect**. A cause is an act or event that makes something happen, and an effect is the thing that happens as a result of the cause. A cause-and-effect relationship is not always explicit, but there are some terms in English that signal causes, such as *since, because,* and *due to*. Furthermore, terms that signal effects include *consequently, therefore, this lead(s) to*. As an example, consider the sentence *Because the sky was clear, Ron did not bring an umbrella*. The cause is the clear sky, and the effect is that Ron did not bring an umbrella. However, readers may find that sometimes the cause-and-effect relationship will not be clearly noted. For instance, the sentence *He was late and missed the meeting* does not contain any signaling words, but the sentence still contains a cause (he was late) and an effect (he missed the meeting). Be aware of the possibility for a single cause to have multiple effects (e.g., *Single cause*: Because you left your homework on the table, your dog engulfs the assignment. *Multiple effects*: As a result, you receive a failing grade; your parents do not allow you to visit your friends; you miss out on the new movie and holding the hand of a potential significant other).

Also, the possibility of a single effect to have multiple causes (e.g.. *Single effect*: Alan has a fever. *Multiple causes*: An unexpected cold front came through the area, and Alan forgot to take his multi-vitamin to avoid being sick.)

Additionally, an effect can in turn be the cause of another effect, in what is known as a cause-and-effect chain. (e.g., As a result of her disdain for procrastination, Lynn prepared for her exam. This led to her passing her test with high marks. Hence, her resume was accepted and her application was approved.)

Review Video: <u>Rhetorical Strategy of Cause-and-Effect Analysis</u>
Visit mometrix.com/academy and enter code: 725944

Point of View

The **point of view** of a text is the perspective from which a passage is told. An author will always have a point of view about a story before he or she draws up a plot line. The author will know what events they want to take place, how they want the characters to interact, and how they want the story to resolve. An author will also have an opinion on the topic or series of events which is presented in the story that is based on their prior experience and beliefs.

The two main points of view that authors use--especially in a work of fiction--are first person and third person. If the narrator of the story is also the main character, or *protagonist*, the text is written in first-person point of view. In first person, the author writes from the perspective of *I*. Third-person point of view is probably the most common that authors use in their passages. Using third person, authors refer to each character by using *he* or *she.* In third-person omniscient, the narrator is not a character in the story and tells the story of all of the characters at the same time.

> **Review Video: Point of View**
> Visit mometrix.com/academy and enter code: 383336

Topics and Main Ideas

One of the most important skills in reading comprehension is the identification of **topics** and **main ideas.** There is a subtle difference between these two features. The topic is the subject of a text (i.e., what the text is all about). The main idea, on the other hand, is the most important point being made by the author. The topic is usually expressed in a few words at the most while the main idea often needs a full sentence to be completely defined. As an example, a short passage might have the topic of penguins and the main idea could be written as *Penguins are different from other birds in many ways.* In most nonfiction writing, the topic and the main idea will be stated directly and often appear in a sentence at the very beginning or end of the text. When being tested on an understanding of the author's topic, you may be able to quickly skim the passage for the general idea, by reading only the first sentence of each paragraph. A body paragraph's first sentence is often--but not always--the main topic sentence which gives you a summary of the content in the paragraph. However, there are cases in which the reader must figure out an unstated topic or main idea. In these instances, you must read every sentence of the text and try to come up with an overarching idea that is supported by each of those sentences.

> **Review Video: Topics and Main Ideas**
>
> Visit mometrix.com/academy and enter code: 407801

Note: A thesis statement should not be confused with the main idea of the passage. While the main idea gives a brief, general summary of a text, the thesis statement provides a specific perspective on an issue that the author supports with evidence.

Supporting Details

Supporting details provide evidence and backing for the main point. In order to show that a main idea is correct, or valid, authors add details that prove their point. All texts contain details, but they are only classified as supporting details when they serve to reinforce some larger point. Supporting details are most commonly found in informative and persuasive texts. In some cases, they will be clearly indicated with terms like *for example* or *for instance*, or they will be enumerated with terms like *first, second,* and *last.* However, you need to be prepared for texts that do not contain those indicators. As a reader, you should consider whether the author's supporting details really back up his or her main point. Supporting details can be factual and correct, yet they may not be relevant to the author's point. Conversely, supporting details can seem pertinent, but they can be ineffective because they are based on opinion or assertions that cannot be proven.

An example of a main idea is: *Giraffes live in the Serengeti of Africa.* A supporting detail about giraffes could be: *A giraffe in this region benefits from a long neck by reaching twigs and leaves on tall trees.* The main idea gives the general idea that the text is about giraffes. The supporting detail gives a specific fact about how the giraffes eat.

Review Video: Supporting Details
Visit mometrix.com/academy and enter code: 396297

Identifying the Logical Conclusion

When reading informational texts, there is importance in understanding the logical conclusion of the author's ideas. **Identifying a logical conclusion** can help you determine whether you agree with the writer or not. Coming to this conclusion is much like making an inference: the approach requires you to combine the information given by the text with what you already know in order to make a logical conclusion. If the author intended the reader to draw a certain conclusion, then you can expect the author's argumentation and detail to be leading in that direction. One way to approach the task of drawing conclusions is to make brief notes of all the points made by the author. When the notes are arranged on paper, they may clarify the logical conclusion. Another way to approach conclusions is to consider whether the reasoning of the author raises any pertinent questions. Sometimes you will be able to draw several conclusions from a passage. On occasion these will be conclusions that were never imagined by the author. Therefore, be aware that these conclusions must be supported directly by the text.

Review Video: Identifying Logical Conclusions
Visit mometrix.com/academy and enter code: 281653

Text Evidence

The term **text evidence** refers to information that supports a main point or minor points and can help lead the reader to a conclusion. Information used as text evidence is precise, descriptive, and factual. A main point is often followed by supporting details that provide evidence to back-up a claim. For example, a passage may include the claim that winter occurs during opposite months in the Northern and Southern hemispheres. Text evidence based on this claim may include countries where winter occurs in opposite months along with reasons that winter occurs at different times of the year in separate hemispheres (due to the tilt of the Earth as it rotates around the sun).

Review Video: Text Evidence
Visit mometrix.com/academy and enter code: 486236

Directly Stated Information

A reader should always be drawing conclusions from the text. Sometimes conclusions are implied from written information, and other times the information is **stated directly** within the passage. One should always aim to draw conclusions from information stated within a passage, rather than to draw them from mere implications.

At times an author may provide some information and then describe a counterargument. Readers should be alert for direct statements that are subsequently rejected or weakened by the author. Furthermore, you should always read through the entire passage before drawing conclusions. Many readers are trained to expect the author's conclusions at either the beginning or the end of the passage, but many texts do not adhere to this format.

Review Video: Conclusions that are Stated Directly
Visit mometrix.com/academy and enter code: 851825

Implications

Drawing conclusions from information implied within a passage requires confidence on the part of the reader. **Implications** are things that the author does not state directly, but readers can assume based on what the author does say. Consider the following passage: *I stepped outside and opened my umbrella. By the time I got to work, the cuffs of my pants were soaked.* The author never states that it is raining, but this fact is clearly implied. Conclusions based on implication must be well supported by the text. In order to draw a solid conclusion, readers should have multiple pieces of evidence. If readers have only one piece, they must be assured that there is no other possible explanation than their conclusion. A good reader will be able to draw many conclusions from information implied by the text which will be a great help in the exam.

Summarizing

A helpful tool is the ability to **summarize** the information that you have read in a paragraph or passage format. This process is similar to creating an effective outline. First, a summary should accurately define the main idea of the passage though the summary does not need to explain this main idea in exhaustive detail. The summary should continue by laying out the most important supporting details or arguments from the passage. All of the significant supporting details should be included, and none of the details included should be irrelevant or insignificant. Also, the summary should accurately report all of these details. Too often, the desire for brevity in a summary leads to the sacrifice of clarity or accuracy. Summaries are often difficult to read because they omit all of the graceful language, digressions, and asides that distinguish great writing. However, an effective summary, it should contain much the same message as the original text.

Review Video: Summarizing Text
Visit mometrix.com/academy and enter code: 172903

Paraphrasing

Paraphrasing is another method that the reader can use to aid in comprehension. When paraphrasing, one puts what they have read into their words by rephrasing what the author has written, or one "translates" all of what the author shared into their words by including as many details as they can.

Predictions

When reading a good passage, readers are moved to engage actively in the text. One part of being an active reader involves making predictions. A **prediction** is a guess about what will happen next. Readers constantly make predictions based on what they have read and what they already know. Consider the following sentence: *Staring at the computer screen in shock, Kim blindly reached over for the brimming glass of water on the shelf to her side.* The sentence suggests that Kim is agitated, and that she is not looking at the glass that she is going to pick up. So, a reader might predict that Kim is going to knock over the glass. Of course, not every prediction will be accurate: perhaps Kim will pick the glass up cleanly. Nevertheless, the author has certainly created the expectation that the water might be spilled. Predictions are always subject to revision as the reader acquires more information.

> **Review Video: Predictions**
> Visit mometrix.com/academy and enter code: 437248

Inference

Readers are often required to understand a text that claims and suggests ideas without stating them directly. An **inference** is a piece of information that is implied but not written outright by the author. For instance, consider the following sentence: *After the final out of the inning, the fans were filled with joy and rushed the field.* From this sentence, a reader can infer that the fans were watching a baseball game and their team won the game. Readers should take great care to avoid using information beyond the provided passage before making inferences. As you practice drawing inferences, you will find that they require concentration and attention.

> **Review Video: Inference**
> Visit mometrix.com/academy and enter code: 379203

Sequence

Readers must be able to identify a text's **sequence**, or the order in which things happen. Often, when the sequence is very important to the author, the text is indicated with signal words like *first, then, next,* and *last.* However, a sequence can be merely implied and must be noted by the reader. Consider the sentence *He walked through the garden and gave water and fertilizer to the plants.* Clearly, the man did not walk through the garden before he collected water and fertilizer for the plants, so the implied sequence is that he first collected water, then he collected fertilizer, next he walked through the garden, and last he gave water or fertilizer as necessary to the plants. Texts do not always proceed in an orderly sequence from first to last. Sometimes they begin at the end and start over at the beginning. As a reader, you can enhance your understanding of the passage by taking brief notes to clarify the sequence.

> **Review Video: Sequence**
> Visit mometrix.com/academy and enter code: 489027

Drawing Conclusions

In addition to inference and prediction, readers must often **draw conclusions** about the information they have read. When asked for a *conclusion* that may be drawn, look for critical "hedge" phrases, such as *likely, may, can, will often,* among many others. When you are being tested on this knowledge, remember the question that writers insert into these hedge phrases to cover every possibility. Often an answer will be wrong simply because there is no room for exception. Extreme positive or negative answers (such as always or never) are usually not correct. The reader should not use any outside knowledge that is not gathered from the passage to answer the related questions. Correct answers can be derived straight from the passage.

> **Review Video: Identifying Logical Conclusions**
> Visit mometrix.com/academy and enter code: 281653

Fact and Opinion

Readers must always be conscious of the distinction between fact and opinion. A **fact** can be subjected to analysis and can be either proved or disproved. An **opinion**, on the other hand, is the author's personal thoughts or feelings which may not be alterable by research or evidence. If the author writes that the distance from New York to Boston is about two hundred miles, then he or she is stating a fact. If an author writes that New York is too crowded, then he or she is giving an opinion because there is no objective standard for overpopulation. An opinion may be indicated by words like *believe*, *think*, or *feel*. Readers must be aware that an opinion may be supported by facts. For instance, the author might give the population density of New York as a reason for an overcrowded population. An opinion supported by fact tends to be more convincing. On the other hand, when authors support their opinions with other opinions, readers should not be persuaded by the argument to any degree. When you have an argumentative passage, you need to be sure that facts are presented to the reader from reliable sources. An opinion is what the author thinks about a given topic. An opinion is not common knowledge or proven by expert sources, instead the information is the personal beliefs and thoughts of the author. To distinguish between fact and opinion, a reader needs to consider the type of source that is presenting information, the information that backs-up a claim, and the author's motivation to have a certain point-of-view on a given topic. For example, if a panel of scientists has conducted multiple studies on the effectiveness of taking a certain vitamin, then the results are more likely to be factual than a company that is selling a vitamin and claims that taking the vitamin can produce positive effects. The company is motivated to sell their product, and the scientists are using the scientific method to prove a theory. Remember: if you find sentences that contain phrases such as "I think...", then the statement is an opinion.

> **Review Video: Fact or Opinion**
> Visit mometrix.com/academy and enter code: 870899

Biases and Stereotypes

In their attempts to persuade, writers often make mistakes in their thinking patterns and writing choices. These patterns and choices are important to understand so you can make an informed decision. Every author has a point-of-view, but authors demonstrate a bias when they ignore reasonable counterarguments or distort opposing viewpoints. A bias is evident whenever the author is unfair or inaccurate in his or her presentation. Bias may be intentional or unintentional, and readers should be skeptical of the author's argument. Remember that a biased author may still be correct; however, the author will be correct in spite of his or her bias, not because of the bias. A **stereotype** is like a bias, yet a stereotype is applied specifically to a group or place. Stereotyping is considered to be particularly abhorrent because the practice promotes negative generalizations about people. Readers should be very cautious of authors who stereotype in their writing. These faulty assumptions typically reveal the author's ignorance and lack of curiosity.

> **Review Video: Bias and Stereotype**
> Visit mometrix.com/academy and enter code: 644829

Nouns, Common Nouns, and Proper Nouns

When you talk about a person, place, thing, or idea, you are talking about nouns. The two main types of nouns are common and proper nouns. Also, nouns can be abstract (i.e., general) or concrete (i.e., specific).

Common nouns are the class or group of people, places, and things (Note: do not capitalize common nouns). Examples of common nouns:

- *People*: boy, girl, worker, manager
- *Places*: school, bank, library, home
- *Things*: dog, cat, truck, car

Proper nouns are the names of a specific person, place, or thing. (Note: Capitalize all proper nouns) Examples of proper nouns:

- *People*: Abraham Lincoln, George Washington, Martin Luther King, Jr.
- *Places*: Los Angeles, California / New York / Asia
- *Things*: Statue of Liberty, Earth*, Lincoln Memorial

*Note: When you talk about the planet that we live on, you capitalize *Earth*. When you mean the dirt, rocks, or land, you lowercase *earth*.

> **Review Video: What is a Noun?**
> Visit mometrix.com/academy and enter code: 344028

General Nouns, Specific Nouns, and Collective Nouns

General nouns are the names of conditions or ideas. **Specific nouns** name people, places, and things that are understood by using your senses.

General nouns:

- *Condition*: beauty, strength
- *Idea*: truth, peace

Specific nouns:

- *People*: baby, friend, father
- *Places*: town, park, city hall
- *Things*: rainbow, cough, apple, silk, gasoline

Collective nouns are the names for a person, place, or thing that may act as a whole. The following are examples of collective nouns: *class, company, dozen, group, herd, team,* and *public.*

Pronouns and Personal Pronouns

Pronouns are words that are used to stand in for a noun. A pronoun may be grouped as personal, intensive, relative, interrogative, demonstrative, indefinite, and reciprocal.

> **Review Video: Pronouns**
> Visit mometrix.com/academy and enter code: 119325

Personal: Nominative is the case for nouns and pronouns that are the subject of a sentence. Objective is the case for nouns and pronouns that are an object in a sentence. Possessive is the case for nouns and pronouns that show possession or ownership.

Singular

	Nominative	Objective	Possessive
1st Person	I	me	my, mine
2nd Person	you	you	your, yours
3rd Person	he, she, it	him, her, it	his, her, hers, its

Plural

	Nominative	Objective	Possessive
1st Person	we	us	our, ours
2nd Person	you	you	your, yours
3rd Person	they	them	their, theirs

Intensive, relative, interrogative, demonstrative, indefinite, and reciprocal pronouns

Intensive: I myself, you yourself, he himself, she herself, the (thing) itself, we ourselves, you yourselves, they themselves

Relative: which, who, whom, whose

Interrogative: what, which, who, whom, whose

Demonstrative: this, that, these, those

Indefinite: all, any, each, everyone, either/neither, one, some, several

Reciprocal: each other, one another

Verbs and Transitive and Intransitive Verbs

If you want to write a sentence, then you need a verb in your sentence. Without a verb, you have no sentence. The verb of a sentence explains action or being. In other words, the verb shows the subject's movement or the movement that has been done to the subject.

A transitive verb is a verb whose action (e.g., drive, run, jump) points to a receiver (e.g., car, dog, kangaroo). Intransitive verbs do not point to a receiver of an action. In other words, the action of the verb does not point to a subject or object.

Transitive: He plays the piano. | The piano was played by him.

Intransitive: He plays. | John writes well.

A dictionary will let you know whether a verb is transitive or intransitive. Some verbs can be transitive and intransitive.

- 55 -

Action and Linking Verbs

An action verb is a verb that shows what the subject is doing in a sentence. In other words, an action verb shows action. A sentence can be complete with one word: an action verb. Linking verbs are intransitive verbs that show a condition.

Linking verbs link the subject of a sentence to a noun or pronoun, or they link a subject with an adjective. You always need a verb if you want a complete sentence. However, linking verbs are not able to complete a sentence. Common linking verbs include *appear, be, become, feel, grow, look, seem, smell, sound,* and *taste.* However, any verb that shows a condition and has a noun, pronoun, or adjective that describes the subject of a sentence is a linking verb.

Action: He sings. | Run! | Go! | I talk with him every day. | She reads.

Linking:

- Incorrect: I am.
- Correct: I am John. | I smell roses. | I feel tired.

Some verbs are followed by words that look like prepositions, but they are a part of the verb and a part of the verb's meaning. These are known as phrasal verbs and examples include *call off, look up,* and *drop off.*

> **Review Video:** Action Verbs and Linking Verbs
> Visit mometrix.com/academy and enter code: 743142

Active and Passive Voice in Verbs

Transitive verbs come in active or passive voice. If the subject does an action or receives the action of the verb, then you will know whether a verb is active or passive. When the subject of the sentence is doing the action, the verb is active voice. When the subject receives the action, the verb is passive voice.

Active: Jon drew the picture. (The subject *Jon* is doing the action of *drawing a picture.*)

Passive: The picture is drawn by Jon. (The subject *picture* is receiving the action from Jon.)

Verb Tenses

A verb tense shows the different form of a verb to point to the time of an action. The present and past tense are shown by changing the verb's form. An action in the present *I talk* can change form for the past: *I talked.* However, for the other tenses, an auxiliary (i.e., helping) verb is needed to show the change in form. These helping verbs include *am, are, is | have, has, had | was, were, will.*

Present: I talk	Present perfect: I have talked
Past: I talked	Past perfect: I had talked
Future: I will talk	Future perfect: I will have talked

Present, Past, and Future Verb Tenses

Present: The action happens at the current time.

Example: He walks to the store every morning.

To show that something is happening right now, use the progressive present tense: I am walking.

Past: The action happened in the past.

Example: He walked to the store an hour ago.

Future: The action is going to happen later.

Example: I will walk to the store tomorrow.

> **Review Video: Verb Tenses**
> Visit mometrix.com/academy and enter code: 809578

Present Perfect, Past Perfect, and Future Perfect Verb Tenses

Present perfect: The action started in the past and continues into the present.

Example: I *have walked* to the store three times today.

Past perfect: The second action happened in the past. The first action came before the second.

Example: Before I walked to the store (Action 2), I *had walked* to the library (Action 1).

Future perfect: An action that uses the past and the future. In other words, the action is complete before a future moment. Example: When she comes for the supplies (future moment), I *will have walked* to the store (action completed in the past).

> **Review Video: Present Perfect, Past Perfect, and Future Perfect Verb Tenses**
> Visit mometrix.com/academy and enter code: 269472

Verb Conjugation

When you need to change the form of a verb, you are conjugating a verb. The key parts of a verb are first person singular, present tense (dream); first person singular, past tense (dreamed); and the past participle (dreamed). Note: the past participle needs a helping verb to make a verb tense. For example, I *have dreamed* of this day. | I *am dreaming* of this day.

Present Tense: Active Voice

	Singular	Plural
1st Person	I dream	We dream
2nd Person	You dream	You dream
3rd Person	He, she, it dreams	They dream

Indicative, Imperative, and Subjunctive Mood in Verbs

There are three moods in English: the indicative, the imperative, and the subjunctive.

The **indicative mood** is used for facts, opinions, and questions.

Fact: You can do this.

Opinion: I think that you can do this.

Question: Do you know that you can do this?

The **imperative** is used for orders or requests.

Order: You are going to do this!

Request: Will you do this for me?

The **subjunctive mood** is for wishes and statements that go against fact.

Wish: I wish that I were going to do this.

Statement against fact: If I were you, I would do this. (This goes against fact because I am not you. You have the chance to do this, and I do not have the chance.)

Adjectives and Articles

An adjective is a word that is used to modify a noun or pronoun. An adjective answers a question: *Which one?*, *What kind of?*, or *How many?*. Usually, adjectives come before the words that they modify.

Which one?: The *third* suit is my favorite.

What kind?: The *navy blue* suit is my favorite.

How many?: Can I look over the *four* neckties for the suit?

Articles are adjectives that are used to mark nouns. There are only three: the definite (i.e., limited or fixed amount) article *the*, and the indefinite (i.e., no limit or fixed amount) articles *a* and *an*. Note: *An* comes before words that start with a vowel sound (i.e., vowels include *a, e, i, o, u,* and *y*). For example, Are you going to get an **u**mbrella?

Definite: I lost *the* bottle that belongs to me.

Indefinite: Does anyone have *a* bottle to share?

> **Review Video: What is an Adjective?**
> Visit mometrix.com/academy and enter code: 470154

Comparison with Adjectives

Some adjectives are relative and other adjectives are absolute. Adjectives that are relative can show the comparison between things. Adjectives that are absolute can show comparison. However, they show comparison in a different way. Let's say that you are reading two books. You think that one book is perfect, and the other book is not exactly perfect. It is not possible for the book to be more perfect than the other. Either you think that the book is perfect, or you think that the book is not perfect.

The adjectives that are relative will show the different degrees of something or someone to something else or someone else. The three degrees of adjectives include positive, comparative, and superlative.

The positive degree is the normal form of an adjective.

Example: This work is *difficult*. | She is *smart*.

The comparative degree compares one person or thing to another person or thing.

Example: This work is *more difficult* than your work. | She is *smarter* than me.

The superlative degree compares more than two people or things.

Example: This is the *most difficult* work of my life. | She is the *smartest* lady in school.

> **Review Video:** **Unequal Comparison Adjectives**
> Visit mometrix.com/academy and enter code: 751059

Adverbs

An adverb is a word that is used to modify a verb, adjective, or another adverb. Usually, adverbs answer one of these questions: *When?*, *Where?*, *How?*, and *Why?* . The negatives *not* and *never* are known as adverbs. Adverbs that modify adjectives or other adverbs strengthen or weaken the words that they modify.

Examples:

- He walks quickly through the crowd.
- The water flows smoothly on the rocks.

Note: While many adverbs end in *-ly*, you need to remember that not all adverbs end in *-ly*. Also, some words that end in *-ly* are adjectives, not adverbs. Some examples include: *early, friendly, holy, lonely, silly*, and *ugly*. To know if a word that ends in *-ly* is an adjective or adverb, you need to check your dictionary.

Examples:

- He is *never* angry.
- You talk *too* loud.

> **Review Video:** **Adverbs**
> Visit mometrix.com/academy and enter code: 713951

Comparison with Adverbs

The rules for comparing adverbs are the same as the rules for adjectives.

The positive degree is the standard form of an adverb.

Example: He arrives soon. | She speaks softly to her friends.

The comparative degree compares one person or thing to another person or thing.

Example: He arrives sooner than Sarah. | She speaks more softly than him.

The superlative degree compares more than two people or things.

Example: He arrives soonest of the group. | She speaks most softly of any of her friends.

Review Video: Unequal Adverb Comparisons
Visit mometrix.com/academy and enter code: 315825

Prepositions

A preposition is a word placed before a noun or pronoun that shows the relationship between an object and another word in the sentence.

Review Video: What is a Preposition?
Visit mometrix.com/academy and enter code: 946763

Examples:

- The napkin is *in* the drawer.
- The Earth rotates *around* the Sun.
- The needle is *beneath* the haystack.
- Can you find me *among* the words?

Common prepositions:

about	before	during	on	under	about
after	beneath	for	over	until	after
against	between	from	past	up	against
among	beyond	in	through	with	among
around	by	of	to	within	around

Conjunctions, Coordinating Conjunctions, and Correlative Conjunctions

Conjunctions join words, phrases, or clauses, and they show the connection between the joined pieces. There are coordinating conjunctions that connect equal parts of sentences. Correlative conjunctions show the connection between pairs. Subordinating conjunctions join subordinate (i.e., dependent) clauses with independent clauses.

The coordinating conjunctions include: *and, but, yet, or, nor, for,* and *so*

Examples:

- The rock was small, but it was heavy.
- She drove in the night, and he drove in the day.

Review Video: Conjunctions
Visit mometrix.com/academy and enter code: 904603

The correlative conjunctions are: *either...or | neither...nor | not only... but also*

Examples:

- *Either* you are coming, *or* you are staying. | He ran *not only* three miles, *but also* swam 200 yards.

Subordinating Conjunctions

Common subordinating conjunctions include:

after	since	whenever
although	so that	where
because	unless	wherever
before	until	whether
in order that	when	while

Examples:

- I am hungry *because* I did not eat breakfast.
- He went home *when* everyone left.

Interjections

An interjection is a word for exclamation (i.e., great amount of feeling) that is used alone or as a piece to a sentence. Often, they are used at the beginning of a sentence for an introduction. Sometimes, they can be used in the middle of a sentence to show a change in thought or attitude.

Common Interjections: Hey! | Oh,... | Ouch! | Please! | Wow!

Rules for Capitalization

Capitalize the first word of a sentence and the first word in a direct quotation.

Examples:

- First Word: *Football* is my favorite sport.
- Direct Quote: She asked, "*What* is your name?"

Capitalize proper nouns and adjectives that come from proper nouns.

Examples:

- Proper Noun: My parents are from *Europe*.
- Adjective from Proper Noun: My father is *British,* and my mother is *Italian.*

Capitalize the names of days, months, and holidays.

Examples:

- Day: Everyone needs to be here on *Wednesday*.
- Month: I am so excited for *December*.
- Holiday: *Independence Day* comes every July.

Capitalize the names on a compass for specific areas, not when they give direction.

Examples:

- Specific Area: James is from the West.
- Direction: After three miles, turn south toward the highway.

Capitalize the first letter of each word in a title. (Note: Articles, Prepositions, and Conjunctions are not capitalized)

Examples:

- Titles: <u>Romeo and Juliet</u> is a beautiful drama on love.
- Incorrect: <u>The Taming Of The Shrew</u> is my favorite. (Remember that internal prepositions and articles are not capitalized.)

Note: Books, movies, plays (more than one act), newspapers, magazines, and long musical pieces are put in italics. The two examples of Shakespeare's plays are underlined to show their use as an example.

> **Review Video: Capitalization**
> Visit mometrix.com/academy and enter code: 369678

End Punctuation with Declarative and Imperative Sentences and the Use of Periods for Abbreviations

A declarative sentence gives information or makes a statement. Examples: I can fly a kite. | The plane left two hours ago.

An imperative sentence gives an order or command. Examples: You are coming with me. | Bring me that note.

Examples of periods for abbreviations: 3 P.M. | 2 A.M. | Mr. Jones | Mrs. Stevens | Dr. Smith | Bill Jr. | Pennsylvania Ave. Note: an abbreviation is a shortened form of a word or phrase.

Question Marks and Exclamation Marks

Question marks should be used following a direct question. A polite request can be followed by a period instead of a question mark.

Direct Question: What is for lunch today? | How are you? | Why is that the answer?

Polite Requests: Can you please send me the item tomorrow. | Will you please walk with me on the track.

> **Review Video: Question Marks**
> Visit mometrix.com/academy and enter code: 118471

Exclamation marks are used after a word group or sentence that shows much feeling or has special importance. Exclamation marks should not be overused. They are saved for proper exclamatory interjections.

Examples: We're going to the finals! | You have a beautiful car! | That's crazy!

Rules for Commas

Use a comma before a coordinating conjunction joining independent clauses. Example: Bob caught three fish, and I caught two fish.

Use a comma after an introductory phrase or an adverbial clause.

Examples:

- After the final out, we went to a restaurant to celebrate.
- Studying the stars, I was surprised at the beauty of the sky.

Use a comma between items in a series. Example: I will bring the turkey, the pie, and the coffee.

Use a comma between coordinate adjectives not joined with and.

- Incorrect: The kind, brown dog followed me home.
- Correct: The kind, loyal dog followed me home.

Not all adjectives are coordinate (i.e., equal or parallel). There are two simple ways to know if your adjectives are coordinate. One, you can join the adjectives with and: The kind and loyal dog. Two, you can change the order of the adjectives: The loyal, kind dog.

Use commas for interjections and after *yes* and *no* responses.

Examples:

- Interjection: Oh, I had no idea. | Wow, you know how to play this game.
- Yes and No: *Yes,* I heard you. | *No,* I cannot come tomorrow.

Use commas to separate nonessential modifiers and nonessential appositives.

Examples:

- Nonessential Modifier: John Frank, who is coaching the team, was promoted today.
- Nonessential Appositive: Thomas Edison, an American inventor, was born in Ohio.

Use commas to set off nouns of direct address, interrogative tags, and contrast.

Examples:

- Direct Address: You, *John,* are my only hope in this moment.
- Interrogative Tag: This is the last time, *correct?*
- Contrast: You are my friend, *not my enemy.*

- 63 -

Use commas to separate expressions like *he said* and *she said* if they come between a sentence of a quote.

Examples:

- "I want you to know," he began, "that I always wanted the best for you."
- "You can start," Jane said, "with an apology."

Use commas with dates, addresses, geographical names, and titles.

Examples:

- Date: *July 4, 1776,* is an important date to remember.
- Address: He is meeting me at *456 Delaware Avenue, Washington, D.C.,* tomorrow morning.
- Geographical Name: *Paris, France,* is my favorite city.
- Title: John Smith, *Ph. D.,* will be visiting your class today.

> **Review Video: Common Comma Functions**
> Visit mometrix.com/academy and enter code: 644254

Rules for Semicolons

Use a semicolon between closely connected independent clauses that are not connected with a coordinating conjunction.

Examples:

- She is outside; we are inside.
- You are right; we should go with your plan.

Use a semicolon between independent clauses linked with a transitional word.

Examples:

- I think that we can agree on this*; however,* I am not sure about my friends.
- You are looking in the wrong places*; therefore,* you will not find what you need.

Use a semicolon between items in a series that has internal punctuation. Example: I have visited *New York, New York; Augusta, Maine; and Baltimore, Maryland.*

> **Review Video: Semicolon Usage**
> Visit mometrix.com/academy and enter code: 370605

Rules for Colons

Use a colon after an independent clause to make a list. Example: I want to learn many languages: Spanish, French, German, and Italian.

Use a colon for explanations or to give a quote.

Examples:

- Quote: The man started with an idea: "We are able to do more than we imagine."
- Explanation: There is one thing that stands out on your resume: responsibility.

Use a colon after the greeting in a formal letter, to show hours and minutes, and to separate a title and subtitle.

Examples:

- Greeting in a formal letter: Dear Sir: | To Whom It May Concern:
- Time: It is 3:14 P.M.
- Title: The essay is titled "America: A Short Introduction to a Modern Country"

> **Review Video: Colons**
> Visit mometrix.com/academy and enter code: 868673

Parentheses

Parentheses are used for additional information. Also, they can be used to put labels for letters or numbers in a series. Parentheses should not be used very often. If they are overused, parentheses can be a distraction instead of a help.

> **Review Video: Parentheses**
> Visit mometrix.com/academy and enter code: 947743

Examples:

- Extra Information: The rattlesnake (see Image 2) is a dangerous snake of North and South America.
- Series: Include in the email (1) your name, (2) your address, and (3) your question for the author.

Rules for Quotation Marks

Use quotation marks to close off direct quotations of a person's spoken or written words. Do not use quotation marks around indirect quotations. An indirect quotation gives someone's message without using the person's exact words. Use single quotation marks to close off a quotation inside a quotation.

Direct Quote: Nancy said, "I am waiting for Henry to arrive."

Indirect Quote: Henry said that he is going to be late to the meeting.

Quote inside a Quote: The teacher asked, "Has everyone read 'The Gift of the Magi'?"

Quotation marks should be used around the titles of short works: newspaper and magazine articles, poems, short stories, songs, television episodes, radio programs, and subdivisions of books or web sites.

Examples:

- "Rip van Winkle" (short story by Washington Irving)
- "O Captain! My Captain!" (poem by Walt Whitman)

Quotation marks may be used to set off words that are being used in a different way from a dictionary definition. Also, they can be used to highlight irony.

Examples:

- The boss warned Frank that he was walking on "thin ice."
- (Frank is not walking on real ice. Instead, Frank is being warned to avoid mistakes.)

The teacher thanked the young man for his "honesty." (Honesty and truth are not always the same thing. In this example, the quotation marks around *honesty* show that the teacher does not believe the young man's explanation.) Periods and commas are put inside quotation marks. Colons and semicolons are put outside the quotation marks. Question marks and exclamation points are placed inside quotation marks when they are part of a quote. When the question or exclamation mark goes with the whole sentence, the mark is left outside of the quotation marks.

Examples:

- *Period and comma*: We read "The Gift of the Magi," "The Skylight Room," and "The Cactus."
- *Semicolon*: They watched "The Nutcracker"; then, they went home.
- Exclamation mark that is a part of a quote: The crowd cheered, "Victory!"
- *Question mark that goes with the whole sentence*: Is your favorite short story "The Tell-Tale Heart"?

Review Video: Quotation Marks

Visit mometrix.com/academy and enter code: 884918

Apostrophes

An apostrophe is used to show possession or the deletion of letters in contractions. An apostrophe is not needed with the possessive pronouns *his, hers, its, ours, theirs, whose,* and *yours.*

Singular Nouns: David's car | a book's theme | my brother's board game

Plural Nouns with -*s*: the scissors' handle | boys' basketball

Plural Nouns without -*s*: Men's department | the people's adventure

Review Video: Apostrophes
Visit mometrix.com/academy and enter code: 213068

Hyphens

The hyphen is used to separate compound words. The following are the rules for hyphens:

Compound numbers come with a hyphen. Example: This team needs *twenty-five* points to win the game.

Fractions need a hyphen if they are used as an adjective.

- Correct: The recipe says that we need a *three-fourths* cup of butter.
- Incorrect: *One-fourth* of the road is under construction.

Compound words used as adjectives that come before a noun need a hyphen.

- Correct: The *well-fed* dog took a nap.
- Incorrect: The dog was *well-fed* for his nap.

To avoid confusion with some words, use a hyphen. Examples: semi-irresponsible | Re-collect |Re-claim

Note: This is not a complete set of the rules for hyphens. A dictionary is the best tool for knowing if a compound word needs a hyphen.

> **Review Video: Hyphens**
> Visit mometrix.com/academy and enter code: 981632

Dashes

Dashes are used to show a break or a change in thought in a sentence or to act as parentheses in a sentence. When typing, use two hyphens to make a dash. Do not put a space before or after the dash. The following are the rules for dashes:

- To set off parenthetical statements or an appositive that has internal punctuation.
- Example: The three trees--oak, pine, and magnolia--are coming on a truck tomorrow.
- To show a break or change in tone or thought.
- Example: The first question--how silly of me--does not have a correct answer.

> **Review Video: Dash**
> Visit mometrix.com/academy and enter code: 351706

Subjects

Every sentence has two things: a subject and a verb. The subject of a sentence names who or what the sentence is all about. The subject may be directly stated in a sentence, or the subject may be the implied *you*. In imperative sentences, the verb's subject is understood (e.g., |You| Run to the store). So, the subject may not be in the sentence. Normally, the subject comes before the verb. However, the subject comes after the verb in sentences that begin with *There are* or *There was*.

Direct:

John knows the way to the park.

(Who knows the way to the park? Answer: John)

By five o' clock, Bill will need to leave.

(Who needs to leave? Answer: Bill)

Remember: The subject can come after the verb.

There are five letters on the table for him.

(What is on the table? Answer: Five letters)

There were coffee and doughnuts in the house.

(What was in the house? Answer: Coffee and doughnuts)

Implied:

Go to the post office for me.

(Who is going to the post office? Answer: You are.)

Come and sit with me, please?

(Who needs to come and sit? Answer: You do.)

Review Video: <u>Subjects</u>
Visit mometrix.com/academy and enter code: 444771

Complete Subjects

The complete subject has the simple subject and all of the modifiers. To find the complete subject, ask *Who* or *What* and insert the verb to complete the question. The answer is the complete subject. To find the simple subject, remove all of the modifiers in the complete subject. When you can find the subject of a sentence, you can correct many problems. These problems include sentence fragments and subject-verb agreement.

Examples:

- The small red car is the one that he wants for Christmas.
- (The complete subject is *the small red car*.)
- The young artist is coming over for dinner.
- (The complete subject is *the young artist*.)

Predicates

In a sentence, you always have a predicate and a subject. A predicate is what remains when you have found the subject. The subject tells what the sentence is about, and the predicate explains or describes the subject. Think about the sentence: *He sings*. In this sentence, we have a subject (He) and a predicate (sings). This is all that is needed for a sentence to be complete. Would we like more information? Of course, we would like to know more. However, if this all the information that you are given, you have a complete sentence.

Now, let's look at another sentence:

John and Jane sing on Tuesday nights at the dance hall.

What is the subject of this sentence?

Answer: John and Jane.

What is the predicate of this sentence?

- 68 -

Answer: Everything else in the sentence besides John and Jane.

Review Video: What is a Predicate?
Visit mometrix.com/academy and enter code: 511780

Subject-Verb Agreement and Number and Person Agreement

Verbs agree with their subjects in number. In other words, singular subjects need singular verbs. Plural subjects need plural verbs. Singular is for one person, place, or thing. Plural is for more than one person, place, or thing. Subjects and verbs must also agree in person: first, second, or third. The present tense ending *-s* is used on a verb if its subject is third person singular; otherwise, the verb takes no ending.

Review Video: Subject Verb Agreement
Visit mometrix.com/academy and enter code: 479190

Number Agreement Examples:
Single Subject and Verb: *Dan calls home.*

(Dan is one person. So, the singular verb *calls* is needed.)

Plural Subject and Verb: *Dan and Bob call home.*

(More than one person needs the plural verb *call*.)

Person Agreement Examples:
First Person: I *am* walking.

Second Person: You *are* walking.

Third Person: He *is* walking.

Subject-Verb Agreement Problems

Words between Subject and Verb and Compound Subjects

Words between Subject and Verb
The joy of my life returns home tonight.

(**Singular Subject**: joy. **Singular Verb**: returns)

The phrase *of my life* does not influence the verb *returns*.

The question that still remains unanswered is "Who are you?"

(**Singular Subject**: question. **Singular Verb**: is)

Don't let the phrase "*that still remains...*" trouble you. The subject question goes with *is*.

Compound Subjects
You and Jon are invited to come to my house.

(**Plural Subject**: You and Jon. **Plural Verb**: are)

The pencil and paper belong to me.

(**Plural Subject**: pencil and paper. **Plural Verb**: belong)

Words *or* and *nor*

Today or tomorrow is the day.

(**Subject**: Today / tomorrow. **Verb**: is)

Stan or Phil wants to read the book.

(**Subject**: Stan / Phil. **Verb**: wants)

Neither the books nor the *pen is* on the desk.

(**Subject**: Books / Pen. **Verb**: is)

Either the blanket or *pillows arrive* this afternoon.

(**Subject**: Blanket / Pillows. **Verb**: arrive)

Note: Singular subjects that are joined with the conjunction *or* need a singular verb. However, when one subject is singular and another is plural, you make the verb agree with the closer subject. The example about books and the pen has a singular verb because the pen (singular subject) is closer to the verb.

Indefinite Pronouns and the Adjective *every*

Indefinite Pronouns: Either, Neither, and Each
Is either of you ready for the game?

(**Singular Subject**: Either. **Singular Verb**: is)

Each man, woman, and child is unique.

(**Singular Subject**: Each. **Singular Verb**: is)

Adjective Every and compounds: Everybody, Everyone, Anybody, Anyone
Every day passes faster than the last.

(**Singular Subject**: Every day. **Singular Verb**: passes)

Anybody is welcome to bring a tent.

(**Singular Subject**: Anybody. **Singular Verb**: is)

Collective Nouns and *who*, *which*, and *that*

Collective Nouns
The family eats at the restaurant every Friday night.

(The members of the family are one at the restaurant.)

The team are leaving for their homes after the game.

(The members of the team are leaving as individuals to go to their own homes.)

<u>Who, Which, and That as Subject</u>
This is the man that is helping me today.

He is a good man who serves others before himself.

This painting which is hung over the couch is very beautiful.

Nouns that are Plural in Form and Singular in Meaning

Some nouns that are singular in meaning but plural in form: news, mathematics, physics, and economics

The news is coming on now.

Mathematics is my favorite class.

Some nouns that are plural in meaning: athletics, gymnastics, scissors, and pants

Do these pants come with a shirt?

The scissors are for my project.

Note: Look to your dictionary for help when you aren't sure whether a noun with a plural form has a singular or plural meaning.

Addition, Multiplication, Subtraction, and Division are normally singular.

One plus one is two.

Three times three is nine.

Direct and Indirect Objects

A direct object is a noun that takes or receives the action of a verb. Remember: a complete sentence does not need a direct object. A sentence needs only a subject and a verb. When you are looking for a direct object, find the verb and ask *who* or *what*.

Examples:

- I took the blanket. (Who or what did I take? *The blanket*)
- Jane read books. (Who or what does Jane read? *Books*)

An indirect object is a word or group of words that show how an action had an influence on someone or something. If there is an indirect object in a sentence, then you always have a direct object in the sentence. When you are looking for the indirect object, find the verb and ask *to/for whom or what.*

Examples:

- We taught the old dog a new trick.
- (To/For Whom or What was taught? *The old dog*)
- I gave them a math lesson.
- (To/For Whom or What was given? *Them*)

Review Video: Direct and Indirect Objects
Visit mometrix.com/academy and enter code: 817385

Predicate Nouns and Predicate Adjectives

Predicate Nouns are nouns that modify the subject and finish linking verbs.

Example: My father is a lawyer.

Father is the subject. Lawyer is the predicate noun.

Predicate Adjectives are adjectives that modify the subject and finish linking verbs.

Example: Your mother is patient.

Mother is the subject. Patient is the predicate adjective.

Pronoun-Antecedent Agreement

Pronoun - antecedent agreement - The antecedent is the noun that has been replaced by a pronoun. A pronoun and the antecedent agree when they are singular or plural.

Singular agreement: *John* came into town, and *he* played for us.

(The word *He* replaces *John*.)

Plural agreement: *John and Rick* came into town, and *they* played for us.

(The word *They* replaces *John* and *Rick*.)

Review Video: Pronoun Antecedent Agreement
Visit mometrix.com/academy and enter code: 919704

Correct Pronoun for a Compound Subject

To know the correct pronoun for a compound subject, try each pronoun separately with the verb. Your knowledge of pronouns will tell you which one is correct.

Example: Bob and (I, me) will be going.

(Answer: Bob and I will be going.)

Test: (1) *I will be going* or (2) *Me will be going*. The second choice cannot be correct because *me* is not used as a subject of a sentence. Instead, *me* is used as an object.

Pronoun Used with a Noun Immediately after the Pronoun

When a pronoun is used with a noun immediately following (as in "we boys"), try the sentence without the added noun. Example: (We/Us) boys played football last year. (Answer: We boys played football last year.)

Test: (1) *We* played football last year or (2) *Us* played football last year. Again, the second choice cannot be correct because *us* is not used as a subject of a sentence. Instead, *us* is used as an object.

Pronoun Reference

Pronoun reference - A pronoun should point clearly to the antecedent. Here is how a pronoun reference can be unhelpful if it is not directly stated or puzzling.

Unhelpful: Ron and Jim went to the store, and he bought soda.

(Who bought soda? Ron or Jim?)

Helpful: Jim went to the store, and he bought soda.

(The sentence is clear. Jim bought the soda.)

Subjective, Objective, and Possessive Case of Pronouns

Some pronouns change their form by their placement in a sentence. A pronoun that is a subject in a sentence comes in the subjective case. Pronouns that serve as objects appear in the objective case. Finally, the pronouns that are used as possessives appear in the possessive case.

Subjective case: *He* is coming to the show.

(The pronoun *He* is the subject of the sentence.)

Objective case: Josh drove *him* to the airport.

(The pronoun *him* is the object of the sentence.)

Possessive case: The flowers are *mine*.

(The pronoun *mine* shows ownership of the flowers.)

Who and Whom

Who or whom - *Who*, a subjective-case pronoun, can be used as a subject. *Whom*, an objective case pronoun, can be used as an object. The words *who* and *whom* are common in subordinate clauses or in questions.

Subject: He knows who wants to come.

(*Who* is the subject of the verb *wants*.)

Object: He knows whom we want at the party.

(*Whom* is the object of *we want*.)

Which, That, and Who

Which is used for things only.

Example: John's dog, *which was called Max,* is large and fierce.

That is used for people or things.

Example: Is this the only book *that Louis L'Amour wrote?*

Example: Is Louis L'Amour the author *that wrote Western novels?*

Who is used for people only.

Example: Mozart was the composer *who wrote those operas.*

> **Review Video: Use of Which, That, and Who**
> Visit mometrix.com/academy and enter code: 354355

To, Too, and Two

To can be an adverb or a preposition for showing direction, purpose, and relationship. See your dictionary for the many other ways use to in a sentence.

Examples: I went to the store. | I want to go with you.

Too is an adverb that means also, as well, very, or more than enough.

Examples: I can walk a mile too. | You have eaten too much.

Two is the second number in the series of numbers (e.g., one (1), two, (2), three (3)...)

Example: You have two minutes left.

There, Their, and They're

There can be an adjective, adverb, or pronoun. Often, there is used to show a place or to start a sentence. Examples: I went there yesterday. | There is something in his pocket.

Their is a pronoun that is used to show ownership. Examples: He is their father. | This is their fourth apology this week.

They're is a contraction of they are. Example: Did you know that they're in town?

Knew and New

Knew is the past tense of know. Example: I knew the answer.

New is an adjective that means something is current, has not been used, or modern. Example: This is my new phone.

Its and It's

Its is a pronoun that shows ownership. Example: The guitar is in its case.

It's is a contraction of it is. Example: It's an honor and a privilege to meet you.

Note: The h in honor is silent. So, the sound of the vowel o must have the article an.

Your and You're

Your is a pronoun that shows ownership. Example: This is your moment to shine. *You're* is a contraction of you are. Example: Yes, you're correct.

Affect and Effect

Affect can be used as a noun for feeling, emotion, or mood. Effect can be used as a noun that means result. Affect as a verb means to influence. Effect as a verb means to bring about.

- *Affect:* The sunshine affects plants.
- *Effect:* The new rules will effect order in the office.

Independent and Dependent Clauses

There are two groups of clauses: independent and dependent. Unlike phrases, a clause has a subject and a verb. So, what is the difference between a clause that is independent and one that is dependent? An independent clause gives a complete thought. A dependent clause does not share a complete thought. Instead, a dependent clause has a subject and a verb, but it needs an independent clause. Subordinate (i.e., dependent) clauses look like sentences. They may have a subject, a verb, and objects or complements. They are used within sentences as adverbs, adjectives, or nouns.

Examples:

- *Independent Clause*: I am running outside.
- (The sentence has a subject *I* and a verb *am running*.)
- *Dependent Clause*: I am running <u>because I want to stay in shape</u>.

The clause *I am running* is an independent clause. The underlined clause is dependent. Remember: a dependent clause does not give a complete thought. Think about the dependent clause: *because I want to stay in shape*. Without any other information, you think: So, you want to stay in shape. What are you are doing to stay in shape? Answer: *I am running*.

Adjective Clauses

An adjective clause is a dependent clause that modifies nouns and pronouns. Adjective clauses begin with a relative pronoun (*who, whose, whom, which,* and *that*) or a relative adverb (*where, when,* and *why*). Also, adjective clauses come after the noun that the clause needs to explain or rename. This is done to have a clear connection to the independent clause.

Examples:

- I learned the reason *why I won the award.*
- This is the place where I started my first job.

An adjective clause can be an essential or nonessential clause. An essential clause is very important to the sentence. Essential clauses explain or define a person or thing. Nonessential clauses give more information about a person or thing. However, they are not necessary to the sentence.

Examples:

- Essential: A person *who works hard at first* can rest later in life.
- Nonessential: Neil Armstrong, *who walked on the moon*, is my hero.

Adverb Clauses

An **adverb clause** is a dependent clause that modifies verbs, adjectives, and other adverbs. To show a clear connection to the independent clause, put the adverb clause immediately before or after the independent clause. An adverb clause can start with *after, although, as, as if, before, because, if, since, so, so that, unless, when, where,* or *while*.

Examples:

- *When you walked outside*, I called the manager.
- I want to go with you *unless you want to stay*.

Noun Clauses

A **noun clause** is a dependent clause that can be used as a subject, object, or complement. Noun clauses can begin with *how, that, what, whether, which, who,* or *why*. These words can also come with an adjective clause. Remember that the entire clause makes a noun or an adjective clause, not the word that starts a clause. So, be sure to look for more than the word that begins the clause. To show a clear connection to the independent clause, be sure that a noun clause comes after the verb. The exception is when the noun clause is the subject of the sentence.

Examples:

- The fact *that you were alone* alarms me.
- *What you learn from each other* depends on your honesty with others.

> **Review Video: Clauses**
> Visit mometrix.com/academy and enter code: 940170

Phrase

A phrase is not a complete sentence. So, a phrase cannot be a statement and cannot give a complete thought. Instead, a phrase is a group of words that can be used as a noun, adjective, or adverb in a sentence. Phrases strengthen sentences by adding explanation or renaming something.

Prepositional Phrases

Prepositional Phrases - A phrase that can be found in many sentences is the prepositional phrase. A prepositional phrase begins with a preposition and ends with a noun or pronoun that is used as an object. Normally, the prepositional phrase works as an adjective or an adverb.

Examples:

- The picnic is *on the blanket*.
- I am sick *with a fever* today.
- *Among the many flowers*, a four-leaf clover was found by John.

Verbals and Verbal Phrases

A verbal looks like a verb, but it is not used as a verb. Instead, a verbal is used as a noun, adjective, or adverb. Be careful with verbals. They do not replace a verb in a sentence.

Correct: Walk a mile daily.

(*Walk* is the verb of this sentence. As in, "*You* walk a mile daily.")

Incorrect: To walk a mile.

(*To walk* is a type of verbal. But, verbals cannot be a verb for a sentence.)

A verbal phrase is a verb form that does not function as the verb of a clause. There are three major types of verbal phrases: participial, gerund, and infinitive phrases.

> **Review Video: Verbals**
> Visit mometrix.com/academy and enter code: 915480

Participles and Participial Phrases

A participle is a verbal that is used as an adjective. The present participle always ends with -*ing*. Past participles end with -*d, -ed, -n,* or -*t.* Examples: Verb: *dance* | Present Participle: *dancing* | Past Participle: *danced*

Participial phrases are made of a participle and any complements or modifiers. Often, they come right after the noun or pronoun that they modify.

Examples:

- *Shipwrecked on an island*, the boys started to fish for food.
- *Having been seated for five hours*, we got out of the car to stretch our legs.
- *Praised for their work*, the group accepted the first-place trophy.

Gerunds and Gerund Phrases

A gerund is a verbal that is used as a noun. Gerunds can be found by looking for their -*ing* endings. However, you need to be careful that you have found a gerund, not a present participle. Since gerunds are nouns, they can be used as a subject of a sentence and the object of a verb or preposition.

Gerund Phrases are built around present participles (i.e., -*ing* endings to verbs) and they are always used as nouns. The gerund phrase has a gerund and any complements or modifiers.

Examples:

- We want to be known for *teaching the poor*. (Object of Preposition)
- *Coaching this team* is the best job of my life. (Subject)
- We like *practicing our songs* in the basement. (Object of the verb: *like*)

Infinitives and Infinitive Phrases

An infinitive is a verbal that can be used as a noun, an adjective, or an adverb. An infinitive is made of the basic form of a verb with the word *to* coming before the verb.

Infinitive Phrases are made of an infinitive and all complements and modifiers. They are used as nouns, adjectives, or adverbs.

Examples:

- *To join the team* is my goal in life. (Noun)
- The animals have enough food *to eat for the night*. (Adjective)
- People lift weights *to exercise their muscles*. (Adverb)

> **Review Video: Gerund, Infinitive, and Participle**
> Visit mometrix.com/academy and enter code: 634263

Appositives and Appositive Phrases

An appositive is a word or phrase that is used to explain or rename nouns or pronouns. In a sentence they can be noun phrases, prepositional phrases, gerund phrases, or infinitive phrases.

Examples:

- Terriers, *hunters at heart*, have been dressed up to look like lap dogs.
- (The phrase *hunters at heart* renames the noun *terriers*.)

His plan, *to save and invest his money*, was proven as a safe approach.

(The italicized infinitive phrase renames the plan.)

Appositive phrases can be essential or nonessential. An appositive phrase is essential if the person, place, or thing being described or renamed is too general. Essential: Two Founding Fathers George Washington and Thomas Jefferson served as presidents.

Nonessential: George Washington and Thomas Jefferson, two Founding Fathers, served as presidents.

Absolute Phrases

An absolute phrase is a phrase with a participle that comes after a noun. The absolute phrase is never the subject of a sentence. Also, the phrase does not explain or add to the meaning of a word in a sentence. Absolute phrases are used independently from the rest of the sentence. However, they are still a phrase, and phrases cannot give a complete thought.

Examples:

- *The alarm ringing*, he pushed the snooze button.
- *The music paused*, she continued to dance through the crowd.

Simple and Compound Sentences

Simple sentences have one independent clause with no subordinate clauses. A simple sentence can have compound elements (e.g., a compound subject or verb).

Examples:

- Judy watered the lawn. (Singular Subject & Singular Predicate)
- Judy and Alan watered the lawn. (Compound Subject: Judy and Alan)

Compound sentences have two or more independent clauses with no dependent clauses. Usually, the independent clauses are joined with a comma and a coordinating conjunction, or they can be joined with a semicolon.

Example:

- The time has come, and we are ready.
- I woke up at dawn; then I went outside to watch the sun rise.

Complex and Compound-Complex Sentences

A complex sentence has one independent clause and one or more dependent clauses.

Examples:

- Although he had the flu, Harry went to work.
- Marcia got married after she finished college.

A compound-complex sentence has at least two independent clauses and at least one dependent clause.

Examples:

- John is my friend who went to India, and he brought souvenirs for us.
- You may not know, but we heard the music that you played last night.

Sentence Fragments

A part of a sentence should not be treated like a complete sentence. A sentence must be made of at least one independent clause. An independent clause has a subject and a verb. Remember that the independent clause can stand alone as a sentence. Some fragments are independent clauses that begin with a subordinating word (e.g., as, because, so, etc.). Other fragments may not have a subject, a verb, or both. A sentence fragment can be repaired in several ways. One way is to put the fragment with a neighbor sentence. Another way is to be sure that punctuation is not needed. You can also turn the fragment into a sentence by adding any missing pieces. Sentence fragments are allowed for writers who want to show off their art. However, for your exam, sentence fragments are not allowed.

Fragment: Because he wanted to sail for Rome.

Correct: He dreamed of Europe because he wanted to sail for Rome.

Run-On Sentences

Run-on sentences are independent clauses that have not been joined by a conjunction. When two or more independent clauses appear in one sentence, they must be joined in one of these ways:

- Correction with a comma and a coordinating conjunction.
- *Incorrect*: I went on the trip and I had a good time.
- *Correct*: I went on the trip, and I had a good time.
- Correction with a semicolon, a colon, or a dash. Used when independent clauses are closely related and their connection is clear without a coordinating conjunction.
- *Incorrect*: I went to the store and I bought some eggs.
- *Correct*: I went to the store; I bought some eggs.
- Correction by separating sentences. This correction may be used when both independent clauses are long. Also, this can be used when one sentence is a question and one is not.
- *Incorrect*: The drive to New York takes ten hours it makes me very tired.
- *Correct*: The drive to New York takes ten hours. So, I become very tired.
- Correction by changing parts of the sentence. One way is to turn one of the independent clauses into a phrase or subordinate clause.
- *Incorrect*: The drive to New York takes ten hours it makes me very tired.
- *Correct*: During the ten-hour drive to New York, I become very tired.

> **Review Video: Fragments and Run-on Sentences**
> Visit mometrix.com/academy and enter code: 541989

Dangling Modifiers

A dangling modifier is a verbal phrase that does not have a clear connection to a word. A dangling modifier can also be a dependent clause (the subject and/or verb are not included) that does not have a clear connection to a word.

Examples:

- Dangling: *Reading each magazine article*, the stories caught my attention.
- Corrected: Reading each magazine article, *I* was entertained by the stories.

In this example, the word *stories* cannot be modified by *Reading each magazine article*. People can read, but stories cannot read. So, the pronoun *I* is needed for the modifying phrase *Reading each magazine article*.

Dangling: Since childhood, my grandparents have visited me for Christmas.

Corrected: Since childhood, I have been visited by my grandparents for Christmas.

In this example, the dependent adverb clause *Since childhood* cannot modify grandparents. So, the pronoun *I* is needed for the modifying adverb clause.

Misplaced Modifiers

In some sentences, a modifier can be put in more than one place. However, you need to be sure that there is no confusion about which word is being explained or given more detail.

Incorrect: He read the book to a crowd that was filled with beautiful pictures.

Correct: He read the book that was filled with beautiful pictures to a crowd.

The crowd is not filled with pictures. The book is filled with pictures.

Incorrect: John only ate fruits and vegetables for two weeks.

Correct: John ate *only* fruits and vegetables for two weeks.

John may have done nothing else for two weeks but eat fruits and vegetables and sleep. However, it is reasonable to think that John had fruits and vegetables for his meals. Then, he continued to work on other things.

Split Infinitives

A split infinitive is when something comes between the word *to* and the verb that pairs with *to*.

Incorrect: To *clearly* explain | To *softly* sing

Correct: *To explain* clearly | *To sing* softly

Double Negatives

Standard English allows two negatives when a positive meaning is intended. For example, "The team was not displeased with their performance." Double negatives that are used to emphasize negation are not part of Standard English. Negative modifiers (e.g., never, no, and not) should not be paired with other negative modifiers or negative words (e.g., none, nobody, nothing, or neither). The modifiers *hardly, barely*, and *scarcely* are also considered negatives in Standard English. So, they should not be used with other negatives.

Parallelism in Sentence Structure

Parallel structures are used in sentences to highlight similar ideas and to connect sentences that give similar information. Parallelism pairs parts of speech, phrases, or clauses together with a matching piece. To write, *I enjoy reading and to study* would be incorrect. An infinitive does not match with a gerund. Instead, you should write *I enjoy reading and studying*.

Be sure that you continue to use certain words (e.g., articles, linking verbs, prepositions, infinitive sign (to), and the introductory word for a dependent clause) in sentences.

Incorrect: Will you bring the paper and pen with you?

Correct: Will you bring *the* paper and *a* pen with you?

Incorrect: The animals can come to eat and play.

Correct: The animals can come *to* eat and *to* play.

Incorrect: You are the person who remembered my name and cared for me.

Correct: You are the person *who* remembered my name and *who* cared for me.

Subordination in Sentence Structure

When two items are not equal to each other, you can join them by making the more important piece an independent clause. The less important piece can become subordinate. To make the less important piece subordinate, you make it a phrase or a dependent clause. The piece of more importance should be the one that readers want or will need to remember.

Example:

- The team had a perfect regular season. (2) The team lost the championship.
- Despite having a perfect regular season, *the team lost the championship.*

Selecting the Correct Answer for Grammar Questions

Read each sentence carefully and put the answer choices into the blanks. Don't stop at the first answer choice if you think that you have the right answer. Read through the choices and think about each choice to know which one is best. At first you may have an answer choice that you think is correct. Then, you may have a different idea after you have read each choice. Don't allow your ear to decide what sounds right. Instead, use your knowledge and think about each answer choice. You may think that some answer choices can be ruled out because they sound incorrect. However, those are the answer choices that may be correct.

Context Clues

To decide on the best answer, you can use context clues as you read through the answer choices. Key words in the sentence will allow you to decide which answer choice is the best to fill in the blank.

Example: Archeology has shown that some of the ruins of the ancient city of Babylon are approximately 500 years <u>as old as their supposed</u> Mesopotamian predecessors.

- as old as their supposed
- older than their supposed

In this example, the key word is *supposed*. Archaeology would confirm that the predecessors to Babylon were more ancient or disprove that supposition. Since supposed was used, the word implies that archaeology had disproved the accepted belief. So, this would make Babylon older. Thus, answer choice B correct. Furthermore, the use of *500 years* in the sentence can rule out answer choice A. Years are used to show absolute or relative age. If two objects are as old as each other, then years are not necessary to describe that relationship. So, you could say, "The ancient city of Babylon is approximately as old as their supposed Mesopotamian predecessors." So, the term *500 years* is not needed in the sentence.

Watching out for Simplicity

When your answer choices seem simple, you need to be careful with the question. Don't pick an answer choice because one choice is long or complicated. A simple or short sentence can be correct.

However, not every simple or short sentence will be correct. An answer that is simple and does not make sense may not be correct. The phrases *of which [...] are* in the below examples are wordy and unnecessary. They should be removed. You can place a colon after the words *sport* and *following*.

Examples:

- There are many benefits to running as a sport, *of which the top advantages are*:
- The necessary school supplies were the following, *of which a few are*:

Special Report: GMAT Secrets in Action

This section will walk you through techniques that can help you to answer specific types of questions. The following section will provide you with the opportunity to practice these skills in a practice test modeled after the GMAT.

Verbal Subtest

Sample Sentence Correction Question

Choose which of five ways of writing the underlined part of the sentence is correct.

<u>While a leader, one can decide</u> to allow the group to determine its course by a simple vote of majority, or we can choose to guide the group without allowing the opportunity for discussion.

> A. While a leader, one can decide
> B. While leaders, we can decide
> C. While a leader, we can decide
> D. While leaders, one can decide
> E. While leading, one can decide

Let's look at a couple of different methods and steps to solving this problem.

Agreement in Pronoun Number

All pronouns have to agree in number to their antecedent or noun that they are representing. In the underlined portion, the pronoun "one" has as its antecedent the noun "leader".

Go through and match up each of the pronouns in the answer choices with their antecedents:

> A. leader, one – correctly matches singular antecedent to singular pronoun
> B. leaders, we – correctly matches plural antecedent to plural pronoun
> C. leader, we – incorrectly matches singular antecedent to plural pronoun
> D. leaders, one – incorrectly matches plural antecedent to singular pronoun
> E. one – no antecedent

Based on pronoun number agreement, you can eliminate choices C and D from consideration, because they fail the test.

Parallelism

Not only do the pronouns and antecedents in the underlined portion of the sentence have to be correct, but the rest of the sentence has to match as well. The remainder of the sentence has to be parallel to the underlined portion. Part of the sentence that is not underlined has the phrase "we can choose." Notice how this phrase uses the plural pronoun "we". This means that the underlined portion of the sentence has to be plural to agree with the rest of the sentence and have matching plural pronouns and nouns as well.

Quickly review the answer choices and look for whether the nouns and pronouns in the answer choices are singular or plural:

> A. leader, one – singular noun, singular pronoun
> B. leaders, we – plural noun, plural pronoun
> C. leader, we – singular noun, plural pronoun
> D. leaders, one – plural noun, singular pronoun
> E. one – singular pronoun

Only choice B has both a plural noun and a plural pronoun, making choice B correct.

Sample Reading Comprehension Question

Mark Twain was well aware of his celebrity. He was among the first authors to employ a clipping service to track press coverage of himself, and it was not unusual for him to issue his own press statements if he wanted to influence or "spin" coverage of a particular story. The celebrity Twain achieved during his last ten years still reverberates today. Nearly all of his most popular novels were published before 1890, long before his hair grayed or he began to wear his famous white suit in public. We appreciate the author but seem to remember the celebrity.

Based on the passage above, Mark Twain seemed interested in:

> A. maintaining his celebrity
> B. selling more of his books
> C. hiding his private life
> D. gaining popularity
> E. writing the perfect novel

Let's look at a couple of different methods of solving this problem.

Key Words

Identify the key words in each answer choice. These are the nouns and verbs that are the most important words in the answer choice:

> A. maintaining, celebrity
> B. selling, books
> C. hiding, life
> D. gaining, popularity
> E. writing, novel

Now try to match up each of the key words with the passage and see where they fit. You're trying to find synonyms and/or exact replication between the key words in the answer choices and key words in the passage:

> A. maintaining – no matches; celebrity – matches in sentences 1, 3, and 5
> B. selling – no matches; books – matches with "novels" in sentence 4.
> C. hiding – no matches; life – no matches
> D. gaining – no matches; popularity –matches with "celebrity" in sentences 1, 3, and 5, because they can be synonyms
> E. writing – no matches; novel – matches in sentence 4

- 85 -

At this point there are only two choices that have more than one match, choices A and D, and they both have the same number of matches, and with the same word in the passage, which is the word "celebrity" in the passage. This is a good sign, because the exam will often have two answer choices that are close. Having two answer choices pointing towards the same key word is a strong indicator that those key words hold the "key" to finding the right answer.

Now let's compare choice A and D and the unmatched key words. Choice A still has "maintaining" which doesn't have a clear match, while choice D has "gaining" which doesn't have a clear match. While neither of those have clear matches in the passage, ask yourself what are the best arguments that would support any kind of connection with either of those two words.

- "Maintaining" makes sense when you consider that Twain was interested in tracking his press coverage and that he was actively managing the "spin" of certain stories.
- "Gaining" makes sense when you consider that Twain was actively issuing his own press releases, however one key point to remember is that he was only issuing these press releases after another story was already in existence.

Since Twain's press releases were not being released in a news vacuum, but rather as a response mechanism to ensure control over the angle of a story, his releases were more to maintain control over his image, rather than gain an image in the first place.

Furthermore, when comparing the terms "popularity" and "celebrity", there are similarities between the words, but in referring back to the passage, it is clear that "celebrity" has a stronger connection to the passage, being the exact word used three times in the passage.

Since "celebrity" has a stronger match than "popularity" and "maintaining" makes more sense than "gaining," it is clear that choice A is correct.

Process of Elimination

The process of elimination for this passage could follow these lines:

A. maintaining his celebrity – The passage discusses how Mark Twain was both aware of his celebrity status and would take steps to ensure that he got the proper coverage in any news story and maintained the image he desired. This is the correct answer.

B. selling more of his books – Mark Twain's novels are mentioned for their popularity and while common sense would dictate that he would be interested in selling more of his books, the passage makes no mention of him doing anything to promote sales.

C. hiding his private life – While the passage demonstrates that Mark Twain was keenly interested in how the public viewed his life, it does not indicate that he cared about hiding his private life, not even mentioning his life outside of the public eye. The passage deals with how he was seen by the public.

D. gaining popularity – At first, this sounds like a good answer choice, because Mark Twain's popularity is mentioned several times. The main difference though is that he wasn't trying to gain popularity, but simply ensuring that the popularity he had was not distorted by bad press.

E. writing the perfect novel – Though every author of fiction may strive to write the perfect novel, and Mark Twain was a famous author, the passage makes no mention of any quest of his to write a perfect novel.

Sample Critical Reasoning Question

The cost of producing radios in Country Q is ten percent less than the cost of producing radios in Country Y. Even after transportation fees and tariff charges are added, it is still cheaper for a company to import radios from Country Q to Country Y than to produce radios in Country Y.

The statements above, if true, best support which of the following assertions?

> A. Labor costs in Country Q are ten percent below those in Country Y.
> B. Importing radios from Country Q to Country Y will eliminate ten percent of the manufacturing jobs in Country Y.
> C. The tariff on a radio imported from Country Q to Country Y is less than ten percent of the cost of manufacturing the radio in Country Y.
> D. The fee for transporting a radio from Country Q to Country Y is more than ten percent of the cost of manufacturing the radio in Country Q.
> E. It takes ten percent less time to manufacture a radio in Country Q than it does in Country Y.

Let's look at a couple of different methods of solving this problem.

Eliminate Choices

When in doubt, eliminate what you can first. Go through each answer choice and see if you can eliminate it from consideration:

- Answer choice A mentions labor costs, although labor costs are not even mentioned in the question. Rarely will GMAT try to trick you by bringing up an unmentioned variable, therefore answer choice A can be eliminated.
- Answer choice B mentions manufacturing jobs, and answer choice E mentioned manufacturing time, neither of which were mentioned in the question, and both answer choices can be eliminated.

Now you're down to just answer choice C and D, making your task much easier.

- Answer choice D states that the transportation fee is more than ten percent of the cost of manufacturing the radio. However, if that were true, then the total cost of importing a radio from Country Q would exceed the manufacturing cost in Country Y, making choice D incorrect, because the question clearly states that the importing cost is still less, even after the transportation and tariff costs are added in.

This makes answer choice C the default correct answer.

Plug and Chug

Take some sample numbers and plug them into the problem. Rather than having to remember the relationships, writing them down with real numbers helps a lot of students understand the problem better. Use round number like 100 that are easy to use in calculations, especially with percents.

In this case, you could write:

Country Y - $100 is the cost to produce 1 radio

Country Q - $90 is the cost to produce 1 radio (10% less)

The question states that even if transportation fees and tariff charges are added to the cost of producing radios in Country Q, radios are still cheaper to import. Since that would mean that the total cost from Country Q could not exceed $100 (the cost in Country Y), then the transportation and tariff costs could not exceed $10, because the manufacturing cost is already $90, and $90 + any number greater than $10 would exceed $100.

Since the upper limit of the transportation and tariff costs of $10 is 10% of $100, that means that the tariff costs alone would definitely have to be less than 10%, which makes answer choice C correct.

Quantitative Subtest

Sample Problem Solving Question

Three coins are tossed up in the air. What is the probability that two of them will land heads and one will land tails?

> A. 0
> B. 1/8
> C. 1/4
> D. 3/8
> E. 1/2

Let's look at a few different methods and steps to solving this problem.

Reduction and Division

Quickly eliminate the probabilities that you immediately know. You know to roll all heads is a 1/8 probability, and to roll all tails is a 1/8 probability. Since there are in total 8/8 probabilities, you can subtract those two out, leaving you with 8/8 – 1/8 – 1/8 = 6/8. So after eliminating the possibilities of getting all heads or all tails, you're left with 6/8 probability. Because there are only three coins, all other combinations are going to involve one of either head or tail, and two of the other. All other combinations will either be 2 heads and 1 tail, or 2 tails and 1 head. Those remaining combinations both have the same chance of occurring, meaning that you can just cut the remaining 6/8 probability in half, leaving you with a 3/8 chance that there will be 2 heads and 1 tail, and another 3/8 chance that there will be 2 tails and 1 head, making choice D correct.

Run through the Possibilities for That Outcome

You know that you have to have two heads and one tail for the three coins. There are only so many combinations, so quickly run through them all.

You could have:

> H, H, H
> H, H, T
> H, T, H
> T, H, H
> T, T, H
> T, H, T
> H, T, T
> T, T, T

Reviewing these choices, you can see that three of the eight have two heads and one tail, making choice D correct.

Fill in the Blanks with Symbology and Odds

Many probability problems can be solved by drawing blanks on a piece of scratch paper (or making mental notes) for each object used in the problem, then filling in probabilities and multiplying them out. In this case, since there are three coins being flipped, draw three blanks. In the first blank, put an "H" and over it write "1/2". This represents the case where the first coin is flipped as heads. In that case (where the first coin comes up heads), one of the other two coins must come up tails and one must come up heads to fulfill the criteria posed in the problem (2 heads and 1 tail). In the second blank, put a "1" or "1/1". This is because it doesn't matter what is flipped for the second coin, so long as the first coin is heads. In the third blank, put a "1/2". This is because the third coin must be the exact opposite of whatever is in the second blank. Half the time the third coin will be the same as the second coin, and half the time the third coin will be the opposite, hence the "1/2". Now multiply out the odds. There is a half chance that the first coin will come up "heads", then it doesn't matter for the second coin, then there is a half chance that the third coin will be the opposite of the second coin, which will give the desired result of 2 heads and 1 tail. So, that gives 1/2*1/1*1/2 = 1/4.

But, now you must calculate the probabilities that result if the first coin is flipped tails. So draw another group of three blanks. In the first blank, put a "T" and over it write "1/2". This represents the case where the first coin is flipped as tails. In that case (where the first coin comes up tails), both of the other two coins must come up heads to fulfill the criteria posed in the problem. In the second blank, put an "H" and over it write "1/2". In the third blank, put an "H" and over it write "1/2". Now multiply out the odds. There is a half chance that the first coin will come up "tails", then there is a half chance that the second coin will be heads, and a half chance that the third coin will be heads. So, that gives 1/2*1/2*1/2 = 1/8.

Now, add those two probabilities together. If you flip heads with the first coin, there is a 1/4 chance of ultimately meeting the problem's criteria. If you flip tails with the first coin, there is a 1/8 chance of ultimately meeting the problem's criteria. So, that gives 1/4 + 1/8 = 2/8 + 1/8 = 3/8, which makes choice D correct.

Sample Data Sufficiency Question

If a real estate agent received a commission of 6 percent of the selling price of a certain house, what was the selling price of the house?
(1) The selling price minus the real estate agent's commission was $84,600.
(2) The selling price was 250 percent of the original purchase price of $36,000.
    A. Statement (1) ALONE is sufficient, but statement (2) alone is not sufficient.
    B. Statement (2) ALONE is sufficient, but statement (1) alone is not sufficient.
    C. BOTH statements TOGETHER are sufficient, but NEITHER statement ALONE is sufficient.
    D. EACH statement ALONE is sufficient.
    E. Statements (1) and (2) TOGETHER are NOT sufficient.

Let's look at a few different methods and steps to solving this problem.

Use Algebra

If the answer isn't immediately apparent, creating an algebra problem allows you to logically dissect the problem and statements into pieces that can be put together to solve whether or not the statement is sufficient to find the answer to the question.

Create an algebra problem out of both statements.

First Statement: The first statement is that "The selling price minus the real estate agent's commission was $84,600." You can convert this into:

$$x \text{ (the selling price)} - y \text{ (the commission)} = \$84,600.$$

This alone doesn't tell you enough, yet you do have another piece of information that you can plug in. The question told you that the real estate agent's commission was 6% of the selling price. Since we set the variable "x" as the selling price, that makes the agent's commission ".06*x". This allows us to replace "y" in the equation above, with ".06*x".

Our equation is now:

$$x - .06 * x = \$84,600.$$

"x" can be factored out, leaving x(1–.06) = $84,600 or .94*x = $84,600.

Solving for x gives us:

$$.94 * x / .94 = \$84,600 / .94 \text{ or } x = \$90,000$$

This is the selling price, meaning that statement 1 is sufficient to answer the question, but what about statement 2?

Second Statement: The second statement is that "The selling price was 250 percent of the original purchase price of $36,000." You can convert this into:

$$x \text{ (the selling price)} = 250\% * \$36,000.$$

This becomes:

$$x = 2.5 * \$36,000 \text{ or } x = \$90,000$$

This is the selling price, meaning that statement 2 is also sufficient to answer the question, making answer choice D correct.

Single Variable Logic

A method that works even faster than setting up equations is using simple logic. Whenever you are able to create an equation, if you know that you will only have a single variable to work with, then you can solve for that variable. In the first statement, you have, "The selling price minus the real estate agent's commission was $84,600." Quickly looking at this statement it appears that you will have two variables. However, once you realize that you can substitute the variable for the agent's commission with a 6% multiplier based on the selling price (using the information in the question) then you know that you are actually down to just a single variable, meaning this statement alone is sufficient to solve for the answer.

In the second statement, you have, "The selling price was 250 percent of the original purchase price of $36,000." A quick view of this statement reveals that you are going to have a simple equation with only a single variable and will be able to solve for the answer, meaning that this statement is also sufficient.

Warning: Make sure that the single variable you've identified is the variable asked about in the question. In this question, you are asked for the selling price. Therefore, the single variable in each statement must be the selling price. Don't make this simple mistake!

Analytical Writing Subtest

Sample Analysis of an Issue Topic

Possessions can be extremely difficult to give up or lose. Some people believe that is an evolutionary adaptation to cling to assets which are necessary for survival. Others feel that it is due to a personal attachment that develops over the years as emotional memories become linked to inanimate objects.

Which do you find more compelling, the belief that attachment to possessions is an evolutionary adaptation for survival or that the attachment stems from a more human element of emotions? Explain your position, using relevant reasons and/or examples from your own experience, observations, or reading.

Let's look at a few different methods and steps to writing your analysis.

What's the Goal?

Remember that on the essay portion of the GMAT, there isn't a "correct" answer. The response you choose to give to the topic provided does not have to be the first thing that comes to your mind. In fact, the side or response you pick doesn't even have to support the side of the topic that you actually believe in. It is better to have a good explanation for the position, rather than to actually believe in the position on the topic. However, typically you will find that the side you believe in is also the side that you have the most information that you can write about.

To go through some of the steps that you could walk through as you develop your response, let's choose to support the belief that the attachment develops from emotional memories slowly becoming linked to inanimate objects.

As you consider some good examples of possessions, your first thought might be the importance of your home or car, which are necessary for the basic functions of life, such as providing a roof over your head and a method of transportation. Yet, what would be your supporting answer about why your car is important and would be difficult to give up? Some possibilities might be: "it gets me where I need to go, it is brand new, it is expensive, I like it a lot, it would be difficult to replace, it's shiny."

These answer choices may fill up some space, but don't have much meaning. There are other possessions in your life that have much more meaning and priority in other ways that would be better to write about.

Think of possessions that have meaning beyond the mere basics of shelter or transportation. You want examples that you could potentially write pages and pages about, filling each of them with depths of passionate detail. While you probably won't have time to write pages and pages, it's good to have a examples that have plenty of room to be expanded upon.

Make a Short List

The best way to think of examples you would want to include might be to create a short list of possibilities. What are some that you would truly hate to give up? What are things that you would regret and miss for years to come? What are items that would fit the description of having an emotional attachment develop over the years? Perhaps a precious heirloom, a family antique, or a faded photograph would be suitable examples. After you've made your list, look back over it and see which possessions you could write the most information about. Those are the ones you would want to include as examples.

Answer "Why"

Notice that choosing possessions and writing about them is not the only thing that you have to do. You have to explain your position. You have to answer the "Why." That is an all-important question. If you wrote a sentence as part of your response and one of the essay scorers looked over your shoulder and said, "but why?" would your next sentence answer their question. For example, suppose you wrote, "The old chair that used to belong to my grandfather has a lot of meaning." If someone asked why, would your next sentence answer it? Your next sentence should say, "It has meaning because it was the one chair that my grandfather would sit in every day and tell stories from." Answering the "Why" question is crucial to your success at writing a great essay. It doesn't do any good to write a good essay if it doesn't answer that question.

GMAT Practice Test

Analytical Writing Assessment

Analysis of an Issue

This writing task is designed to test your ability to present a position on an issue effectively and persuasively. Your task is to analyze the issue presented, considering various perspectives, and to develop your own position on the issue. In scoring your issue essay, readers will consider how effectively you: recognize and deal with the complexities and implications of the issue; organize, develop, and express your ideas; support your ideas with reasons and examples; control the elements of standard written English. You are given 30 minutes to write the response. You must not write on any other subject than the one expressed in the prompt. You are allowed to accept, reject, or qualify the statement made by the prompt, though you must be sure to support whatever position you take with reasons and examples from your experience, observation, reading, and/or academic studies. You should take a few minutes to plan your response before typing.

Issue: Although elementary education proposals have typically emphasized math and science, there is a growing movement to restore fine arts education in the early grades. Many education experts assert that neglecting music, dance, and painting produces students who have a great deal of knowledge but little capability of expression. Furthermore, they argue, the creativity and free-thinking required for the practice of the fine arts leads to innovation and progress in other areas. Critics of these proposals argue that the United States still lags behind other countries in science and mathematics test scores, and should focus on improving performance in these areas before allocating extra funds to arts programs.

Analysis of an Argument

This writing task is designed to test your critical reasoning skills as well as your writing skills. Your task is to critique the stated argument in terms of its logical soundness and in terms of the strength of the evidence offered in support of the argument. In scoring your argument essay, the reader will consider how effectively you: identify and analyze the key elements of the argument; organize, develop, and express your critique; support your ideas with reasons and examples; control the elements of standard written English.

You are not being asked to agree or disagree with any of the statements in the argument. You should only consider the argument's line of reasoning. Specifically, you should consider: questionable assumptions underlying the argument; the extent to which the evidence presented supports the conclusion of the argument; what additional evidence would help to strengthen or refute the argument; and what additional information if any would help you to evaluate the argument's conclusion.

Argument: According to the author of a recent editorial, most of the problems in the United States are a consequence of the national dependence on oil. Oil consumption is expensive, damaging to the environment, and requires the United States to do business with some unsavory regimes. The United States should therefore impose strict gas-mileage requirements on automobiles, effective immediately. Although this would pose some temporary problems for the economy, in the long run it would be the best solution to American oil addiction.

Integrated Reasoning

1. The table below shows the percentage of students at several local high schools that are failing each subject.

School	Math	English	Science	Social Studies
Candlewood	12%	6%	11%	4%
Ridgecrest	13%	5%	10%	6%
Woodlands	9%	5%	10%	5%
West Hills	12%	7%	12%	3%
North Forest	8%	4%	9%	4%

For each of the following statements select *Would help explain* if it would, if true, help explain some of the information in the table. Otherwise select *Would not help explain.*

Would help explain	Would not help explain	
○	○	Ridgecrest is a private school with high tuition costs.
○	○	North Forest has a 1 hour study block built into their schedule.
○	○	Woodlands has the highest percentage of students participating in extracurricular activities.

2. A coach is dividing up players on his basketball team for a scrimmage. There should be 5 players on each team. The coach currently has 4 players assigned to each team. He wants team 1 to be stronger at shooting than team 2. He wants team 2 to have better dribbling skills and passing skills than team 1. Players are rated 1-10 in each of the three categories. Listed below is Player name (shooting rating, dribbling rating, passing rating).

       <u>Team 1</u>

       Isaac (7, 8, 6)

       Timothy (7, 5, 7)

       Steve (8, 6, 8)

       Jordan (6, 8, 7)

       <u>Team 2</u>

       Michael (6, 6, 7)

       Tony (8, 8, 7)

       Chris (6, 7, 9)

       John (9, 5, 6)

Select the player that could be added to team 1 to meet the coach's criteria and the select the player that could be added to team 2 to meet the coach's criteria. He averages each of the players rating to get a team rating. When selecting a player only take into account the opposite team's current rating (not the rating they will have after selecting a player for that team).

Team 1	Team 2	Player
○	○	Gordon (9, 9, 5)
○	○	James (9, 5, 4)
○	○	Caleb (8, 8, 7)
○	○	Howard (6, 8, 7)
○	○	Ben (5, 8, 8)

3. Refer to the pictograph below of a survey of students at a local elementary school. Each symbol represents 10 students in a sample of 200 students.

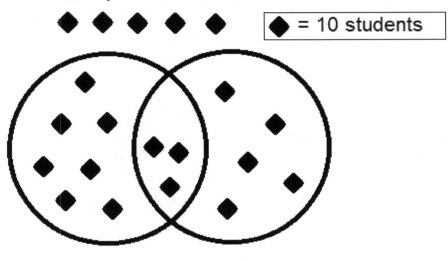

8 years of age   Own a dog

or older

If one student is selected at random, the chance that student will be under 8 years of age is

    a. 3 out of 4
    b. 1 out of 3
    c. 1 out of 2
    d. 4 out of 5

If one student is selected at random, the chance that student will be both under 8 and not own a dog is

    a. 1 out of 3
    b. 1 out of 4
    c. 4 out of 5
    d. 2 out of 3

4. The graph models Derrick's bank account for a 6 month period. Points *A, B,* and *C* represent the account balance in month 1, 3, and 5 respectively.

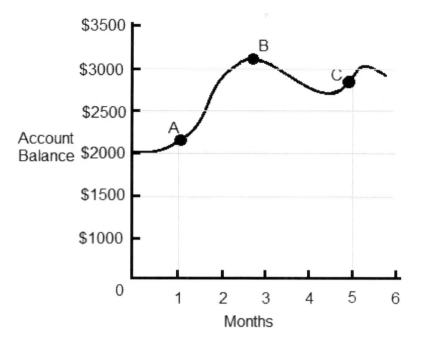

The amount that Derrick's account increases from point *B* is roughly _____ as much as the amount that it decreases from point *B* to point *C*.

a. Twice as much
b. Three times as much
c. Half as much
d. One third as much

For months from point *A* to point *C* the average (arithmetic mean) balance in Derrick's account was approximately...

a. $2000-$2200
b. $2250-$2450
c. $2550-$2750
d. $2800-$3000

For questions 5 and 6 use the following texts.

Comets

Comets are bodies that orbit the sun. They are distinguishable from asteroids by the presence of coma or tails. In the outer solar system, comets remain frozen and are so small that they are difficult to detect from Earth. As a comet approaches the inner solar system, solar radiation causes the materials within the comet to vaporize and trail off the nuclei. The released dust and gas forms a fuzzy atmosphere called the coma, and the force exerted on the coma causes a tail to form, pointing away from the sun.

Comet nuclei are made of ice, dust, rock and frozen gases and vary widely in size: from 100 meters or so to tens of kilometers across. The comas may be even larger

- 97 -

than the Sun. Because of their low mass, they do not become spherical and have irregular shapes.

There are over 3,500 known comets, and the number is steadily increasing. This represents only a small portion of the total comets existing, however. Most comets are too faint to be visible without the aid of a telescope; the number of comets visible to the naked eye is around one a year.

Comets leave a trail of solid debris behind them. If a comet's path crosses the Earth's path, there will likely be meteor showers as Earth passes through the trail of debris.

Many comets and asteroids have collided into Earth. Some scientists believe that comets hitting Earth about 4 billion years ago brought a significant proportion of the water in Earth's oceans. There are still many near-Earth comets.

Most comets have oval shaped orbits that take them close to the Sun for part of their orbit and then out further into the Solar System for the remainder of the orbit. Comets are often classified according to the length of their orbital period: short period comets have orbital periods of less than 200 years, long period comets have orbital periods of more than 200 years, single apparition comets have trajectories which cause them to permanently leave the solar system after passing the Sun once.

Stars

There are different life cycle possibilities for stars after they initially form and enter into the main sequence stage. Small, relatively cold red dwarfs with relatively low masses burn hydrogen slowly, and will remain in the main sequence for hundreds of billions of years. Massive, hot supergiants will leave the main sequence after just a few million years. The Sun is a mid-sized star that may be in the main sequence for 10 billion years. After the main sequence, the star expands to become a red giant. Depending upon the initial mass of the star, it can become a black dwarf (from a medium-sized star), and then a small, cooling white dwarf. Massive stars become red supergiants (and sometimes blue supergiants), explode in a supernova, and then become neutron stars. The largest stars can become black holes.

A nebula is a cloud of dust and gas that is composed primarily of hydrogen (97%) and helium (3%). Gravity causes parts of the nebula to clump together. This accretion continues adding atoms to the center of an unstable protostar. Equilibrium between gravity pulling atoms and gas pressure pushing heat and light away from the center is achieved. A star dies when it is no longer able to maintain equilibrium. A protostar may never become a star if it does not reach a critical core temperature. It may become a brown dwarf or a gas giant instead. If nuclear fusion of hydrogen into helium begins, a star is born. The "main sequence" of a star's life involves nuclear fusion reactions. During this time, the star contracts over billions of years to compensate for the heat and light energy lost. In the star's core, temperature, density, and pressure increase as the star contracts and the cycle continues.

5. For each of the following descriptions give either a *yes* or a *no* as to whether or not it describes a comet.

Yes	No	Description
◯	◯	Have collided with Earth
◯	◯	Have an orbital period of only 150 years
◯	◯	Are formed when gravity causes parts of the nebula to clump together

6. Decide whether or not the following statements are true or false based on the text.

True	False	Statement
◯	◯	Both stars and comets can be seen with the naked eye.
◯	◯	Comets have an oval shaped orbit while stars have a circular shaped orbit.
◯	◯	A nebula and a comet are both composed of 97% hydrogen.

7. The flowchart below represents a mathematical algorithm that takes two positive integers as the input and returns a positive integer as the output. Processes are indicated in the symbols in the flowchart.

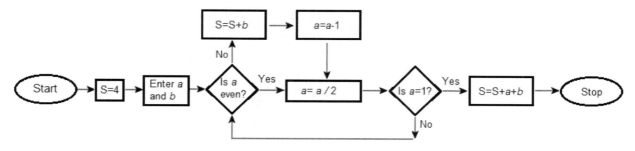

If 9 and 11 are entered as values for *a* and *b* respectively, then what is the value for S when you get to Stop?

    a. 20
    b. 27
    c. 28
    d. 32

If 19 and 4 are entered as values for *a* and *b* respectively, then what is the value for S when you get to Stop?

    a. 13
    b. 14
    c. 17
    d. 18

8. The table below displays 5 toy companies production for dolls, action figures, and toy cars for the year 2014. Assume that these are the only toys the company produces.

Company	Total Dolls	Total Action Figures	Total Toy Cars
Pop Toys	2800	3500	3700
Wild West Toys	3000	3400	3200
Tots Toys	3500	3100	3500
Lots of Toys	3000	2900	3400
Uptown Toys	2700	2800	3100

For each of the following statements, select *Yes* if it the statement can be shown to be true based on the information in the table. Otherwise select *No*.

Yes	No	Statement
◯	◯	No one company produces more than 25% of the total dolls produced
◯	◯	Wild West Toys produced the largest volume of toys overall
◯	◯	Lots of Toys produced more toy cars as a percentage of total production than Tots Toys

9. The following excerpt is from a fictitious story that discusses a type of location called *Laziguny*.

It was a Friday afternoon and Billy was sitting in math class waiting on the bell to ring so that he could leave for the day. The bell finally rings and he walks out of class and heads for the *Laziguny*. On his way he runs into his neighbors Jim and Chris. They continue to walk to the *Laziguny* while making plans for what they should do when they get home.

Based on the context of the imaginary word *Laziguny* in the previous paragraph, which of the following is the best description of the location?
   a. Where the children eat lunch
   b. Where the children play at recess
   c. Where the children wait for the bus
   d. Where the children play their instruments in music class

10. Below is a chart of 5 employees and the number of hours they work per month. The number under their name is their salary per month.

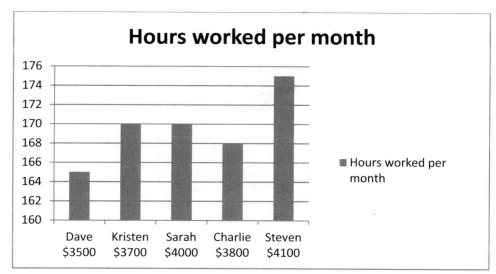

Below select the expression that best represents the calculation of their hourly wage. Then select the employee that is paid the most per hour. H = hourly wage, M= monthly salary, T= # of hours per month.

Calculation of hourly wage	
○	$M = \dfrac{H}{T}$
○	$H = \dfrac{M}{T}$
○	$H = M \times T$
○	$T = \dfrac{H}{M}$

Paid most per hour	
○	Dave
○	Kristen
○	Sarah
○	Charlie
○	Steven

11. A study done on 500 cats yielded the following results. Each symbol represents 20 cats.

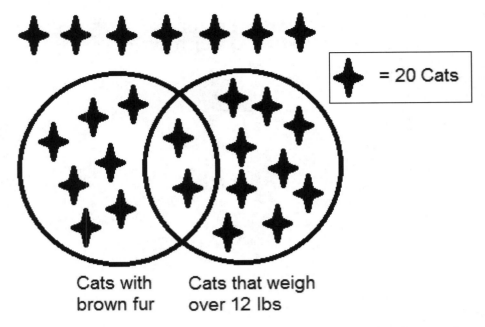

For the following statements select either *possible* if the statement is possible according to the results or *not possible* if it is not.

Possible	Not Possible	Statement
○	○	There were 210 cats with black fur
○	○	There were 190 cats that weighed 13-15 lbs
○	○	There were 195 cats that weighed 9-11 lbs and had brown fur

12. Daniel went for a walk through some woods near his house. For the first hour of the walk he tracked his distance from home via a handheld GPS. The results are graphed below.

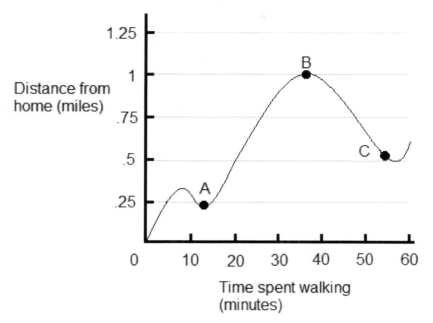

From point *A* to point *B*, Daniel moves approximately (1) _____ more mile(s) away from his house. From point *B* to point *C* he gets approximately (2)_____ closer to his house.

(1) A. 0.25
B. 0.5
C. 0.75
D. 1
(2) A. 40%
B. 50%
C. 60%
D. 70%

Quantitative

Problem Solving

1. The number 2 + 0.4 is how many times the number 1 − 0.2?

 a. $1\frac{1}{3}$
 b. 2
 c. $2\frac{2}{5}$
 d. $2\frac{1}{2}$
 e. 3

2. If a movie reached the 90-minute mark 12 minutes ago, what minute mark had it reached m minutes ago?

 a. $m - 102$
 b. $m - 78$
 c. $102 - m$
 d. $78 - m$
 e. $90 - m$

3. A bull's-eye with a 4-inch diameter covers 20 percent of a circular target. What is the area, in square inches, of the target?

 a. 0.8π
 b. 32π
 c. 10π
 d. 20π
 e. 80π

4. Which of the following is less than $\frac{5}{8}$?

 a. $\frac{7}{10}$
 b. $\frac{4}{5}$
 c. $\frac{6}{11}$
 d. 0.625
 e. 0.65

5. A wholesale bakery marks up the price of a loaf of bread by 20 percent. The grocery store that resells that bread then marks up the increased price by 20 percent. This series of successive markups is equivalent to what single markup?

 a. 20 percent
 b. 22 percent
 c. 30 percent
 d. 40 percent
 e. 44 percent

6. If line AB perpendicularly bisects line CD at point O, which of the following is true of Δ AOD?

    a. 40° < Δ AOD ≤ 50°

    b. 80° < Δ AOD ≤ 90°

    c. 170° < Δ AOD ≤ 180°

    d. 215° < Δ AOD ≤ 225°

    e. 260° < Δ AOD ≤ 270°

7. The volume in a water drum is halved every 2 days of a drought. If the volume of water in the drum was initially 10^6 gallons, what was the volume after 10 days?

    a. $(\frac{1}{2})^{10}(10^6)$

    b. $(\frac{1}{2})^5(10^6)$

    c. $2^5(10^6)$

    d. $2^{10}(10^6)$

    e. $(10^6)^5$

8. At a wedding reception, only 60 percent of the 750 invited guests show up. Of those in attendance, 46 percent are males. How many of the guests in attendance are female?

    a. 207

    b. 243

    c. 345

    d. 405

    e. 450

9.

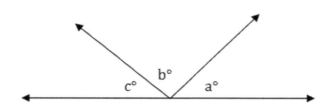

In the figure above, if $\frac{b}{a+b+c} = \frac{3}{5}$, then b = ?

    a. 60

    b. 72

    c. 108

    d. 120

    e. 180

10. Abby is selling magazine subscriptions. She has turned in 3 order forms totaling $75, $40, and $107. She has 1 additional order pending. If Abby's average (arithmetic mean) order is to be exactly $80 on 4 forms, the fourth order must total how much?

    a. $18

    b. $74

    c. $80

    d. $98

    e. $101

11. $3y - 2x = 9$

$2x + y = -5$

In the system of equations above, what is the value of y?

    a. −3
    b. $-\frac{1}{7}$
    c. −1
    d. 1
    e. 3

12.

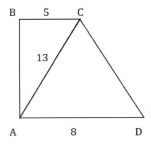

In the figure above, what is the area of triangular region ACD?

    a. 13
    b. 30
    c. 48
    d. 60
    e. 96

13. What is the maximum number of $6\frac{3}{4}$-inch strips that can be cut from a spool of ribbon that is 10 yards long?

    a. 1
    b. 17
    c. 18
    d. 53
    e. 54

14. A pilot traveled the first 1,500 miles of a 3,000-mile journey with an average speed of 400 miles per hour. At what speed must the pilot travel the remaining 1,500 miles to record an average speed of 500 miles per hour for the entire flight?

    a. $261\frac{2}{3}$ MPH
    b. 600 MPH
    c. $666\frac{2}{3}$ MPH
    d. 800 MPH
    e. 5,625 MPH

15. If the radius of circle O is one-quarter the diameter of circle P, what is the ratio of the circumference of circle O to the circumference of circle P?

    a. $\frac{1}{4}$

    b. $\frac{1}{2}$

    c. 1

    d. 2

    e. 4

16. If $\frac{3}{8}$ of the money in a certain college fund was spent on tuition, $\frac{1}{4}$ was spent on room and board, $\frac{1}{5}$ was spent on books, and the remaining $7,000 remained in the fund, what was the total amount of the college fund?

    a. $7,000

    b. $8,485

    c. $33,000

    d. $40,000

    e. $47,000

17. If $x^2 + 3x - 18 = 0$ and $x < 0$, which of the following must equal 0?

    I. $x^2 - 36$
    II. $x^2 - 2x - 3$
    III. $x^2 + 5x - 6$

    a. I only

    b. II only

    c. III only

    d. I and III only

    e. I, II, and III

18. The length of the edge of cube A is three-quarters the length of the edge of cube B. What is the ratio of the volume of cube B to the volume of cube A?

    a. $\frac{1}{64}$

    b. $\frac{1}{4}$

    c. $\frac{27}{64}$

    d. $\frac{3}{4}$

    e. $\frac{64}{27}$

19. If the fractions $\frac{5}{9}, \frac{6}{11}, \frac{1}{2}, \frac{9}{16}$, and $\frac{3}{5}$ are numbered from least to greatest, the second fraction of the resulting sequence would be?

    a. $\frac{5}{9}$

    b. $\frac{6}{11}$

    c. $\frac{1}{2}$

    d. $\frac{9}{16}$

    e. $\frac{3}{5}$

20. If x > 2500, then the value of $\frac{x}{1-2x}$ is closest to

    a. −1

    b. $-\frac{50}{99}$

    c. $-\frac{1}{2}$

    d. $\frac{50}{99}$

    e. $\frac{1}{2}$

21. If the area of a rectangular game board is 336 square inches and its perimeter is 76 inches, what is the length of each of the shorter sides?

    a. 10 inches

    b. 14 inches

    c. 19 inches

    d. 24 inches

    e. 65 inches

22. In a spelling bee, Anish's placement is both the 11th highest and the 25th lowest among all the spellers who participated. How many spellers participated in the spelling bee?

    a. 33

    b. 34

    c. 35

    d. 36

    e. 37

23. If c is to be chosen at random from the set {1, 2, 3, 4} and d is to be chosen at random from the set {1, 2, 3, 4}, what is the probability cd will be odd?

    a. $\frac{1}{4}$

    b. $\frac{1}{3}$

    c. $\frac{3}{4}$

    d. 4

    e. 12

24. The length (l) of a rectangle is three times its width. What is the length of the diagonal in terms of the length (l)?

    a. $\frac{\sqrt{10}}{3}l$

    b. $\frac{10}{3}l$

    c. $\frac{10}{9}l$

    d. $\sqrt{10}\, l$

    e. $10l$

Data Sufficiency

This Data Sufficiency problem consists of a question and two statements, labeled (1) and (2), in which certain data are given. You have to decide whether the data given in the statements are sufficient for answering the question, using only the data given in the statements and your knowledge of mathematics and everyday facts (such as the number of days in July or the meaning of counterclockwise).

  A. Statement (1) ALONE is sufficient, but statement (2) is not sufficient.
  B. Statement (2) ALONE is sufficient, but statement (1) is not sufficient.
  C. BOTH statements TOGETHER are sufficient, but NEITHER statement ALONE is sufficient.
  D. EACH statement ALONE is sufficient.
  E. Statements (1) and (2) TOGETHER are NOT sufficient.

25. What is the value of $\frac{q}{5} - \frac{r}{5}$?

(1) $\frac{q-r}{5} = 3$
(2) $q - r = 15$
a.   b.   c.   d.   e.

26. If Barry is y years old and Charisse is z years old, what is their combined age?

(1) Barry is 16 years older than Charisse.
(2) Ten years from now, Barry will be twice Charisse's age.
a.   b.   c.   d.   e.

27. If l, w, and h represent the length, width, and height respectively of a rectangular solid, what is the volume of the solid?

(1) $lw = 40$
(2) $\frac{1}{2}lwh = 30$
a.   b.   c.   d.   e.

28. What were the net proceeds from a fundraiser on the third day it was held?

(1) Net proceeds on the third day were $50,000 more than the first day.
(2) Net proceeds on the third day were three-quarters the second day's net proceeds.
a.   b.   c.   d.   e.

29. What is the value of x?

(1) $1 - 3x = 7x + 5$
(2) $\frac{4}{x} = -10$
a.   b.   c.   d.   e.

30.

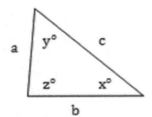

Is the triangle above a right triangle?
(1) $a = 5, b = 12, c = 13$
(2) $x = 45$
a.   b.   c.   d.   e.

31. If a total of 1,500 Democrats, Republicans, and Independents participated in a voters' survey, how many Independents were surveyed?

(1) 40 percent of the voters were Republicans.
(2) The number of Independents surveyed was 25 percent of the combined total of Democrats and Republicans surveyed.
a.   b.   c.   d.   e.

32. Is the value of p closer to 10 than to 25?

(1) $25 - p < p - 10$
(2) $p < 20$
a.   b.   c.   d.   e.

33. What is the radius of circle O?

(1) The ratio of circle O's area to its circumference is 2.
(2) The area of circle O is 16π.
a.   b.   c.   d.   e.

34. If the average (arithmetic mean) of m consecutive integers is 7, what is the greatest of the integers?

(1) The range of the m integers is 8.
(2) The least of the m integers is 3.
a.   b.   c.   d.   e.

35. Janika buys fabric in each of her three school colors: black, white, and red. If the total yardage of the fabric is 19, how much white fabric did she buy?

(1) The amount of white fabric is 1.5 times the amount of black fabric and two-thirds the amount of red fabric.
(2) The sum of the amounts of white and black fabric is 1 yard more than the amount of red fabric.
a.   b.   c.   d.   e.

36.

What is the measure of x in the circle with center O above?
(1) The circumference of the circle is 6π.
(2) The length of arc AB is 2π.
a.   b.   c.   d.   e.

37. If q is an integer between 2 and 9 inclusive and q is also the square root of an integer, what is the value of q?

(1) q is even.
(2) The cube root of q is an integer.
a.   b.   c.   d.   e.

Verbal

Reading Comprehension

Questions 1 – 4 pertain to the following passage:

One of the key features of the music scene in the past decade has been the increasing popularity of outsiders, especially those with a career. In previous decades, amateur status was seen as a lower calling or, at best, a step on the way to professional status, but many musical insiders now believe that amateurs actually constitute an elite group within the music scene, with greater chances of eventual success. Professionals, once able to fully devote themselves to the advancement of their musical careers, now find themselves hamstrung by a variety of factors that were not issues even a decade ago, giving the edge to people who do not depend on music for a livelihood. A number of technological, demographic, and economic factors are to blame for this change.

Full-time musicians always had difficulties making ends meet, but these difficulties have been vastly increased by a changing music scene. The increased popularity of electronic music, mega-bands, and other acts that rely heavily on marketing, theatrics, and expensive effects has made it harder than ever for local acts to draw crowds. The decreasing crowds at coffee houses, bars, and other small venues leave the owners without the ability to pay for live music. Amateurs can still play the same coffee houses as ever, and the lack of a hundred-dollar paycheck at the end of the night is hardly noticed. Professionals, however, have to fight more desperately than ever for those few lucrative gigs.

An even bigger factor has been the rise of digital media in general and digital file sharing in particular. People have been trading copies of music for decades, but in the days of analog tapes there was always a loss. The tape one fan burned for another would be of lesser quality than the original, prompting the recipient to go out and buy the album. Now that music fans can make full-quality copies for little or nothing and distribute them all over the world, it can be very hard for bands to make any money on music sales. Again, this does not make much difference to amateurs, but it robs the professionals of what has traditionally been one of their biggest sources of revenue.

All of this results in a situation so dire for professional musicians that their extra experience often doesn't balance out their lack of economic resources. The amateurs are the only ones who can afford to buy new gear and fix broken equipment, keep their cars in working order to get to shows, and pay to promote their shows. The professionals tend to have to fall back on "day jobs," typically at lower rates and with less opportunity for advancement. Even those professional musicians who are able to supplement their incomes with music lessons, wedding shows, and other traditional jobs are often living at such a low level that they cannot afford to buy the professional equipment they need to keep the higher-paying gigs. A fairly skilled amateur, by contrast, may not have the same level of virtuosity but will be able to fake his way through most of what a professional does at a more competitive rate, which will allow him to play professional shows.

1. The author of this essay is mainly

    a. arguing for a return to a climate more favorable to professional musicians
    b. examining the causes of the increasing success of amateur musicians over professionals
    c. revealing the psychological toll the current economy takes on professional musicians
    d. disputing the claim that unsuccessful professional musicians simply don't work hard enough
    e. comparing the relative contributions of professional and amateur musicians

2. Which of the following statements about musicians does the essay most directly support?

    a. Bars and coffee houses should be willing to pay a fair wage to professional musicians
    b. The most popular professional bands have not been affected by the changes that plague most professional musicians
    c. It is much easier for amateur musicians to book shows than it was a decade ago
    d. Professional musicians have recently lost some of their most important sources of income
    e. With the shrinking music scenes, it is nearly impossible for a modern musician to support himself on music alone

3. In his discussion of professional musicians in the last paragraph, the author

    a. indicates that amateurs deserve their new, higher status
    b. shows that in the current climate, professionals may not have the ability to purchase and maintain the tools that they need
    c. points out the decrease in the market for wedding gigs and lessons
    d. questions an assumption about the status of professional musicians
    e. predicts a decline in the number of professional musicians

4. According to the essay, amateur musicians are becoming more successful at both amateur and professional gigs because professionals

    a. exclusively performs high-paying gigs and are unwilling to play in clubs
    b. are not able to relate to ordinary people as well as amateurs can
    c. have financial needs that they are not able to meet in the current musical climate
    d. are in an industry that is particularly susceptible to economic changes
    e. don't receive the same respect as people with more lucrative careers

Questions 5 – 7 pertain to the following passage:

A meeting of the High Tribal Council of Urk in the year 5543 addressed parliamentary critiques of the 5542 Freedom of Thought Law. The law's complete exemption of any thoughts believed to be libelous or licentious from protection—e.g., negative opinions about major political and religious figures or daydreams about taboo or illegal subjects—caused the Council to redraft portions of the law and overturn convictions of many currently incarcerated under it. Supreme councilor Snort McGuinn stated that the law provided "no way to selectively pardon thoughts thought in the pursuit of artistic creativity or legitimate political activity." Members of Parliament also testified that the overly broad provisions of the law were sometimes used by corrupt bureaucrats as a way to stifle political dissent and to dispossess wealthy artists for personal gain.

As a reply, the Terrestrial House of Parliament drafted PT 5x23, which included numerous proposed changes to the text of the law. A section was written to ensure the liberty to ponder even controversial ideas if the thinker was able to furnish a general explanation as to how his thought process could lead to the betterment of society without compromising social order. In this version, citizens would no longer be required to specifically catalog, register, and answer for each thought they had, but they would instead be able to defend ideas and avenues of inquiry as a whole. Both the Low and High Tribal Councils would be empowered to review these defenses, speeding up the review process considerably. The Orbiting House of Parliament bill, PO 2D54 included all of the changes in the Terrestrial bill but went even further. It provided a legal process to punish bureaucrats using thought restrictions for personal gain, designated free thought zones within personal residences, and a special Civilian Thought Review Council with the ability to permanently legalize new ideas on a case-by-case basis.

The Urk Homeland Security Department strongly objected to the proposed changes, calling them "dangerous, unenforceable, and ill-defined." They argued that the new laws might actually limit protections for freedom of thought by moving many previously illegal thoughts into a gray area where they could be found either legal or illegal, hampering the efforts of citizens to restrict their thought-processes to wholly legal topics. The elite Department of Friendly and Secret Enforcement further stated that the review of thoughts set up in the new laws could pose a threat to Urk national safety and security.

Both parliamentary laws were passed later that year after a considerable amount of further negotiation and discussion. One key amendment added to the bill was the Sol amendment, which required that bureaucrats detail any possible personal benefit before dispossessing a thought criminal unless detailing those benefits could cause a breach in state security. The president himself objected strongly to this, saying that the amendment would potentially expose huge numbers of government contacts and connections to public view unless the bureaucrats were able to show that each individual secret was exempt from the law.

Before the law was submitted to the president and the High Tribal Council for ratification, the two versions of the bill were combined into one compromise bill. It addressed the president's concern by making it somewhat easier for bureaucrats to gain exemptions to the disclosure law. It also worked with the Urk Homeland Security Department to tighten the definitions of what constituted thought crime. The bill passed by an overwhelming majority, and the council and president had no choice but to ratify it.

5. The Urk Homeland Security Department opposed the bill because its members felt that the bill would

    a. curtail the public's right to security
    b. undermine existing national security laws
    c. pose legal problems for ordinary citizens
    d. weaken their own power in enforcing security measures
    e. undermine the authority of the High Tribal Council

6. Of the statements below, which best supports that "the review of thoughts set up in the new laws could pose a threat to Urk national safety and security"?

    a. Civilians do not have the knowledge required to judge whether a thought is dangerous or not
    b. Some of the thoughts that are currently labeled dangerous are actually no longer threatening to the political establishment
    c. A civilian board would need a huge amount of resources to review all of the thoughts currently labeled illegal
    d. Civilians can be influenced by government pressure not to legalize a thought
    e. The High Tribal Council has the power to veto all Civilian Thought Review Council decisions

7. Judging by the president's statement on the Sol amendment, with which statement would he most likely agree?

    a. Bureaucratic conflicts of interest should be exempt from any public scrutiny
    b. Bureaucratic conflicts of interest should be released into the public eye unless doing so would threaten national security
    c. It would be impractical for bureaucrats to have to justify withholding each individual secret from public disclosure
    d. Protection of public safety comes before protection of bureaucratic secrets
    e. Bureaucratic secrets should not be examined individually before being released

Questions 8 – 11 pertain to the following passage:

Current theories of linguistic evolution state that language change, rather than being the result of incorrect language use or sloppy speech, is part of the continual evolution and progression of the structure of language. As languages are influenced by other cultures they come into contact with, dialectical variations occur. It can take anywhere from a century in intensely multicultural areas to millennia in isolated communities for the standard spoken language to change so much that it would be unrecognizable to speakers of the original tongue. In either case, the accumulation of new words is accompanied by the proliferation of subtle grammatical variations that indicate a deeper language change.

Language changes in multicultural regions—like the Balkans of Europe—are quite drastic and rapid; linguists studying language change in these areas can observe the process as it occurs much more readily. When the language seems to be evolving much more gradually, however, as in Iceland and the other Scandinavian countries, locating current linguistic trends is just the surface. Verb morphology irregularities, vowel shifts, and recently introduced words all help to show how the language may change next, as do areas where the language has remained surprisingly consistent over the past several centuries. When the historical record is available, linguists rely on it. Early writings can vary from fragments of stories on scraps of parchment to well-preserved, detailed accounts of the proper use and pronunciation of the ancient tongue, as is the case with the ancient Romans.

Once the boundaries and characteristics of a language community are established, linguistic scholars can gather data from subcultures within that community. The linguists must attempt to study every group within a community, while staying within a linguistically well-defined area. Changes in the speech of young or marginalized subcultures or groups that have an unusual amount of contact with outsiders are great early indicators of looming language shifts. Phonological drift—a gradual change in the way certain sounds or combinations of sound are pronounced by speakers within the community—can be accurately measured and recorded through computer voice analysis measuring the pronunciations of hundreds of volunteers saying the same sentences. In theory, if the linguists posit a definition of a critical language shift—the amount of change in a given language before it would become unrecognizable to current speakers—they can predict when this will occur by extrapolating current rates of change. All things being equal, this can predict the time it will take for a completely new language to evolve.

Massive migrations, occupations, and social collapse are some phenomena that can trigger a more rapid language change. Many are only just being investigated as modern linguists observe cultures in crisis. Watching for these sorts of drastic upheavals helps linguists select potential regions for current studies. The effects of these events are still being discovered. For example, linguists are currently studying the declines of Meso-American languages under the influence of Spanish-speaking Mexican linguistic and cultural hegemony.

8. The text says that a main difference between multicultural regions like the Balkans and isolated regions like Iceland is that in multicultural regions
    a. there are no precursors to change
    b. there are fewer language changes
    c. languages change more rapidly
    d. there are no subtle changes before big language shifts
    e. the cultural forces that underlie language change are less powerful

9. The essay is written to
    a. show how languages change in isolated areas
    b. argue that language change is a normal thing
    c. examine the phenomena that cause language change in multicultural areas
    d. assert that it is impossible to predict when a language will change
    e. describe how linguists study language change

10. The third paragraph serves primarily to
    a. describe the relationship between phonological drift and language change
    b. explain the difficulty of studying language change in a given community
    c. contrast language communities in isolated and multicultural areas
    d. examine some of the ways linguists study language change in different parts of a community to get a picture of the community as a whole
    e. suggest that language change is a much more pervasive phenomenon than most scholars think

11. According to the essay, information about phonological drift within a community can help linguists
    a. predict when a new language will evolve
    b. assess how important a new word is in the evolution of the language
    c. measure social and cultural upheaval
    d. come up with more accurate ways to measure language change
    e. estimate the rate of language change in similar cultures

Questions 12 – 14 pertain to the following passage:

Although technological tools like polygraph tests, psychological theories, and interrogation techniques have resulted in slightly greater accuracy for law enforcement agents catching liars, it is still important to understand the nature of lies and check unfounded assumptions that can lead to unquestioning acceptance of false statements. Because intentional deception is one of the biggest obstacles to a successful criminal investigation, developing the ability to separate dubious or outright false statements from true ones has to be one of the main goals of every police officer and law enforcement investigator. In addition, an officer must be able to quickly sort out the possible repercussions of a false statement and the ways it can affect the rest of an investigation, should one slip by police screening. This is the only way to punish the guilty, exonerate the innocent, and do the most possible good in preventing future crimes.

The most difficult lie to catch is the half-truth. Half-truths are distortions constructed by using a seed of truth as a way to sprout a more convincing lie. A half-truth may incorporate intentional exaggeration or understatement, lies of omission, false implications, or outright lies mixed in with actual facts. Half-truths that slip past the detectives investigating a case are classified as either "smoke" lies or "mirror" lies. Smoke refers to half-truths that slow down an investigation by casting doubt on otherwise promising leads or angles of investigation. Mirrors are lies that manage to send the detective off in the wrong direction altogether, usually by linking a fact to a false supposition.

Most other lies are overt and intentional. Usually, they are told as a way for a suspect or witness to protect himself or his friends or, more rarely, to cast suspicion on a rival. In some cases, these sorts of lies can be compounded by overzealous or corrupt police who want to earn a conviction of a supposed perpetrator at any cost. Particularly in high-profile cases with gruesome details, this sort of lie results in more false convictions than any other type of distortion.

12. Which statement most accurately conveys the essay's main idea?

    a. New police techniques have been ineffective at helping investigators catch liars
    b. The worst lies aren't outright lies, but sneaky half-truths
    c. People in law enforcement need to be able to recognize lies to be effective and just
    d. There are only two primary types of lies
    e. Most overt lies are told to protect a suspect or a witness

13. The essay's writer would be most likely to say that a police officer's ability to recognize both lies and half-truths is

    a. indispensable in a criminal investigation
    b. difficult because of the sophistication of some liars
    c. the most important tool that law enforcement has
    d. important only when investigating a crime
    e. crucial, but beyond the abilities of most officers

14. According to the essay, "smoke"

    a. is the most frequently told type of half-truth

    b. never contains outright lies mixed in with truth

    c. can slow down an investigation

    d. is used to protect the guilty

    e. sends detectives off in the wrong direction altogether

Sentence Correction

These questions present a sentence, all or part of which is underlined. Beneath each sentence you will find five ways of phrasing the underlined part. The first of these repeats the original; the other four are different. If you think the original is best, choose the first answer; otherwise, choose one of the other answers.

These questions test correctness and effectiveness of expression. In choosing your answer, follow the requirements of standard written English; that is, pay attention to grammar, choice of words, and sentence construction. Choose the answer that produces the most effective sentence; this answer should be clear and exact, without awkwardness, ambiguity, redundancy, or grammatical error.

15. Skeptical visitors often dismiss the Castle Blood hauntings on the basis of the lack of a tangible experience, such as spirit knockings, that are called conclusive evidence of the occult, and ignore less obvious phenomena, such as faint whisperings and cold mists.

    a. a tangible experience, such as spirit knockings, that are called conclusive evidence of the occult, and ignore less obvious phenomena, such as

    b. a tangible experience, such as spirit knockings, that are called conclusive evidence of the occult, and ignore less obvious phenomena, such as what is experienced as

    c. a tangible experience, such as spirit knockings, that is called conclusive evidence of the occult, and ignore less obvious phenomena, such as

    d. what they think of as tangible experience, such as spirit knockings, that are called conclusive evidence of the occult, and ignore less obvious phenomena, such as what is experienced as

    e. what they think of as tangible experience, such as spirit knockings, that are called conclusive evidence of the occult, and ignore less obvious phenomena, such as

16. A frequent source of stress for entering freshmen happens <u>when students enroll in out-of-state schools, and it makes them grow apart</u> from their high school friends.

    a. when students enroll in out-of-state schools, and it makes them grow apart

    b. by a student enrolling in an out-of-state school, which makes him grow apart

    c. when students enroll in out-of-state schools, thereby growing apart

    d. when a student who enrolls in out-of-state schools, and so grows apart

    e. if a student enrolls in an out-of-state school, he would grow apart

17. Egyptologists believe that the desiccated bodies recently found in an Egyptian tomb, <u>evidently those of servants who are believed to have been buried</u> nearly 4,000 years ago, remained intact and undisturbed by rot or scavengers because of their dry, stable, and isolated environment

    a. evidently those of servants who are believed to have been buried

    b. those of servants, evidently, who were believed to have been buried

    c. those of evident servants who were believed to have been buried

    d. those of servants who are believed to have been evidently buried

    e. those of servants who were evidently believed to have been buried

18. Unlike Hakim Bey, <u>Robert Anton Wilson felt how late 20th-century technology not as an inherently alienating force, and</u> something that could potentially liberate people from their hang-ups, isolation, and prejudices.

    a. Robert Anton Wilson felt how late 20th-century technology not as an inherently alienating force, and

    b. Robert Anton Wilson saw late 20th-century technology not as an inherently alienating force, but as

    c. Robert Anton Wilson felt that late 20th-century technology was not as an inherently alienating force, and

    d. it was felt by Robert Anton Wilson that late 20th-century technology was not an inherently alienating force, but

    e. late 20th-century technology was felt by Robert Anton Wilson to be not an inherently alienating force, and be

19. Federal investigators surveying the crash scene noted that only one-third of the passengers on board the plane had been issued life jackets. <u>At the least as many as 80 or more other ones had not been given any</u> flotation device whatsoever.

    a. At the least as many as 80 or more other ones had not been given any

    b. At the least as many as more than 80 other ones had not been given any

    c. More than 80 other ones had not been given any

    d. At least 80 had not been given any

    e. There were at the least 80 or even more who had not been given any

20. Historians have discovered that fighting was a popular sport for ancient cultures, <u>as that of modern civilizations</u>.

    a. as that of modern civilizations

    b. like that for modern civilizations

    c. exactly like modern civilizations do

    d. as modern people do

    e. as it still is for modern civilizations

21. Born John Joseph Lydon in North London in 1956, Johnny Rotten's first number 1 song, *God Save the Queen* was released during the week of Queen Elizabeth II's Silver Jubilee when the musician was 21.

    a. Johnny Rotten's first number 1 song, *God Save the Queen* was released during the week of Queen Elizabeth II's Silver Jubilee when the musician was 21

    b. Johnny Rotten's first number 1 song, *God Save the Queen*, released during the week of Queen Elizabeth II's Silver Jubilee when the musician was 21

    c. Johnny Rotten's *God Save the Queen*, his first number 1 song was released during the week of Queen Elizabeth II's Silver Jubilee when the musician was 21

    d. Johnny Rotten released his first number 1 song, *God Save the Queen*, during the week of Queen Elizabeth II's Silver Jubilee when the musician was 21

    e. during the week of Queen Elizabeth II's Silver Jubilee, Johnny Rotten released his first number 1 song, *God Save the Queen* when the musician was 21

22. In musical recording, one advantage of simultaneous multi-track recording over recording one musician at a time is that the harmonies are blended as the music is played <u>rather than </u>a digital simulation requiring extra processing and remixing.

    a. rather than
    b. rather than in
    c. as opposed to
    d. and not
    e. instead of having been with

23. The Discordian Society believes that, since the untimely demise of their leader Kerry Thornley, <u>they did and will keep continuing the chaotic goals of Thornley and his cabal, the Legion of Dynamic Discord</u>, who have begun to sow the seeds of worldwide anarchy.

    a. they did and will keep continuing the chaotic goals of Thornley and his cabal, the Legion of Dynamic Discord
    b. they did and will keep continuing Thornley's, and his cabal the Legion of Discord's, chaotic goals
    c. it did and will keep continuing the chaotic goals of Thornley and his cabal, the Legion of Dynamic Discord
    d. it has maintained and will continue to maintain the chaotic goals of Thornley and his cabal, the Legion of Dynamic Discord
    e. it has continued the chaotic goals of Thornley and his cabal, the Legion of Dynamic Discord

24. Environmentalists studying global climate change have scientifically determined that global warming is accelerating, and the Kyoto protocols and other environmental treaties of the latter half of the 20th century is only slowing, rather than stopping, the acceleration of climate change.

    a. the Kyoto protocols and other environmental treaties of the latter half of the 20th century is only slowing, rather than stopping, the acceleration of climate change
    b. in the latter half of the 20th century, the Kyoto protocols and other environmental treaties is only slowing, rather than stopping, the acceleration of climate change
    c. the Kyoto protocols and other environmental treaties of the latter half of the 20th century have only slowed, rather than stopped, the acceleration of climate change
    d. in the latter half of the 20th century, the Kyoto protocols and other environmental treaties have only been slowing, rather than stopped, the acceleration
    e. the latter half of the 20th century's Kyoto protocols and other environmental treaties only were slowing, rather than stopping, climate change's acceleration

25. All of Lloyd Kaufman's most successful movies—*Class of Nuke 'em High*, *Toxic Avenger*, and *Tromeo and Julliet*—takes place in a high school setting, a fact that suggests that his high school experiences may have played a formative role in his film-making career.

    a. All of Lloyd Kaufman's most successful movies—*Class of Nuke 'em High*, *Toxic Avenger*, and *Tromeo and Julliet*—takes place in a high school setting
    b. *Class of Nuke 'em High*, *Toxic Avenger*, and *Tromeo and Julliet*—each of them among Lloyd Kaufman's most successful movies—takes place in a high school setting
    c. Lloyd Kaufman's most successful movies—*Class of Nuke 'em High*, *Toxic Avenger*, and *Tromeo and Julliet*—all take place in a high school setting
    d. The movies by Lloyd Kaufman—*Class of Nuke 'em High*, *Toxic Avenger*, and *Tromeo and Julliet*—each one of these successful movies takes place in a high school setting
    e. Movies Lloyd Kaufman made—*Class of Nuke 'em High*, *Toxic Avenger*, and *Tromeo and Julliet*—all of them successful, take place in a high school setting

26. Still using classic forms dating from before the age of Shakespeare, new metric forms and approaches to rhythm allow 21st-century poets not only to write artful verse, but also to express the rhythms of modern life.

   a. new metric forms and approaches to rhythm allow 21st-century poets not only to write artful verse, but also to express
   b. 21st-century poets using new metric forms and approaches to rhythm write not only artful verse, but also can express
   c. employing new metric forms and approaches to rhythm allows 21st-century poets not only to write artful verse, but also to express
   d. employing new metric forms and approaches not just for artful verse, 21st-century poets are able to express
   e. the poets of the 21st century are empowered by new metric forms and approaches not just for writing artful verse, but also for expressing

27. Unlike their Scandinavian counterparts, British teens have force to compete from an early age, with no regard given to the value of cooperation.

   a. have force to compete
   b. are forced to compete
   c. are forced of competing
   d. are under force to compete
   e. have force that they must compete

28. In the early 1960s, when the Scratching Post was a small, recently opened, hole-in-the-wall pub, the club booked as many local bands in a typical month as they do now, despite the fact that they are a much more popular club in a better location.

   a. when the Scratching Post was a small, recently opened, hole-in-the-wall pub, the club booked as many local bands in a typical month as they do now, despite
   b. when the Scratching Post was a small, recently opened, hole-in-the-wall pub, the club booked as many local bands in a typical month as they do in a typical month now, despite
   c. when the Scratching Post was a small, recently opened, hole-in-the-wall pub, the club booked a quantity of local bands in a typical month as so they do now, despite
   d. whereas the Scratching Post was a small, recently opened, hole-in-the-wall pub, the club booked such a number of local bands in a typical month as do they now, in spite of
   e. when the Scratching Post was a small, recently opened, hole-in-the-wall pub, the club booked a quantity of local bands just as great in a typical month as the number that they do now, despite

29. The writing of novelist Philip K. Dick works as an interrogation of consensus reality and the category of the real more than it does as a response to the particular wars and struggles of late 20th-century society.

   a. more than it does as a response to the particular wars and struggles of late 20th-century society.
   b. more than it did as a response to the particular wars and struggles of late 20th-century society.
   c. more than it did respond, during the late 20th century, to the particular wars and struggles of society.
   d. more than it was responsive to the particular wars and struggles of late 20th-century society.
   e. more than, in late 20th-century society, responding to the particular wars and struggles.

30. Just as the rarity of musical all-ages venues contributes to the dullness of life for teens in the Detroit suburbs, so the absence of public transportation further restricts the ability of young people to enjoy an active and varied social life.

  a. so the absence of public transportation further restricts the ability of young people to enjoy an active and varied social life.

  b. just the same, public transportation being absent further restricts the ability of young people to enjoy an active and varied social life.

  c. so the absence of public transportation further restricting the ability of young people to enjoy an active and varied social life.

  d. in identical manner, potentials for an active and varied social life are restricted by the absence of public transportation.

  e. so it is in other aspects of life, where the absent public transportation aids the further restricting of the ability of young people to enjoy an active and varied social life.

Critical Reasoning

31. A recent exposé reported that a new series of television commercials makes deceptive claims about the health benefits of a new cereal. The reporter drew the conclusion that the commercials could cause consumers to actually choose a less healthful cereal for its supposed health benefits. *Which of the following choices would best reinforce the reporter's conclusion?*

  a. Television stations rely heavily on food commercials as a source of revenue

  b. Television executives have little idea whether a particular commercial is true or false

  c. Viewers depend on commercials as a way to understand the health benefits of new foods

  d. Television commercials tend to distort information more than print ads do

  e. All food ads are carefully screened by a panel of experts for accuracy before they are put on the air

32. A state senator asserts that her state's ban on smoking marijuana is unprincipled and backwards, since more dangerous drugs like nicotine and alcohol are legal. She argues that instead of futilely struggling to enforce the ban, the government should lift all drug prohibition. She asserts that legalization would provide a further benefit by reducing crime. *Assuming the following statements are true, which does the most to weaken the senator's argument?*

  a. Many people use drugs because of the thrill of getting away with it. Therefore, legalizing drug use would drive these people away, lowering the rate of drug use.

  b. The senator's state already makes drug enforcement a low priority. Therefore, legalization wouldn't have much effect on the law enforcement budget.

  c. Since marijuana was first outlawed, the number of users has increased substantially every year.

  d. If drugs were legalized, users from neighboring states would be drawn in. Many of them are involved in racketeering and other serious illegal activities.

  e. Many illegal drug users argue that they can get high on cough syrup and other legal pharmaceuticals.

33. Scientists studying the CPUs (equivalent to the brains) of killer robots discovered that the robots receive just as many commands to crush humans when recharging as when actively crushing. In order to discover why the robot's massive steel claws don't respond to the crush command when the bot recharges, a scientist removed a chip in the primary sympathetic processor (PSC), a module that connects the robot's body to the CPU. Without leaving recharge mode, the robot grabbed the scientist, threw him to the ground, stomped him repeatedly, and then proceeded to crush several imaginary people while stomping around the room. *In combination with the account above, which statement lends most support to the conclusion that the recharging robot was acting out some sort of evil robot dream?*

    a. The chip that was removed from the primary sympathetic processor normally triggers the robotic recharge state and the diminished activity that accompanies it
    b. The PSC can pass on data even if the robot is recharging
    c. The chip that was extracted normally transmits commands from the CPU to the robot body
    d. The chip that was extracted normally stops commands from moving from the CPU to the robot body
    e. The CPU seems to select different targets for crushing when asleep than when awake

34. A widely believed anthropological theory states that the Hill People, an early culture on Mucky Muck Island, fought with and were eventually wiped out by the Lothars whose culture dominates the island today. More recently, however, anthropologists have proposed that modern Mucky Muck culture is more complex than they previously thought. The theory states that the Lothars, the Hill People, and several other tribes lived side-by-side for a long time and that the modern culture shows influences from several societies. *Which piece of evidence would most strongly support the more modern theory about the culture of the Mucky Muck Islanders?*

    a. Archaeological evidence shows that both the Hill People and the Lothars originated in Central Europe at least 10,000 years before they arrived on Mucky Muck Island
    b. The Hill People and the Lothars had similar height, build, and facial features
    c. A modern Mucky Muck myth incorporates a Hill People hero, one of the gods of the Lothars, as well as fertility rituals used by other cultures in the area
    d. The Hill People culture remained a primitive hunter-gatherer culture, while the Lothars learned agriculture and advanced tool-making skills
    e. The Lothars were willing to trade with strangers, while the Hill People were culturally insular and suspicious

35. Radiation is not the cause of the increase in mutations in the area around the abandoned weapons testing facility. Instead, the increase is caused by the fact that more thrill-seekers have recently moved to the area. Statistics show that thrill-seekers are more likely to undergo genetic mutations, and these thrill-seekers comprise a greater proportion of the population around the facility than ever. *A flaw in this argument is that it fails to account for the possibility that*

    a. thrill-seekers were born as normal, non-thrill-seeking children
    b. there are plenty of citizens around the plant who are not thrill-seekers
    c. the increase in radiation may just be a fluke
    d. thrill-seekers are not statistically more likely to have drastic mutations than other people
    e. thrill-seekers are more likely to expose themselves to radioactive environments such as the abandoned facility than other people are

36. Until Congress began offering bailouts to insolvent lenders, risky loans were limited by the fear that corporate directors had of becoming insolvent. Since the bailouts began, however, high risk strategies have boomed and corporate bankruptcies have crippled the economy. *Assuming that all of the following solutions are possible to carry out, which would have the best chance of stopping the problem of corporate bankruptcy?*

    a. stopping companies from expanding current high-risk loan programs
    b. using economic modeling software to predict how likely risky loans are to lead to lender bankruptcy
    c. requiring the establishment of a low-risk loan program for every new high-risk loan program
    d. offering to buy high-risk loans from lenders and passing a law to ban further bailouts
    e. requiring lenders to adopt a more diverse economic program in exchange for eligibility for future bailouts

37. Victims of Marah's disease, a virtually unknown neurological condition, appear pain-free and content. Often, they also have a desire to engage in vigorous physical activities such as contact sports. Beneath it all, they are in great physical pain but have an inability to express it or act to reduce it, making diagnosis difficult. As a result, they are inaccurately diagnosed as very low on the pain scale, their discomfort level much lower than victims of severe sprains, despite the fact that sprains, although more painful, are temporary and comparatively easy to manage nature. *This passage makes the argument that*

    a. the pain scale is not an accurate or adequate way to measure the physical discomfort of certain people, such as those suffering from Marah's disease
    b. sprain victims have more intense pain than Marah's sufferers, but they can manage their pain more easily
    c. the pain scale seems to put more emphasis on intensity of pain than duration
    d. victims of Marah's syndrome are often unable to deal effectively with their discomfort
    e. there needs to be more public awareness of Marah's syndrome

38. Ignatius II believed that gravity was not a force but actually the result of "falling demons" pulling on all objects. His friend Dot Matrix disagreed, and she set up an experiment to prove that the falling demons do not have anything to do with falling. She invoked the falling demons and dropped a ball from five feet in the air, timing how long it took to reach the ground. She then dispelled the falling demons and dropped the ball again, measuring exactly the same time. Ignatius argued that she had proven nothing since falling demons, once invoked, cannot be quickly expelled. *Which statement provides the best evidence to support Ignatius' argument, assuming the statement is true?*

    a. Excessive heaviness, often present in objects that have had the falling demons summoned into them, is often a cause of quicker acceleration toward the ground.
    b. Dot Matrix was actually an expert in demonology, and she was able to keep the falling demons from leaving despite appearing to dispel them.
    c. Falling demons are more common in places with substantial religious communities who are more likely to invoke them.
    d. Although gravity is a force common to all objects, the falling demons still manage to affect some objects.
    e. If the invoker waits at least twenty-four hours before dispelling the falling demons, the object is likely to take longer to reach the ground.

39. Citing the progress made in literacy since compulsory education was instituted in the United States, legislators have now proposed compulsory job education for young adults. Eighteen- to twenty-year-old mechanics, secretaries, salespeople, and all other workers not currently enrolled in schools will have to undergo at least five hours of class a week if the new legislation is instituted. Employers, who will have to pay for this education, argue that this is a one-size-fits-all solution that will not work well for some businesses. *Of the following statements, which casts the most doubt on the prudence of the legislative proposal?*

> a. Reading needs to be taught in an academic setting, but not all job skills do. In some businesses, on-the-job training is sufficient without outside instruction.
> b. The program will actually help businesses, which will no longer have to provide job training themselves.
> c. The reason some workers are not sufficiently educated in how to perform their jobs is that many companies do not provide sufficient training.
> d. Not being able to read is a much more serious problem than not being good at your job.
> e. More investigation is needed concerning the number of people who don't have enough job training.

40. Between 1980 and 1985, the incarceration rate of the poorest 20% of Americans decreased from 70% of the total prison population to 60%. During the same period, however, the incarceration rate for the poorest 8% increased from 18% to 35%. *Which of the factors below helps to explain this discrepancy?*

> a. Between 1980 and 1985, an estimated 20,000 more cops were put on the street.
> b. Between 1980 and 1985, prosecution of crimes of desperation such as petty theft increased by more than 50%.
> c. Between 1980 and 1985, many of the working poor were able to climb out of poverty.
> d. Between 1980 and 1985, prosecution of white collar crime declined, leaving more rich criminals out of the justice system.
> e. Between 1980 and 1985, the incarceration rate for Americans overall was below 1%.

41. The economic boom of the late 1950s affected the different states of a certain country in very different ways. Although the refrigerator factories of state Alpha and the television factories of state Beta both saw demand drastically increase during the boom, the border state of Alpha was able to quickly scale up production to meet the demand and so reap the rewards, while the inland state of Beta was not. *Of the possible explanations below, which best accounts for the fact that Beta was unable to benefit fully from the economic boom?*

> a. Beta manufactured televisions, which were far more cutting-edge consumer items than refrigerators in the 1950s.
> b. Alpha was able to draw on foreign workers from neighboring countries to work extra shifts in its factories, whereas Beta was nowhere near the border and could not as easily recruit new workers.
> c. Televisions are a luxury item, whereas refrigerators are a necessity. An economic boom naturally favors luxury items.
> d. Many neighboring countries also had factories that could produce refrigerators similar to those made in Alpha's factories.
> e. Because Beta had a diversified economy, it could do reasonably well, even with an inefficient manufacturing base.

Answer Key and Explanations

Integrated Reasoning

1.

Would help explain	Would not help explain	
○	●	Ridgecrest is a private school with high tuition costs.
●	○	North Forest has a 1 hour study block built into their schedule.
○	●	Woodlands has the highest percentage of students participating in extracurricular activities.

The fact that Ridgecrest is a private school or has high tuition costs has no correlation to student's grades. Since North Forest has a built in study block this would help explain why they have some of the lowest failure rates in the area. Having more students participate in extracurricular activities could take away from their study time but since Woodlands still has low failure rates there seems to be no correlation.

2. **James should be added to Team 1 and Ben should be added to Team 2**. James will get Team 1's shooting average higher than Team 2 while getting their passing and dribbling average lower. Ben will raise Team 2's passing and dribbling average while keeping their shooting average lower than Team 1.

3. C, B: To find the chance that a student will be 8 years of age or under, first count all of the symbols not contained in the 8 years of age or older circle. There 10 are of the 20 not in the 8 years of age or older circle. This can be reduced to 1 out of 2. To find the chance that a student is both under 8 years of age and does not own a dog, count all of the symbols outside of both circles. There are 5 of the 20 that are not in either circle. This can be reduced to 1 out of 4.

4. B, C: Point A can be approximated at $2200, while Point B can be approximated at $3100, and Point C at $2800. This means that the increase from Point A to Point B is approximately $900, and the decrease from Point B to Point C is approximately $300. This means that the account increases by approximately three times as much from Point A to Point B as it decreases from Point B to Point C. The months from point A to point C are months 1-5. The approximations for each of these months are $2200, $2500, $3100, $2800, $2800. The average of all of these amounts comes out to:

$$\$2200 + \$2500 + \$3100 + \$2800 + \$2800 = \$13,400$$

$$\$13400 \div 5 = \$2680$$

This means that it is approximately between $2550-$2750.

5.

Yes	No	Description
●	○	Have collided with Earth
○	●	Have an orbital period of only 150 years
○	●	Are formed when gravity causes parts of the nebula to clump together

This can be determined from reading both of the passages. At the beginning of paragraph 5 in the text about comets it states that they have collided with earth. In the next paragraph it discusses their orbital period. It says they can have both a short and long orbital period so there is no one specific length of their orbital period. The part about gravity causing parts of a nebula to clump together is discussed in the text about stars.

6.

True	False	Statement
●	○	Both stars and comets can be seen with the naked eye.
○	●	Comets have an oval shaped orbit while stars have a circular shaped orbit.
○	●	A nebula and a comet are both composed of 97% hydrogen.

Even though it states that there is only around one comet visible to the naked eye per year that still makes the first statement true. It does state that comets have an oval shaped orbit but does not say anything about a star having a circular shaped orbit or even orbiting at all. It is stated that a nebula is composed of 97% hydrogen but there is no mention of the composition of a comet.

7. B, C: In the first problem a is 9 and b is 11. If you follow the diagram you should perform the following operations:

$$S = 4 + 11 = 15$$
$$a = 9 - 1 = 8$$
$$a = 8 \div 2 = 4$$
$$a = 4 \div 2 = 2$$
$$a = 2 \div 2 = 1$$
$$S = 15 + 1 + 11 = 27$$

In the second problem a is 19 and b is 4. If you follow the diagram you should perform the following operations:

$$S = 4 + 4 = 8$$
$$a = 19 - 1 = 18$$
$$a = 18 \div 2 = 9$$
$$S = 8 + 4 = 12$$
$$a = 9 - 1 = 8$$
$$a = 8 \div 2 = 4$$
$$a = 4 \div 2 = 2$$
$$a = 2 \div 2 = 1$$
$$S = 12 + 1 + 4 = 17$$

8.

Yes	No	Statement
●	○	No one company produces more than 25% of the total dolls produced
○	●	Wild West Toys produces the largest volume of toys overall
●	○	Lots of Toys produces more toy cars as a percentage of their total production than Tots Toys

The total number of dolls produced can be found by adding up each company's production to get 15,000 total dolls produced. Since Tots Toys produced the most dolls they are the only company that needs to be checked. $\left(\frac{3500}{15000}\right) \times 100 = 23.33\%$. So, they produce less than 25% and this statement is true. To check the next statement first find Wild West Toys total production, which is 9600. Then compare that to the total production of all other companies. If even one of them produced more toys then the statement is false. Tots Toys produced 10,100 so this statement is false. For the last statement first find the percentage of total production for toy cars for both companies. Lots of Toys would be $\left(\frac{3400}{9300}\right) \times 100 \approx 36.56\%$, and Tots Toys would be $\left(\frac{3500}{10100}\right) \times 100 \approx$ 34.65%. So, this would be a true statement.

9. C: The word *Laziguny* was a made up word to represent a location. From the text it can be inferred that this location is at a school. Since it is the end of the day and Billy is walking to the location with his neighbors in can be inferred that they are all headed to the bus pick up area.

10.

Calculation of hourly wage			Paid most per hour	
○	$M = \dfrac{H}{T}$		○	Dave
●	$H = \dfrac{M}{T}$		○	Kristen
○	$H = M \times T$		●	Sarah
○	$T = \dfrac{H}{M}$		○	Charlie
			○	Steven

The hourly wage is the amount of money they make per hour. So, the calculation should be total money divided by total hours, or $H = \frac{M}{T}$. Then, once you have this calculation you can perform it on each employee to see who make the most per hour. It will show that Sarah at approximately $23.53 makes the most per hour.

11.

Possible	Not Possible	Statement
●	○	There were 210 cats with black fur
●	○	There were 190 cats that weighed 13-15 lbs
○	●	There were 155 cats that weighed 9-11 lbs and had brown fur

The only information given about fur color is that there were 180 cats with brown fur. This means that there were 320 cats with some other color fur. So it is possible that 210 cats had black fur. The only information given about weight is that 220 cats weighed over 12 lbs and the remaining 280 weigh less than 12 lbs. This means that of those 220 cats that weighed over 12 lbs it is possible for 190 of them to weigh between 13 and 15 lbs. It is shown that there are 280 cats that weigh less than 12 lbs but only 140 of those had brown fur. So it is not possible for 155 cats to weigh between 9 and 11 lbs and have brown fur.

12. C, B: From Point A to Point B he moves from approximately 0.25 miles away to approximately 1 mile away. This means that he moves approximately 0.75 more miles away from his house. From Point B to Point C he moves from approximately 1 mile away to approximately 0.5 miles away. There is a difference of approximately 0.5 miles. So, $\frac{.5}{1} \times 100 = 50\%$.

Quantitative

Problem Solving

1. E: First perform the operations:

$2 + 0.4 = 2.4$

$1 - 0.2 = 0.8$

Next, solve the equation:

$$2.4 = x(0.8)$$
$$x = 3$$

2. C: The movie is now at the $90 + 12 = 102$-minute mark. Therefore, m minutes ago, it had reached the $102 - m$ mark.

3. D: First calculate the area of the bull's-eye:

$A = \pi r^2 = \pi(4/2)^2 = \pi 2^2 = 4\pi$

Then, let x = the area of the target.

20 percent of $x = 4\pi$

$$0.2x = 4\pi$$
$$x = 20\pi$$

4. C: First, find the decimal equivalent for $\frac{5}{8}$ by dividing. $5 \div 8 = 0.625$. D is equal to $\frac{5}{8}$ and E is greater than $\frac{5}{8}$, so the answer must be A, B, or C. Divide to find the decimal equivalent of each.

   A. $\frac{7}{10} = 0.70$
   B. $\frac{4}{5} = 0.80$
   C. $\frac{6}{11} = 0.5454...$

Only C is less than 0.625.

5. E: After the first markup, the bread costs 1.2 times its original price of x, or $1.2x$. After the second markup, the bread costs 1.2 times the marked up price, or $1.2(1.2x) = 1.44x$.

1.44 is equivalent to a 44 percent markup.

6. B: The perpendicular bisector cuts a line into 90° angles.

7. B: If the volume halves every 2 days, it halves 5 times after 10 days. This halving action can be expressed as $(\frac{1}{2})(\frac{1}{2})(\frac{1}{2})(\frac{1}{2})(\frac{1}{2})$ or $(\frac{1}{2})^5$. Therefore, if the initial volume is (10^6), then the volume will be $(\frac{1}{2})^5(10^6)$ after 10 days.

8. B: The total number of guests in attendance is 0.6(750) = 450. If 46 percent of the attendees are male, then 54 percent are female. Therefore, the number of females in attendance is 0.54(450) = 243.

9. C: The angles a, b, and c form a straight line, so $a + b + c = 180$. Substituting 180 for $a + b + c$ in the proportion, we have:

$$\frac{b}{180} = \frac{3}{5}$$

By cross-multiplying, we can solve for b:$5b = 3(180)$ or $b = 108$.

10. D: Let x equal the amount of the fourth order. Then using the formula Avg = (sum of values)/(# of values), the given information can be expressed in the following equation:

$(75 + 40 + 107 + x)/4 = 80$. Cross-multiplying, we get $75 + 40 + 107 + x = 320$, or x = 98.

11. D: First, solve the second equation for y: $y = -2x - 5$. Next, substitute that expression for y in the first equation:

$$\begin{aligned}
3(-2x - 5) - 2x &= 9 \\
-6x - 15 - 2x &= 9 \\
-8x &= 24 \\
x &= -3
\end{aligned}$$

Finally, substitute -3 for x in either equation in order to solve for y:

$$\begin{aligned}
2(-3) + y &= -5 \\
-6 + y &= -5 \\
y &= 1
\end{aligned}$$

12. C: Using the Pythagorean Theorem, we first find AB.

$$\begin{aligned}
AB^2 + BC^2 &= AC^2 \\
AB^2 + 5^2 &= 13^2 \\
AB^2 + 25 &= 169 \\
AB^2 &= 144 \\
AB &= 12
\end{aligned}$$

Next, we draw a perpendicular bisector from C to AD, forming segment CE, which is the height of triangle ACD and is equal to segment AB. Thus, the height of the triangle is 12.

We know the base of triangle ACD, AD, equals 8. So, we use the area formula.

$A = \frac{1}{2}bh = \frac{1}{2}(8)(12) = 48$

13. D: Justifications:

First, convert 10 yards to inches: 1 yard = 36 inches, so 10 yards = 360 inches.

Next, convert the mixed fraction $6\frac{3}{4}$ to a decimal: 6.75.

Finally, divide: 360/6.75 = 53.3333...

So, the maximum number of strips that can be cut is 53.

14. C: Use the Distance Formula: distance = rate × time   AND   time = distance/rate.

1. First half of trip: 1,500 = 400 × time, so time = $\frac{15}{4}$.

2. Second half of trip: 1,500 = rate × distance/rate = rate × $\frac{1500}{r}$.

3. Total trip: 3,000 = 500 × time, so total time = 6.

The total time of the trip is the sum of the times for the first 1,500 miles and the second 1,500 miles. So, $\frac{15}{4} + \frac{1500}{r} = 6$. Solving for r, we multiply both sides of the equation by $4r$ and get:

$$15r + 6{,}000 = 24r$$
$$6{,}000 = 9r$$
$$r = 666\frac{2}{3}.$$

15. B: The radius of circle O is one-fourth the diameter of circle P. The diameter is twice the radius, or d = 2r. So $r_o = \frac{1}{4}(2r_p) = \frac{1}{2}r_p$.

The circumference of circle P = $2\pi\, r_p$.

The circumference of circle O = $2\pi\, r_o = 2\pi\,(\frac{1}{2}r_p) = \pi\, r_p$.

The ratio of circle O's circumference to circle P's is $(\pi r_p)/(2\pi r_p) = \frac{1}{2}$.

16. D: Let F equal the total amount in the college fund. Then the amount spent on tuition, room and board, and books is $\frac{3}{8}F + \frac{1}{4}F + \frac{1}{5}F$. Finding the LCD, $\frac{3}{8}F + \frac{1}{4}F + \frac{1}{5}F =$

(15 +10 + 8)F/40 = 33/40 F. The remainder of the fund is therefore 1 – 33F/40, or 7F/40.

We are told 7F/40 = $7,000, so F = $40,000.

17. D: If $x^2 + 3x - 18 = 0$, then $(x + 6)(x - 3) = 0$. So $x = -6$ or 3. We are told $x < 0$, so x must equal –6.

I. $(-6)^2 - 36 = 0$ True

II. $(-6)^2 - 2(-6) - 3 \neq 0$ False

III. $(-6)^2 + 5(-6) - 6 = 0$ True

18. E: Using the formula for volume $V = e^3$, where e represents the length of an edge of a cube, let the volume of cube B equal e^3 and so the volume of cube A is $\left(\frac{3}{4}e\right)^3 = \frac{27}{64}e^3$.

The ratio of the volume of cube B to the volume of cube A is $e^3 / \frac{27}{64}e^3 = \frac{64}{27}$.

19. B: We find the decimal equivalent of each fraction by dividing.

5/9 = 0.555..., 6/11 = 0.5454..., 1/2 = 0.50, 9/16 = 0.5625, and 3/5 = 0.60.

When we order these decimals from least to greatest, we find the second equivalent fraction to be 6/11.

20. E: Justifications:

For all large values of x, the value of $\frac{x}{1-2x}$ will be very close to the value of $\frac{x}{-2x} = -\frac{1}{2}$.

21. B: Using the formula for the perimeter of a rectangle, we know that P = 2*l* + 2*w*. Substituting the value given, we get 76 = 2*l* + 2*w* or 38 = *l* + *w*. We can now solve for *l*: 38 − *w* = *l*.

Using the formula for the area of a rectangle, we know that A = *lw*. Substituting the value given, we get 336 = *lw*.

If we substitute the 38 − *w* we found in the first step for *l*, we get (38−*w*)*w* = 336. Thus:

$38w - w^2 = 336$

$0 = w^2 - 38w + 336$

$0 = (w - 14)(w - 24)$

$w = 14$ or 24

The shorter of these two possibilities is 14.

22. C: If Anish was the 11th highest speller, 10 participants placed higher. If Anish was the 25th lowest speller, 24 participants placed lower. Therefore, the total number of participants was 10 + 24 + 1 (Anish) = 35

23. A: There are 4 members of the first set and 4 members of the second set, so there are 4(4) = 16 possible products for *cd*. *cd* is odd only when both *c* and *d* are odd. There are 2 odd numbers in the first set and two in the second set, so 2(2) = 4 products are odd and the probability *cd* is odd is 4/16 or 1/4.

24. A: We are given *l* = 3*w*, so $w = \frac{1}{3}l$. The diagonal is the hypotenuse of the triangle with sides *l* and *w*, so we use the Pythagorean Theorem.

$l^2 + w^2 = d^2$ $\qquad$ $l^2 + (\frac{1}{3}l)^2 = d^2$ $\qquad$ $l^2 + \frac{1}{9}l^2 = d^2$ $\qquad$ $\frac{10}{9}l^2 = d^2$

$d = \sqrt{\frac{10}{9}}\, l = \frac{\sqrt{10}}{3}l$

Data Sufficiency

25. D: Justifications:

Since $\frac{q}{5} - \frac{r}{5} = \frac{1}{5}(q - r)$, we can cross-multiply (1) to get $q - r = 15$ and then substitute 15 into $\frac{1}{5}(q - r)$. $\frac{1}{5}(15) = 3$, so (1) alone is sufficient.

We can do the same substitution for (2). $\frac{1}{5}(15) = 3$, so (2) alone is also sufficient. In fact, both statements (1) and (2) are essentially the same. One could simply multiply both sides of equation

(1) by 5 to obtain equation (2). Therefore, the correct answer is D; EACH statement ALONE is sufficient

26. C: Justifications:

We are trying to find $y + z$. (1) tells us that $y = z + 16$. Substituting, we get $(z + 16) + z = 2z + 16$. This expression can vary in value, so (1) is not sufficient.

(2) tells us that $y + 10 = 2(z + 10)$ or $y + 10 = 2z + 20$. Thus, $y = 2z + 10$.

This expression can also vary in value, so (2) is not sufficient.

Given (1) and (2): $y = z + 16$ and $y = 2z + 10$, we can solve the equations simultaneously to obtain values of y and z.

Therefore, the correct answer is C; BOTH statements TOGETHER are sufficient, but NEITHER statement ALONE is sufficient.

27. B: Justifications:

The volume of a rectangular solid is lwh.

(1) gives us $lw = 40$. Substituting that into the volume formula, we get $V = 40h$. This expression can vary in value, so (1) is not sufficient.

(2) gives us $\frac{1}{2}lwh = 30$. Multiplying both sides by 2, we get $lwh = 60$. The volume is therefore 60 and (2) is sufficient.

Therefore, the correct answer is B; Statement (2) ALONE is sufficient, but statement (1) alone is not sufficient.

28. E: Justifications:

(1) does not give us the net proceeds total for the first day, so it is not sufficient.

(2) does not give us the net proceeds total for the second day, so it is not sufficient.

Without the total net proceeds for either the first or the second day, we are unable to find the net proceeds for the third day.

Therefore, the correct answer is E; Statements (1) and (2) TOGETHER are not sufficient.

29. D: Justifications:

(1) Transposing like terms gives the equivalent equation $-4 = 10x$, or $x = -\frac{4}{10}$. So, (1) is sufficient.

(2) Cross-multiplying gives $-10x = 4$ or $x = -\frac{4}{10}$. So (2) is also sufficient.

Therefore the correct answer is D; EACH statement ALONE is sufficient.

30. A: Justifications:

(1) Using the Pythagorean Theorem, if $a^2 + b^2 = c^2$ then the triangle is a right triangle.

- 134 -

$5^2 + 12^2 = 13^2$ or $25 + 144 = 169$ is true, so (1) is sufficient.

(2) We know that $x + y + z = 180$. We are told that $x = 45$. Substituting, we get $45 + y + z = 180$, or $y + z = 135$. If either y or z is 90 then the triangle is a right triangle, but we are not given enough information to determine this. So (2) is not sufficient.

Therefore, the correct answer is A; Statement (1) ALONE is sufficient, but statement (2) alone is not sufficient.

31. B: Justifications:

If we let d, r, and i be the number of Democrats, Republicans, and Independents surveyed respectively, then $d + r + i = 1,500$.

(1) We are told that 40 percent of the voters are Republicans, so $r = 0.40(1,500) = 600$. Plugging that into the equation $d + r + i = 1,500$, we get $d + 600 + i = 1,500$, or $d + i = 900$ and $i = 900 - d$. The value of this expression varies, so (1) is not sufficient.

(2) We are told $i = 0.25(d + r)$, or $4i = d + r$. By substituting $4i$ for $d + r$ in the original equation, we get $4i + i = 1,500$, or $i = 300$. So (2) is sufficient.

Therefore, the correct answer is B; Statement (2) ALONE is sufficient, but statement (1) alone is not sufficient.

32. A: Justifications:

First we find the midpoint of 10 and 25: $(10 + 25)/2 = 17.5$. So any number greater than 17.5 is closer to 25 and any number less than 17.5 is closer to 10.

(1) $25 - p < p - 10$

$35 < 2p$ or $17.5 < p$, so (1) is sufficient.

(2) We are told $p < 20$, but it could be, for example, 19 (closer to 25), or 11 (closer to 10). So (2) is not sufficient.

Therefore, the correct answer is A; Statement (1) ALONE is sufficient, but statement (2) alone is not sufficient.

33. D: Justifications:

(1) The formula for the area of a circle is $A = \pi r^2$ and the formula for the circumference of a circle is $C = 2\pi r$. So the ratio of A to C is $\frac{\pi r^2}{2\pi r} = \frac{r}{2}$. Setting this ratio equal to 2, we get $r = 4$, so (1) is sufficient.

(2) The formula for the area of a circle is $A = \pi r^2$. Setting this equal to 16π, we get $16\pi = \pi r^2$, or $r^2 = 16$. So $r = 4$ or -4, but the radius must be positive. Thus, $r = 4$ and (2) is also sufficient.

Therefore, the correct answer is D; EACH statement ALONE is sufficient.

34. D: Justifications:

If we let i be the greatest of the consecutive integers, then the set of integers is

$\{i - (m - 1)$ or $i - m + 1, ..., i - 3, i - 2, i - 1, i\}$.

- 135 -

(1) The range is the difference between the greatest and least members of the set, so

8 = i – (i – m + 1), which simplifies as 8 = m – 1, or m = 9. And, we are given that [(i – 9 + 1) + (i – 1) + (i – 2) ... + i]/9 = 7, or [(i – 9 + 1) + (i – 1) + (i – 2) ... + i] = 63. A unique value of i can be determined so (1) is sufficient.

(2) Because the integers are consecutive, they form a data set that is symmetric about its average. So, the average of the integers is the average of the least and greatest numbers: (3 + i) / 2 = 7, or 3 + i = 14, or i = 11. So (2) is sufficient.

Therefore, the correct answer is D; EACH statement ALONE is sufficient.

35. A: Justifications:

(1) If there are x yards of black fabric then there are 1.5x yards of white fabric and (3/2)(1.5)x, or 2.25x yards of red fabric.

So x + 1.5x + 2.25x = 19 or 4.75x = 19 or x = 4. So, the amount of white fabric can be determined: 1.5(4) = 6 yards. Thus, (1) is sufficient.

(2) If the sum of the amounts of the white and black fabrics is y, then the amount of red fabric is y – 1.So y + (y – 1) = 19 or 2y = 20, or y = 10. But we don't know how much of this quantity is black and how much is white. Thus, (2) is not sufficient.

Therefore, the correct answer is A; Statement (1) ALONE is sufficient, but statement (2) alone is not sufficient.

36. C: Justifications:

(1) The formula for circumference is 2πr. Setting that equal to 6π, we get r = 3, but the radius does not tell us anything about x. So (1) is not sufficient.

(2) The length of arc AB = 2π, but without knowing the circumference, we can't find x. So (2) is not sufficient.

Taking both (1) and (2) together, we know that AB = 2π and C = 6π and so arc AB is one-third the circumference. Thus, angle x is one-third of the circle, or (1/3)(360) = 120.

Therefore, the correct answer is C; BOTH statements TOGETHER are sufficient, but NEITHER statement ALONE is sufficient.

37. B: Justifications:

(1) The even integers between 2 and 9 inclusive that are the square root of some integer are 2, 4, 6, and 8. So (1) is not sufficient.

(2) Of the integers 2 through 9, only 8 has a cube root that is an integer, so (2) is sufficient.

Therefore, the correct answer is B; Statement (2) ALONE is sufficient, but statement (1) alone is not sufficient.

Verbal

Reading Comprehension

1. B: In the first paragraph of the essay, the author characterizes amateurs as "an elite group within the music scene" and states that there are several "technological, demographic, and economic factors" that account for them doing better than professionals. The tone of the essay is documentary—the author doesn't make any judgments about whether this is a good development or a bad one. He simply states that amateurs are more successful relative to professionals than they have been before and goes on to examine the reasons for this.

2. D: The key is the phrase "directly support." The essay needs to come right out and say the correct answer, not imply that it is true. Paragraph 3 says that digital file sharing "robs the professionals of what has traditionally been one of their biggest sources of revenue." Paragraph 2 provides less direct evidence, saying that many clubs that were once able to pay professionals now can't. Professionals have lost most of their income from both small clubs and recordings.

3. B: The second sentence in the final paragraph is a giveaway. If the "amateurs are the only ones who can afford to buy new gear and fix broken equipment, keep their cars in working order to get to shows, and pay to promote their shows," then the professionals must not be able to do any of those things.

4. C: The essay as a whole discusses how the current musical scene negatively affects professional musicians while leaving amateurs unharmed. The second paragraph, for example, discusses how professionals are no longer able to make a living playing small venues and must "fight more desperately than ever for those few lucrative gigs." The final paragraph states that, because of the effect on their finances, professionals are unable to maintain the gear and transportation they need to "keep the higher-paying gigs." It goes on to say that "a fairly skilled amateur . . . will be able to fake his way through most of what a professional does . . . to play professional shows." Therefore, professionals are falling behind amateurs at small venues (which professionals can't afford to play because of the lack of pay) and at professional gigs (where professionals can't play because they can't afford professional gear).

5. C: The third paragraph states that the Department of Homeland Security "argued that the new laws might actually limit protections for freedom of thought by . . . hampering the efforts of citizens to restrict their thought-processes to wholly legal topics." In other words, the laws would pose a legal problem for ordinary citizens by making it harder for them to precisely understand and obey the law.

6. A: The "review of thoughts" refers to the provision in the law that sets up a Civilian Thought Review Council with the power to legalize new thoughts. If that council "does not have the knowledge required to judge whether a thought is dangerous or not" as in choice A, a dangerous thought could be made legal, compromising national security.

None of the other choices has the potential to threaten security. Keeping threatening illegal thoughts that are no longer threatening, choice B, won't endanger security, since all threatening thoughts would still be illegal. Similarly, the amount of resources the civilian board needs, choice C, doesn't have any bearing on the impact of its decision. The government pressuring civilians not to legalize a thought, choice D, will not lead to dangerous risks, but rather to more conservative decisions. The veto power of the High Tribal Council, choice E, could actually be used to curtail anything dangerous the Civilian Thought Review Council does.

7. C: The fourth paragraph says "the president himself objected strongly to this, saying that the amendment would potentially expose huge numbers of government contacts and connections to public view unless the bureaucrats were able to show that each individual secret was exempt from the law." Clearly, he feels that having to show that "each individual secret" is exempt is impractical.

8. C: Language change in multicultural areas is characterized as "drastic and rapid." These areas are contrasted with isolated communities. The implication is that languages change much more quickly in multicultural areas than isolated regions.

9. E: This question asks for the main purpose of the essay. The correct answer must not only refer to one part of the essay, but to the essay as a whole. Choice D is incorrect, since the author spends much of the essay talking about ways that language change can be predicted. Choices A, B, and C refer to things the author discusses in part of the essay, but only in part. The whole essay, however, discusses "how linguists study language change."

10. D: The first sentence of the paragraph is a giveaway (it often is). It states that "once . . . a language community is established, linguistic scholars can gather data from subcultures within that community." The paragraph then shows how they study those subcultures by observing and recording changes in speech of "young or marginalized subcultures" as a source of "early indicators of looming language shifts." The paragraph even examines some of the things linguists look for—phonological drift, for example—and discusses the way they catalog language change—"computer voice analysis."

11. A: The third paragraph says that "if the linguists posit a definition of a critical language shift. . . . [they can] predict the time it will take to evolve a completely new language."

12. C: The tricky thing about this question is that all the choices are true statements about things said in the essay. Only one, however, is the main idea. The best way to find it is to go to the first paragraph. In it, the author calls the ability to tell true and false statements apart "one of the main goals of every police officer." He goes further, calling this ability "the only way to punish the guilty, exonerate the innocent, and do the most possible good in preventing future crimes."

13. A: If there is one point that the author has repeated many times in this article, it is that police need to be able to investigate lies to conduct investigations. This is exactly the point explored in the explanation to question 33.

14. C: In paragraph 2, the author states that "smoke" lies "slow down an investigation."

Sentence Correction

15. C: The question contains an error of agreement. "a tangible experience . . . that are called" should be "a tangible experience . . . that is called".

16. C: The "and it" is an awkward way of joining the two clauses. Does "it" refer to enrolling or to out-of-state schools? The "thereby" in choice C connects the ideas much more nicely. By the act of enrolling in out-of-state schools, students grow apart from their friends.

17. A: There are two things going on in the answer choices. First, the word "evidently" is being moved around. As the word works perfectly well where it begins, there is no need to move it—a clue that choice A is probably correct. More important is the change of "are believed" to "were believed." Although the servants were buried in the past, the belief about their burial—that it

- 138 -

occurred nearly 4,000 years ago—occurs in the present. The servants are currently believed—presumably by the Egyptologists—to have been buried nearly 4,000 years ago.

18. B: Since Robert Anton Wilson is being contrasted directly to Hakim Bey, his name has to directly follow the first comma. We can therefore rule out D and E right off the bat. Notice, however, that the original sentence doesn't make sense. The phrase "felt how late 20th-century technology not as" seems awkward and ungrammatical. Sentence C corrects this error, but leaves the "and" at the end. Since we are trying to draw a contrast between Hakim Bey's view of late 20th-century technology as "an inherently alienating force" and Robert Anton Wilson's view of it as "something that could potentially liberate people," we need to use a "but" to draw the contrast.

19. D: The statement "at the least as many as 80 or more other ones had not been given any" is painfully awkward and clearly wrong. The phrase "at least as many" implies that there could be more. Therefore, the phrase "at least as many . . . or more" is redundant. Choice D succinctly expresses the idea that at least 80 passengers were not given flotation devices.

20. E: This question is about parallel structure. If fighting "was" a popular sport in the past, then it "is" in the present.

21. D: The original sentence contains incorrect pronoun reference. It implies that "Johnny Rotten's first number 1 song" was "born John Joseph Lydon." The correct answer should show that it was Johnny Rotten who was born as John Joseph Lydon.

22. B: This question requires parallel structure. The phrase "as the music is played" means "at the same time." It should be contrasted with "in a digital simulation" meaning "at another time after the music is played."

23. E: The sentence contains an error of agreement. The Discordian Society is a collective group, and therefore takes the pronoun "it" and not "they." In addition, "they did and will keep continuing" is an extremely awkward construction.

24. C: The subject "Kyoto protocols" is plural, so the singular "is" does not agree with it. Choices C, D, and E correct this error. Choice E has the awkward possessives "20th century's" and "climate change's." In choice D, the verb phrases "have only been slowing" and "rather than stopped" are not parallel.

25. C: The word "all" does not agree with the verb "takes." Choice C corrects this error without making the sentence excessively convoluted as in choices D and E.

26. B: The subject complement "still using . . . from Shakespeare" has to be followed by the subject, "21st-century poets." Both choices B and E do this, but B is a simpler, less awkward sentence.

27. B: The phrase "have force to compete" should strike you as odd when you hear it, because the verb "force" does not take the auxiliary verb "have." Choice B corrects this problem while leaving the correct "to compete" in its original form.

28. A: There is nothing wrong with the original sentence. All of the other choices either complicate the sentence or make it incorrect.

29. A: The original sentence represented by choice A, works fine. The verb phrase "works as an interrogation" is parallel to "does as a response." Both are also in the same tense, and the sentence is easy to read and understand.

30. A: The original sentence, represented by choice A, is the clearest version. The conjunction "so" joins the phrases "the rarity of musical all-ages venues" and "the absence of public transportation," creating parallel structure. All of the other choices make the sentence more convoluted and more difficult to understand.

Critical Reasoning

31. C: The question asks us to reinforce the conclusion that deceptive television commercials could cause consumers to be tricked into making a poorer health choice. For this to be true, we need to know that consumers actually believe what the ad says.

32. D: The correct answer will contradict the senator's argument that legalization will reduce crime. Choices A and C address the rate of drug use, not the crime rate. Choice B talks about the budget. Choice E talks about legal alternatives to illegal drugs. Only choice D argues that more crime might be committed as a result of legalization.

33. D: The robot was thinking about crushing humans but in a passive recharging state. When the chip was removed, the robot began crushing humans without leaving the recharging state. This obviously implies that it was acting out a dream in the recharging state. If the chip removed were stopping commands from getting to the robot's body, then without it the robot will act out its evil robot dreams.

34. C: The modern theory states that the Lothars, the Hill People, and other cultures influenced each other, and that modern Mucky Muck shows the influence of more than one society. Therefore, we are looking for evidence of cultural cross-pollination. Choice A doesn't say that the cultures influenced each other, only that they both came from Central Europe. Choice B shows that the two peoples looked similar, but that doesn't mean that they had similar cultures or even a lot of contact—they may have evolved similar physical traits because they occupied the same environment. Choice D shows the two cultures diverging, not influencing each other. Choice E shows a difference between the two cultures but does not show them influencing each other. Only choice C shows cultural cross-influence. If a Mucky Muck myth incorporates a Hill People hero and a Lothar god, presumably the two cultures influenced each other to create the myth.

35. E: There are two possible causes for the increase in mutations: radiation and a higher population of thrill-seekers. The original statement argues that thrill-seekers are more prone to mutations, and therefore the rise in their population is the cause of the rise in mutations. If the factor that causes thrill-seekers to be prone to mutation is the radiation, it undermines the argument.

36. D: The question poses a problem (bankruptcy) and a cause (the promise of bailouts leading to high-risk loans) and asks for a solution. The solution should stop the bailouts as a way to stop the risky loans and, in turn, prevent insolvency. Choice A stops current high-risk loan programs from expanding, but it doesn't stop them from existing, nor does it stop companies from making new ones. Choice B is irrelevant—we already know that risky loans lead to bankruptcy. Choice C might help and might not, but it doesn't directly address the cause. Choice E has the same problem as choice C. Only choice D attempts to do away with high-risk loans by both buying back current ones and removing bailouts, the cause of future ones.

37. A: The author says that victims of Marah's disease "appear" to be comfortable but "beneath it all" are in pain. He says that they are "inaccurately" diagnosed as low on the pain scale. This shows that the pain scale is not an accurate way to measure Marah's disease.

38. E: We are not looking for an answer that supports the existence of falling demons in general, but one that supports the specific statement of Ignatius that "falling demons, once invoked, cannot be quickly expelled." Choice E provides evidence that falling demons can be dispelled 24 hours later, indicating that the results of Dot's initial experiment may have been the result of her not waiting long enough to dispel the demons.

39. A: The proposal draws an analogy between improving literacy through compulsory education and improving work performance through compulsory training outside work. We are asked to undermine this argument. Choice A shows that illiteracy and lack of job skills are not the same sort of problems. Whereas teaching literacy requires an educational program, job skills can often simply be taught on the job.

40. B: While poor Americans were being incarcerated at a lower rate, the poorest Americans were being incarcerated more. Since the poorest are the most likely to commit "crimes of desperation" as a means to feed their families or take care of basic needs, it makes sense that increased prosecution would target them, while leaving the slightly less-poor unaffected.

41. B: We are asked to account for the fact that two states with similar industries are affected to much different degrees by an economic boom. We know that Alpha, which is located on the border, is able to scale up production much more quickly than Beta, which is an inland state. The location is our clue. A more ready supply of foreign workers is a plausible explanation for why Alpha might be able to scale up production more quickly.

Additional Quantitative Practice

Problem Solving

Solve these problems and indicate the best of the answer choices given. All numbers used are real numbers.

1. If $a = 3$ and $b = -2$, what is the value of $a^2 + 3ab - b^2$?

    a. 5
    b. -13
    c. -4
    d. -20
    e. 13

2. 34 is what percent of 80?

    a. 34%
    b. 40%
    c. 42.5%
    d. 44.5%
    e. 52%

3. Jack and Kevin play in a basketball game. If the ratio of points scored by Jack to points scored by Kevin is 4 to 3, which of the following could NOT be the total number of points scored by the two boys?

    a. 7
    b. 14
    c. 16
    d. 28
    e. 35

4. Factor the following expression: $x^2 + x - 12$

    a. $(x - 4)(x + 4)$
    b. $(x - 2)(x + 6)$
    c. $(x + 6)(x - 2)$
    d. $(x - 4)(x + 3)$
    e. $(x + 4)(x - 3)$

5. The average of six numbers is 4. If the average of two of those numbers is 2, what is the average of the other four numbers?

    a. 5
    b. 6
    c. 7
    d. 8
    e. 9

6. What is the next-highest prime number after 67?

  a. 68
  b. 69
  c. 71
  d. 73
  e. 76

7. Solve: 0.25 × 0.03 =

  a. 75
  b. 0.075
  c. 0.75
  d. 0.0075
  e. 7.5

8. Dean's Department Store reduces the price of a $30 shirt by 20%, but later raises it again by 20% of the sale price. What is the final price of the shirt?

  a. $24.40
  b. $32
  c. $30
  d. $28.80
  e. $26.60

9. How many 3-inch segments can a 4.5-yard line be divided into?

  a. 15
  b. 45
  c. 54
  d. 64
  e. 84

10. Sheila, Janice, and Karen, working together at the same rate, can complete a job in 3 1/3 days. Working at the same rate, how much of the job could Janice and Karen do in one day?

  a. 1/5
  b. 1/4
  c. 1/3
  d. 1/9
  e. 1/8

11. Dave can deliver four newspapers every minute. At this rate, how many newspapers can he deliver in 2 hours?

  a. 80
  b. 160
  c. 320
  d. 400
  e. 480

12. $4^6 \div 2^8$

    a. 2

    b. 8

    c. 16

    d. 32

    e. 64

13. If $a = 4$, $b = 3$, and $c = 1$, then $\frac{a(b-c)}{b(a+b+c)} =$

    a. 4/13

    b. 1/3

    c. 1/4

    d. 1/6

    e. 2/7

14. What is 20% of 12/5, expressed as a percentage?

    a. 48%

    b. 65%

    c. 72%

    d. 76%

    e. 84%

15. Archie's gas tank is 1/3 full. If Archie adds 3 gallons of gas to the tank, it will be ½ full. What is the capacity in gallons of Archie's tank?

    a. 28

    b. 12

    c. 20

    d. 16

    e. 18

16. Given the triangle shown in the figure, what is the length of the side B?

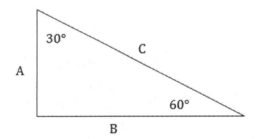

    a. $C/2$

    b. $A/2$

    c. $(A + C)/2$

    d. $2A$

    e. $2C$

17. If the two lines 2x + y = 0 and y = 3 are plotted on a typical *xy* coordinate grid, at which point will they intersect?

    a. -1.5, 3
    b. 1.5, 3
    c. -1.5, 0
    d. 4,1
    e. 4.5, 1

18. What is the surface area, in square inches, of a cube if the length of one side is 3 inches?

    a. 9
    b. 27
    c. 54
    d. 18
    e. 21

19. Which of the following values is closest to the diameter of a circle with an area of 314 square inches?

    a. 20 inches
    b. 10 inches
    c. 100 inches
    d. 31.4 inches
    e. 2π inches

20. Two angles of a triangle measure 15 and 70 degrees, respectively. What is the size of the third angle?

    a. 90 degrees
    b. 80 degrees
    c. 75 degrees.
    d. 125 degrees
    e. 95 degrees

21. The triangle shown in the figure has angles A, B, and C, and sides *a, b*, and *c*. If $a = 14$ cm and $b = 12$ cm, and if angle $\angle B = 35$ degrees, what is angle $\angle A$?

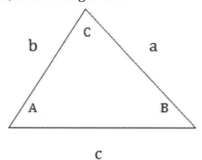

    a. 35 degrees
    b. 42 degrees
    c. 64 degrees
    d. 18 degrees
    e. 28 degrees

22. The town of Fram will build a water storage tank on a hill overlooking the town. The tank will be a right circular cylinder of radius R and height H. The plot of ground selected for the installation is large enough to accommodate a circular tank 60 feet in diameter. The planning commission wants the tank to hold 1,000,000 cubic feet of water, and they intend to use the full area available. Which of the following is the minimum acceptable height?

    a. 655 ft
    b. 455 ft
    c. 355 ft
    d. 255 ft
    e. 155 ft

23. Given the equation $\frac{3}{y-5} = \frac{15}{y+4}$, what is the value of y?

    a. 45
    b. 54
    c. 29/4
    d. 4/29
    e. 4/45

24. In the figure, pictured below, the distance from A to D is 48. The distance from A to B is equal to the distance from B to C. If the distance from C to D is twice the distance of A to B, how far apart are B and D?

    a. 12
    b. 16
    c. 24
    d. 26
    e. 36

25. Which of the following is NOT less than .33?

    a. 4/15
    b. 13/45
    c. 26/81
    d. 8/27
    e. 4/9

26. If $a - 16 = 8b + 6$, what does $a + 3$ equal?

    a. b + 3
    b. 8b + 9
    c. 8b + 22
    d. 8b + 25
    e. 25

27. In the figure, pictured below, angles *b* and *d* are equal. What is the degree measure of angle *d*?

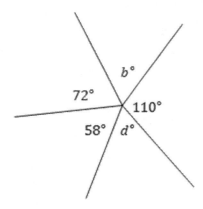

 a. 240°
 b. 120°
 c. 80°
 d. 60°
 e. 30°

28. Janice weighs *x* pounds. Elaina weighs 23 pounds more than Janice. June weighs 14 pounds more than Janice. In terms of *x*, what is the sum of their weights minus 25 pounds?

 a. 3x + 37
 b. 3x + 12
 c. x + 12
 d. 3x - 25
 e. x = 4

29. A bag contains 14 blue, 6 red, 12 green and 8 purple buttons. 25 buttons are removed from the bag randomly. How many of the removed buttons were red if the chance of drawing a red button from the bag is now 1/3?

 a. 0
 b. 1
 c. 3
 d. 5
 e. 6

30. A washing machine makes 85 revolutions per minute on the spin cycle. If the washing machine spends 15 minutes on the spin cycle per wash, about how many washes will it take to reach 100,000 revolutions (rounded to the nearest whole number)?

 a. 1,275
 b. 1,175
 c. 100
 d. 78
 e. 35

31. There are 80 mg / 0.8 ml in Acetaminophen Concentrated Infant Drops. If the proper dosage for a four year old child is 240 mg, how many milliliters should the child receive?

    a. 0.8 ml
    b. 1.6 ml
    c. 2.4 ml
    d. 3.2 ml
    e. 5.2 ml

32. Solve the following equation: $(y + 1)(y + 2)(y + 3)$

    a. $y^2 + 3y + 2$
    b. $3y^2 + 6y + 3$
    c. $2y^2 + 11y$
    d. $y^3 + 6y^2 + 11y + 6$
    e. $8y^3 + 6y + 8$

33. What is the area of the parallelogram in the figure, pictured below?

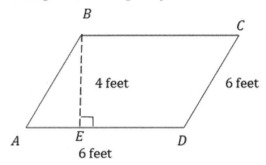

    a. 10 square feet
    b. 12 square feet
    c. 16 square feet
    d. 24 square feet
    e. 36 square feet

34. 50 students are enrolled in both English and Math. 90 students are enrolled in either English or Math. If 25 students are enrolled in English, but not Math, how many students are enrolled in Math but not English?

    a. 15
    b. 25
    c. 50
    d. 65
    e. 90

35. If a savings account earns 3.75% simple interest, how much interest will a deposit of $2,500 earn in one month?

    a. $93.75
    b. $666.67
    c. $2,503.75
    d. $2,593.75
    e. $9,375.00

36. In the figure, pictured below, *AD* = 5 and *AB* = 12, what is the length of *AC* (not shown)?

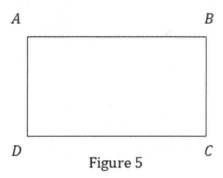

A   B

D   C
Figure 5

    a. 10
    b. 13
    c. 17
    d. 60
    e. 169

37. Convert 12.5% to a fraction.

    a. 1/3
    b. 1/8
    c. 3/8
    d. 5/8
    e. 7/8

38. Rick scores 95%, 68%, 86%, 83%, 64%, 92%, and 79% on his math tests over the semester. When calculating students' semester averages, Rick's teacher disregards each student's highest and lowest score. What is Rick's average test score?

    a. 57.71%
    b. 75.5%
    c. 80.8%
    d. 81%
    e. 81.6%

39. Five dice are rolled together one time. What is the probability of rolling five 6s?

    a. 1/30
    b. 5/6
    c. 3/4
    d. 1/1,000
    e. 1/7,776

40. Simplify the following equation: $4(6 - 3)^2 - (-2)$

    a. 34
    b. 38
    c. 42
    d. 48
    e. 62

41. In the number 6,502,104.9738, what digit is in the thousandths place?

    a. 3
    b. 5
    c. 6
    d. 8
    e. 9

42. A square and an equilateral triangle have the same perimeter. If one side of the triangle measures 4 inches, how long is one side of the square?

    a. 10
    b. 8
    c. 6
    d. 4
    e. 3

43. Which of the following fractions, when entered into the triangle, makes the statement true?

$$3/8 < \Delta < 13/24$$

    a. 7/8
    b. 5/8
    c. 5/12
    d. 1/3
    e. 1/4

44. Using the chart below, which equation describes the relationship between x and y?

x	y
2	6
3	9
4	12
5	15

    a. x = 3y
    b. y = 3x
    c. y = 1/3x
    d. x/y = 3
    e. y/x = 3

45. What is the product of four squared and six?

    a. 22
    b. 28
    c. 55
    d. 96
    e. 106

46. Solve the following equation: $(y + 2)(y + 3)(y + 4)$

    a. $y^2 + 3y + 2$
    b. $3y^2 + 6y + 3$
    c. $y^3 + 9y^2 + 26y + 24$
    d. $8y^3 + 6y + 8$
    e. $y^3 + 6y^2 + 11y + 6$

Data Sufficiency

This Data Sufficiency problem consists of a question and two statements, labeled (1) and (2), in which certain data are given. You have to decide whether the data given in the statements are sufficient for answering the question, using only the data given in the statements and your knowledge of mathematics and everyday facts (such as the number of days in July or the meaning of counterclockwise).

A. Statement (1) ALONE is sufficient, but statement (2) is not sufficient.
B. Statement (2) ALONE is sufficient, but statement (1) is not sufficient.
C. BOTH statements TOGETHER are sufficient, but NEITHER statement ALONE is sufficient.
D. EACH statement ALONE is sufficient.
E. Statements (1) and (2) TOGETHER are NOT sufficient.

47. Does Jonathan get paid more than Deborah?

(1) Alice gets paid more than Deborah.
(2) Jonathan makes less money than Alice.
a.   b.   c.   d.   e.

48. Is the integer a less than the integer b?

(1) $a^3 < b^3$
(2) $a^2 < b^2$
a.   b.   c.   d.   e.

49. Is the perimeter of a given rectangle greater than 8 inches?

(1) The two shorter sides of the rectangle are 2 inches long.
(2) The length of the rectangle is 2 inches greater than the width of the
a.   b.   c.   d.   e.

50. Is a an integer?

(1) $a > 0$
(2) $4^2 + 3^2 = a^2$
a.   b.   c.   d.   e.

51. What is the value of the integer P?

(1) P is an integer multiple of 2, 4, and 5.
(2) $40 < P < 70$
a.   b.   c.   d.   e.

52. Brian is dividing 50 marbles into 3 groups. How many marbles are in the largest of the three groups?

(1) The sum of the two smaller groups of marbles is equal to the largest group of marbles.
(2) The smallest group contains 6 marbles.
a.   b.   c.   d.   e.

53. Is b a positive number?

(1) $1,452(b) > 0$
(2) $-b < 0$
a.   b.   c.   d.   e.

54. Is x greater than y?

(1) $x > 2y$
(2) $x - y > 0$
a.   b.   c.   d.   e.

55. What is the average test score of Angela, Barry, Carl, Dennis, and Edward?

(1) The average of the test scores of Barry, Carl, and Edward is 87.
(2) The average of the test scores of Angela and Dennis is 84.
a.   b.   c.   d.   e.

56. If y is an integer, is it an odd number?

(1) $y^3 \geq 0$
(2) y is either an odd number or a negative number
a.   b.   c.   d.   e.

57. Is Set C closed under subtraction?

(1) Set A is a subset of Set C.
(2) Set A is not closed under subtraction.
a.   b.   c.   d.   e.

58. In Triangle ABC, is $\overline{AB}$ longer than $\overline{AC}$?

(1) $\overline{AC}$ is opposite angle B.
(2) $\overline{BC}$ is longer than $\overline{AC}$.
a.   b.   c.   d.   e.

59. Is Triangle DEF a right triangle?

(1) The measure of angle D is 45 degrees.
(2) The side lengths of Triangle DEF measure 12 units, 16 units, and 20 units.
a.   b.   c.   d.   e.

60. Is $\overline{AB}$ perpendicular to $\overline{CD}$?

(1) The slope of $\overline{AB}$ is the negative reciprocal of the slope of $\overline{CD}$.
(2) $\overline{AB}$ and $\overline{CD}$ intersect at four right angles.
a.   b.   c.   d.   e.

61. Is the integer, a, greater than the integer, c?

(1) The integer, c, is less than the integer, b
(2) The integer, a, is greater than the integer, b
a.   b.   c.   d.   e.

62. What is the sum of the first 100 natural numbers?

(1) There are 50 pairs of numbers, for which a sum can be determined for each pair.
(2) The sum of each pair is 101.
a.   b.   c.   d.   e.

63. Given the sequences produced by the functions, $a_n = 2^n$ and $a_n = 2^{n+1}$, which sequence has a larger value for the 11th term?

(1) n is a real number
(2) n is a positive integer

a.　　　　b.　　　　c.　　　　d.　　　　e.

64. Does Alexander finish more miles than Bruce?

(1) Bruce finishes fewer miles than Eric.
(2) Eric finishes fewer miles than Alexander.

a.　　　　b.　　　　c.　　　　d.　　　　e.

65. Given the same value for the first term, does infinite geometric series A converge to a larger number than geometric series B?

(1) The common ratio in the infinite geometric series A is smaller than the common ratio in the infinite geometric series B.
(2) The difference between the common ratio and 1 in series A is larger than the difference between the common ratio and 1 in series B.

a.　　　　b.　　　　c.　　　　d.　　　　e.

66. Does y vary directly with x?

(1) The y-intercept of the linear equation, relating x and y, is 0.
(2) There is a constant rate of change in the value of y for each subsequent x-value.

a.　　　　b.　　　　c.　　　　d.　　　　e.

67. Is Triangle ABC similar to Triangle DEF?

(1) The corresponding side lengths of Triangles ABC and DEF are proportional.
(2) The corresponding angles of Triangles ABC and DEF are congruent.

a.　　　　b.　　　　c.　　　　d.　　　　e.

68. Is line AB parallel to line CD?

(1) A transversal, intersecting the two lines, forms congruent corresponding angles.
(2) A transversal, intersecting the two lines, forms congruent alternate interior angles.

a.　　　　b.　　　　c.　　　　d.　　　　e.

69. How many positive integers less than 100 are prime?

(1) There are 48 positive multiples of 2, less than 100.
(2) There are 50 odd, positive integers, less than 100.

a.　　　　b.　　　　c.　　　　d.　　　　e.

70. Is Relation A also a function?

(1) Relation A forms a parabola, when graphed.
(2) Each y-value in Relation A is mapped to a unique x-value.

a.　　　　b.　　　　c.　　　　d.　　　　e.

71. Is the range of a data set less than the mode of a data set?

(1) The median is greater than the mode.
(2) The range is less than the median.

a.　　　　b.　　　　c.　　　　d.　　　　e.

72. Is the value of the nth term of arithmetic sequence A greater than the value of the nth term of arithmetic sequence B?

(1) The value of the initial term of arithmetic sequence A is less than the value of the initial term of arithmetic sequence B.
(2) The difference in value in subsequent terms for arithmetic sequence A is greater than the difference in value in subsequent terms for arithmetic sequence B.

a.   b.   c.   d.   e.

73. What is the tangent of angle A?

(1) The cosine of angle A is $\frac{4}{5}$.

(2) The sine of angle A is $\frac{3}{5}$.

a.   b.   c.   d.   e.

74. Is the sum of the first n, even numbers, an even integer?

(1) The rate of change between subsequent even numbers is even.
(2) The rate of change in the sum of the first n, even numbers, is even.

a.   b.   c.   d.   e.

Answers and Explanations

Problem-Solving

1. B: Simply substitute the given values for a and b and perform the required operations.

2. C: This problem is solved by finding x in this equation: $34/80 = x/100$.

3. C: Every possible combination of scores is a multiple of 7, since the two terms of the ratio have a sum of seven.

4. E: To solve this problem, work backwards. That is, perform FOIL on each answer choice until you derive the original expression.

5. A: A set of six numbers with an average of 4 must have a collective sum of 24. The two numbers that average 2 will add up to 4, so the remaining numbers must add up to 20. The average of these four numbers can be calculated: $20/4 = 5$.

6. C: Prime numbers are those that are only evenly divisible by one and themselves.

7. D: Simple Multiplication.

8. D: Multiply 30 by 0.2 and subtract this from the original price of the shirt to find the sale price: $24. Then multiply 24 by 0.2 and add the product to the sale price to find the final price.

9. C: There are 12 inches in a foot and 3 feet in a yard. Four and a half yards is equal to 162 inches. To determine the number of 3-inch segments, divide 162 by 3.

10. A: If it takes 3 people 3 1/3 days to do the job, then it would take one person 10 days: $3 \times 3\frac{1}{3} = 10$. Thus, it would take 2 people 5 days, and one day of work for two people would complete 1/5 of the job.

11. E: There are 60 minutes in an hour, so Dave can deliver 240 newspapers every hour. In 2 hours, then, he can deliver 480 papers.

12. C: Since 4 is the same as 2^2, $4^6 = 2^{12}$. When dividing exponents with the same base, simply subtract the exponent in the denominator from the exponent in the numerator.

13. B: Substitute the given values and solve. Resolve the parenthetical operations first.

14. A: Convert 20% to the fraction 1/5, then multiply by 12/5. The resulting fraction, 12/25, must have both numerator and denominator multiplied by 4 to become a percentage.

15. E: This problem can be solved with the following equation, in which x = the total capacity of the tank: $\frac{1}{2}x = \frac{1}{3}x + 3$.

16. A: This is a right triangle, since the two angles shown add up to 90 degrees, and the remaining angle must therefore be 90 degrees. For a right triangle, the length of a side is related to the hypotenuse by the sine of the opposite angle. Thus $B = C \sin(30°)$ and since the sine of a 30-degree angle is 0.5, $B = C/2$.

17. A: Since the second line, $y = 3$, is a vertical, the intersection must occur at a point where $y = 3$. If $x = 1.5$, the equation describing the line is satisfied: $(2 \times [-1.5] + 3) = 0$

18. C: The surface of a cube is obtained by multiplying the area of each face by 6, since there are 6 faces. The area of each face is the square of the length of one edge.

Therefore, A = $6 \times 3^2 = 6 \times 9 = 54$. Answers A, B, D, and E are incorrect since the surface area is a unique value.

19. A: The area A of a circle is given by $A = \pi \times r^2$, where r is the radius. Since π is approximately

3.14, we can solve for $r = \sqrt{\frac{A}{\pi}} = \sqrt{\frac{314}{3.14}} = \sqrt{100} = 10$. Now, the diameter d is twice the radius, or

$d = 2 \times 10 = 20$.
B. 10 is the value of the radius, not the diameter. C, D, and E are all wrong as they do not equal 20.

20. E: The sum of angles in a triangle equals 180 degrees. Therefore solve for the remaining angle as $180 - (15 + 70) = 95$ degrees. Since this value is unique, all other answers are incorrect.

21. B: This answer may be determined using the Law of Sines, which relates the sides of a triangle and their opposing angles as follows:

Thus we have $\sin A = a \times \frac{\sin B}{b} = 14 \times \frac{\sin(35)}{12} = 14 \times \frac{0.57}{12} = 0.67$, and $\sin^{-1}(0.67) = 42°$.

Since this value is unique, all other answers are incorrect.

22. C: The volume of a right circular cylinder is equal to its height multiplied by the area of its base, A. Since the base is circular, $A = \pi R^2$, where R, the radius, is half the diameter, or 30 feet. Therefore, $V = H \times \pi R^2$

Solving for $H, H = \frac{V}{\pi R^2} = \frac{1,000,000}{\pi \times 30^2} = \frac{1,000,000}{\pi \times 900} \approx 353.7$ ft

A and B are both greater than 355, so they do not represent the minimum acceptable height. D and E are both too low to hold the required volume.

23. C: Rearranging the equation gives

$3(y + 4) = 15(y - 5)$, which is equivalent to

$15y - 3y = 12 + 75$, or

$12y = 87$, and solving for y,

$y = \frac{87}{12} = \frac{29}{4}$.

Since this value is unique, all the other answers are incorrect.

24. E: Segment $AD = 48$. Because the length of CD is 2 times the length of AB, let $AB = x$ and let $CD = 2x$. Since $AB = BC$, let $BC = x$ also. The total length of $AD = AB + BC + CD = x + x + 2x = 4x = 48$. Thus, $x = 12$ and $BC + CD = x + 2x = 3x = 3 \times 12 = 36$.

25. E: .33 is equal to roughly 1/3, so find which choice is NOT less (i.e. greater) than 1/3. Since the "3" in the denominator of 1/3 is a factor of the denominators of all the answer choices, you can compare the fractions with relative ease.

26. D: Isolate a: $a = 8b + 6 + 16$. Thus, $a = 8b + 22$. Next add 3 to both side of the equation: $a + 3 = 8b + 22 + 3 = 8b + 25$.

27. D: Angles around a point add up to 360 degrees. Add the degrees of the given angles: $72° + 110° + 58° = 240°$. Then subtract from $360° - 240° = 120°$. Remember to divide $120°$ in half, since the question is asking for the degree measure of one angle, angle d.

28. B: Translate this word problem into a mathematical equation. Let Janice's weight = x. Let Elaina's weight = $x + 23$. Let June's weight = $x + 14$. Add their weights together and subtract 25 pounds:

$= x + x + 23 + x + 14 - 25$

$= 3x + 37 - 25$

$= 3x + 12$

29. B: Add the 14 blue, 6 red, 12 green and 8 purple buttons to get a total of 40 buttons. If 25 buttons are removed, there are 15 buttons remaining in the bag. If the chance of drawing a red button is now 1/3, divide 15 into thirds to get 5 red buttons remaining in the bag. The original total of red buttons was 6; so $6 - 5 = 1$: one red button was removed, choice (B).

30. D: First, determine how many revolutions the washer makes in one wash by multiplying $85 \times 15 = 1,275$. Then divide 100,000 by 1,275 to determine how many washes it will take to reach 100,000 revolutions $100,000 \div 1,275 = 78.431373$. Round this number to 78, the nearest whole number.

You may not be able to determine the precise answer, but you may be able to solve at least to the tenths decimal place and see that the answer is roughly 78.

31. C: Divide the mg the child should receive by the number of mg in 0.8 ml to determine how many 0.8 ml doses the child should receive: $240 \div 80 = 3$. Multiply the number of doses by 0.8 to determine how many ml the child should receive: $3 \times 0.8 = 2.4$ ml

32. D: This equation is asking you to multiply three algebraic expressions. When multiplying more than two expressions, multiply any two expressions (using the FOIL method), then multiply the result by the third expression. Start by multiplying:

$(y + 1)(y + 2) = (y \times y) + (y \times 2) + (1 \times y) + (1 \times 2)$

$= y^2 + 2y + y + 2$

$= y^2 + 3y + 2$

Then multiply the result by the third expression:

$(y^2 + 3y + 2)(y + 3) = (y^2 + 3y + 2)(y) + (y^2 + 3y + 2)(3)$

$= (y^3 + 3y^2 + 2y) + (3y^2 + 9y + 6)$

$= y^3 + 3y^2 + 2y + 3y^2 + 9y + 6$

$= y^3 + 3y^2 + 3y^2 + 9y + 2y + 6$

$= y^3 + 6y^2 + 11y + 6$

33. D: The area of a parallelogram is base × height or $A = bh$, where b is the length of a side and h is the length of an altitude to that side. In this problem,

$A = 6 \times 4$; $A = 24$. Remember, use the length of BE, not the length of CD for the height.

34. A: There are a total of 90 students that take Math, English, or both. You must avoid counting the same students twice, and you may find it helpful to create a Venn diagram or some sort of chart to keep the different types of students separate.

Total students	90
Students taking both courses:	-50
Students taking just English:	-25
Students taking just Math:	15

35. A: To find the interest earned, multiply the interest rate by the deposit amount. Because this account uses simple interest, you do not need to worry about compounding the interest. Remember to convert the interest rate to a percentage.

$0.0375 \times 2,500 = 93.75$.

Choice (D) might be a tempting answer, since it is the deposit amount added to the interest earned, but the question asks how much interest will be earned, not the total amount of the deposit after earning interest.

36. B: Use the Pythagorean Theorem to solve this problem: $a^2 + b^2 = c^2$ where c is the hypotenuse while a and b are the legs of the triangle.

$5^2 + 12^2 = c^2$

$25 + 144 = 169$

$\sqrt{169} = 13$.

37. B: A percentage is changed into a fraction by first converting the percentage into a decimal, and then changing the decimal to a fraction.

To convert a percentage into a decimal, divide the percentage by 100 by moving the decimal point two places to the left:

$12.5\% = .125$

To convert this decimal into a fraction, the numbers to the right of the decimal point become the numerator. Because the last decimal place is the thousandths place, the numerator of the faction is 1000. Reduce the fraction to the lowest terms:

$125/1000 = 1/8$

Remember that you can reduce the fraction into progressively lower terms until you find the most reduced fraction (ex: 25/200 → 5/40 → 1/8).

38. E: The average of a group of terms is the sum of the terms divided by the number of terms. In this problem, the teacher disregards Rick's highest and lowest scores, so do not use 95% or 64% in your calculation. Add the remaining scores: 68 + 86 + 83 + 92 + 79 = 408

Divide by the number of scores: 408 ÷ 5 = 81.6.

39. E: Use the formula for probability to solve this problem:

Probability =

Number of Desirable Outcomes

Number of Possible Outcomes

Because there are effectively multiple events – the roll of each die is its own event – you must multiply all the possible outcomes for each die. Thus, to determine the number of possible outcomes, multiply the number of sides on dice exponentially by the number dice:

6^5 = (6 × 6 × 6 × 6 × 6) = 7,776

There is one desirable outcome: rolling all sixes. Probability = 1/7,776

40. B: Remember to use the order of operations when simplifying this equation. The acronym *PEMDAS* will help you remember the correct order: Parenthesis, Exponentiation, Multiplication/Division, Addition/Subtraction.

$4(6 – 3)^2 – (-2)$

First, simplify the parentheses: $4 × 3^2 – (-2)$

Next, simplify the exponent: 4 × 9 – (-2)

Then multiply: 36 – (-2)

Finally, subtract: 36 – (-2) = 36 + 2 = 38

The PEMDAS method is used to simplify multiple equations in this practice test.

41. A: You can eliminate choices (B) and (C) since they are to the left of the decimal point. This problem asks for the number in the thousandths place, and the "ths" indicate digits to the right of the decimal point. Of those digits:

- 9 is in the tenths place
- 7 is in the hundredths place
- 3 is in the thousandths place
- 8 is in the ten thousandths place

42. E: An equilateral triangle has three sides of equal length. If each side is 4 inches long, the perimeter of the triangle is 12 inches. A square has four sides of equal length. Since its perimeter also must equal 12 inches, divide 12 by 4: 12 ÷ 4 = 3

43. C: Find the common denominator of $^3/_8$ and $^{13}/_{24}$.

$^3/_8 × ^3/_3 = ^9/_{24}$

- 159 -

$^{13}/_{24} \times {}^1/_1 = {}^{13}/_{24}$

The value in the triangle must be greater than $^9/_{24}$ and less than $^{13}/_{24}$. Choice (C), $^5/_{12}$, when expressed as the equivalent fraction $^{10}/_{24}$, is correct.

44. B: The chart indicates that each x value must be tripled to equal the corresponding y value, so $y = 3x$. One way you can determine this is by plugging corresponding pairs of x and y into the answer choices.

45. D: Turn the word problem into an equation. Remember that product means multiplication:

$4^2 \times 6 = 96$.

46. C: This equation is asking you to multiply three algebraic expressions. When multiplying more than two expressions, multiply any two expressions, (using the FOIL method) then multiply the result by the third expression. Start by multiplying:

$(y + 2)(y + 3) = (y \times y) + (y \times 3) + (2 \times y) + (2 \times 3)$

$= y^2 + 3y + 2y + 6$

$= y^2 + 5y + 6$

Then multiply the result by the third expression:

$(y^2 + 5y + 6)(y + 4) = (y^2 + 5y +6)(y) + (y^2 + 5y +6)(4)$

$= (y^3 + 5y^2 + 6y) + (4y^2 + 20y + 24)$

$= y^3 + 5y^2 + 6y + 4y^2 + 20y + 24$

$= y^3 + 9y^2 + 26y + 24$

Data Sufficiency

47. E: The two statements establish only that Alice is paid more than both Jonathan and Deborah; they do not indicate which of these latter two is paid more.

48. A: Since the cubes of a and b will retain the original sign (whether positive or negative), it will be possible to assess the relative sizes of a and b.

49. A: If the two shorter sides add up to 4 inches in length, the two longer sides must be greater than 4 inches, meaning that the perimeter will be greater than 8 inches.

50. B: The first statement only establishes that a is a positive number; it does not require that a is an integer.

51. C: 60 is the only integer between 40 and 70 that is a multiple of 2, 4, and 5.

52. A: The first statement establishes that the larger group constitutes half of the total amount of marbles, which means it must be equal to 25 marbles.

53. D: For (1), the fact that a positive number multiplied by b has a positive product establishes that b is a positive number. For (2), any positive number with a negative sign placed in front of it will become negative, indicating that b is a positive number.

54. B: It would be possible for x and y to be negative numbers and still satisfy the conditions of (1), but it then would be impossible to satisfy (2).

55. C: As long as the sum of all five test scores can be calculated, it will be possible to calculate the average score.

56. C: In order for (1) to be true, y must be either positive or zero. Therefore, according to the terms of (2), y must be odd.

57. E: The two statements explain that Set A is a subset of Set C, with Set A not being closed under subtraction. These facts do not indicate whether or not Set C is closed under subtraction. For example, the set of natural numbers could represent Set A. In this case, Set A is not closed under subtraction (as the second statement indicates). If Set C were the set of whole numbers, with Set A being a subset of this set, Set C would not be closed under subtraction. However, if Set C were the set of real numbers, with Set A again being a subset of this set, Set C would be closed under subtraction. Since the specifics of Set C are not given, the posed question cannot be answered, using the information in the two statements.

58. E: The statements simply indicate the placement of the vertices of the triangle and the fact that $\overline{BC}$ is longer than $\overline{AC}$. It cannot be determined, from the given information, whether or not $\overline{AB}$ is longer than $\overline{AC}$. In order to make such a deduction, the statements would need to indicate the angle measures of each angle.

59. B: A right triangle has side lengths that adhere to the Pythagorean Theorem, which states: $a^2 + b^2 = c^2$. Statement (1) could possibly describe a 45-45-90 right triangle, but this isn't explicitly stated. Such a triangle could be 45-60-105. The given information only depicts one angle of the triangle to have a measure of 45 degrees. Statement (2) indicates that the triangle has side lengths, in accordance with the Pythagorean Theorem, revealing the Pythagorean Triples of 12, 16, and 20: $12^2 + 16^2 = 20^2$ or $400 = 400$.

60. D: Perpendicular lines have negative reciprocal slopes. Thus, Statement (1) is sufficient. Statement (2) indicates intersect to form four right angles. Perpendicular lines intersect to form four right angles. Thus, either statement is sufficient.

61. C: The relationship described in (1) can be written as: $c < b$. The relationship described in (2) can be written as: $b < a$. If $c < b$ and $b < a$, then $c < a$, by the transitive property.

62. C: The sum of the first 100 natural numbers can be determined by finding the product of the number of pairs of numbers and the sum of each pair. Thus, the sum is equal to $50 \cdot 101$, or 5,050.

63. D: For any real number or positive integer, the sequence, $a_n = 2^{n+1}$, will have a larger value for the 11th term, since the exponent of n, has 1 added to it. The exponent on the base will always be larger in this sequence than in the other sequence, resulting in a larger value of each term.

64. C: The relationship described in (1) can be written as: $b < e$, where b represents the number of miles Bruce finishes and e represents the number of miles Eric finishes. The relationship described in (2) can be written as: $e < a$, where e represents the number of miles Eric finishes and a

represents the number of miles Alexander finishes. If $b < e$ and $e < a$, then $b < a$, by the transitive property. Thus, Bruce finishes fewer miles than Alexander.

65. D: Either statement (1) or statement (2) reveal that infinite geometric series A will converge to a smaller number than infinite geometric series B, given the same value for the first term. The reasoning rests with the fact that the smaller ratio for infinite geometric series A will result in a larger difference in the denominator, thus resulting in division by a larger number, which produces a smaller quotient. For example, suppose each series starts with the first value of 2. A common ratio of $\frac{1}{3}$ shows a convergence of the series to the number, 3. Note $S = \frac{a}{1-r}$, where a represents the value of the first term and r represents the common ratio. Thus, the convergence can be written as: $S = \frac{2}{1-\frac{1}{3}}$, which equals 3. A common ratio of $\frac{1}{2}$ shows a convergence of the series to the number, 4; $\frac{2}{1-\frac{1}{2}} = 4$.

66. A: When y varies directly with x, the relationship is proportional, meaning the graph of the relationship passes through the origin, $(0, 0)$, indicating a y-intercept of 0. In other words, no constant amount is added to or subtracted from the term, containing the slope of the line. Statement (2) simply implies that the relationship is linear, with the constant rate of change noted. However, not all linear relationships are proportional. Such lines have y-intercepts, other than $(0, 0)$. Note. Not all linear relationships are proportional, but all proportional relationships are linear.

67. D: By definition, two triangles are similar if corresponding side lengths are proportional or if corresponding angles are congruent.

68. D: By definition, two lines are parallel, if a transversal, intersecting the lines, forms congruent corresponding angles or congruent alternate interior angles.

69. E: Statement (1) only eliminates composite numbers that are multiples of 2. Statement (2) is not helpful, since odd numbers can be either prime or composite.

70. A: A parabola is a function because each x-value is mapped to one and only one y-value. A vertical line, passing through the graph, will only intersect the parabola at one point. Statement (2) indicates an inverse function. The inverse of a relation can be a function, when the relation itself is not a function. A function maps each x-value to a unique y-value, whereas an inverse function maps each y-value to a unique x-value. For example, given the relation, $R = \{(1,3), (1,5), (2,7)\}$, the relation is not a function, since 1 is mapped to 3 and 5. However, the inverse of the relation is a function, since each y-value is mapped to a unique x-value.

71. E: These statements simply reveal that the median is greater than both the mode and the range. There isn't any information given, relating the mode and the range.

72. E: The formula for finding the nth term of an arithmetic sequence is: $a_n = a_1 + (n-1)d$, where a_n represents the value of the nth term, a_1 represents the value of the first term, n represents the nth term number, and d represents the common difference between the terms. Let the equation for arithmetic sequence A be: $a_n = a_1 + (n-1)d_a$ and let the equation for arithmetic sequence B be: $b_n = b_1 + (n-1)d_b$. The two statements explain that arithmetic sequence A will have a smaller value for the first term $(a_1 < b_1)$ and a larger common difference $(d_a > d_b)$. Substituting $n = 1$, the value of arithmetic sequence A will be less than B. Substituting $n = 2$, the value of arithmetic sequence A is $a_1 + d_a$, and the value of arithmetic sequence B is $b_1 + d_b$. Since no information is provided on whether the first term is greater or less than the difference for each sequence, it cannot be determined whether sequence A or B is greater in this scenario.

73. C: While it might be tempting to pick D since $\tan\left(sin^{-1}\frac{3}{5}\right)$ and $\tan\left(\cos^{-1}\frac{4}{5}\right)$ are the same most of the time (when angle A is between 0 and 90°, for instance), both statements are necessary to know for certain that $\tan A = \frac{3}{4}$ and not $-\frac{3}{4}$.

The tangent of angle A can be represented by the ratio, $\frac{opposite}{adjacent}$. The sine of angle A can be represented by the ratio, $\frac{opposite}{hypotenuse}$. The cosine of angle A can be represented by the ratio, $\frac{adjacent}{hypotenuse}$. Since the cosine of angle A is $\frac{4}{5}$, the adjacent length is 4, and the hypotenuse length is 5. Since the sine of angle A is $\frac{3}{5}$, the opposite length is 3, and the hypotenuse length is 5, as previously determined. Thus, the tangent is $\frac{3}{4}$.

74. D: Considering the even numbers, starting with 0, the sequence can be written: 0, 2, 4, 6, ... Statement (1) indicates that the rate of change between subsequent even integers is even. This statement indicates that each subsequent term will change by an even value, indicating that each subsequent sum will also change by an even value, thus indicating an even sum. Statement (2) actually states that the rate of change in each subsequent sum is even, thus allowing the previous deduction to be made.

Additional Verbal Practice

Reading Comprehension

Questions 1 – 3 pertain to the following passage:

In the United States, where we have more land than people, it is not at all difficult for persons in good health to make money. In this comparatively new field there are so many avenues of success open, so many vocations which are not crowded, that any person of either sex who is willing, at least for the time being, to engage in any respectable occupation that offers, may find lucrative employment.

Those who really desire to attain an independence, have only to set their minds upon it, and adopt the proper means, as they do in regard to any other object which they wish to accomplish, and the thing is easily done. But however easy it may be found to make money, I have no doubt many of my hearers will agree it is the most difficult thing in the world to keep it. The road to wealth is, as Dr. Franklin truly says, "as plain as the road to the mill." It consists simply in expending less than we earn; that seems to be a very simple problem. Mr. Micawber, one of those happy creations of the genial Dickens, puts the case in a strong light when he says that to have annual income of twenty pounds per annum, and spend twenty pounds and sixpence, is to be the most miserable of men; whereas, to have an income of only twenty pounds, and spend but nineteen pounds and sixpence is to be the happiest of mortals.

Many of my readers may say, "we understand this: this is economy, and we know economy is wealth; we know we can't eat our cake and keep it also." Yet I beg to say that perhaps more cases of failure arise from mistakes on this point than almost any other. The fact is, many people think they understand economy when they really do not.

1. Which of the following statements best expresses the main idea of the passage?
   a. Getting a job is easier now than it ever has been before
   b. Earning money is much less difficult than managing it properly
   c. Dr. Franklin advocated getting a job in a mill
   d. Spending money is the greatest temptation in the world
   e. There is no way to predict changes in the economy

2. What would this author's attitude likely be to a person unable to find employment?
   a. descriptive
   b. conciliatory
   c. ingenuous
   d. incredulous
   e. exculpatory

3. According to the author, what is more difficult than making money?

    a. getting a job
    b. traveling to a mill
    c. reading Dickens
    d. understanding the economy
    e. managing money

Questions 4 – 7 pertain to the following passage:

We all know the drill: the consequences of urban sprawl, American's long work hours, and devotion to television and the internet are doing nothing good for American communities.

A new study by sociologists at Duke University and the University of Arizona adds more grist to this mill, noting that Americans in 2004 had smaller networks of people with whom they talk about matters important to them than they did in 1985. (*Social Isolation in America: Changes in Core Discussion Networks Over Two Decades*, American Sociological Review, June 2006.) In 1985, Americans had three confidants, in 2004, we averaged two. The number of Americans who had no one with whom to talk about important matters almost doubled in 2004 to over 25%. Increasingly, most confidants are family: in 2004, 80% of people talked only to family about important matters and about 9% people depended totally on their spouse.

This decrease in confidants is part (a result) of the same trend that's leaving fewer people knowing their neighbors or participating in social clubs or public affairs than in the past (phenomena noted in the book <u>Better Together: Restoring the American Community</u> by Robert Putnam and Lewis Feldstein). We know a lot of people, but not necessarily very well.

Left to our own devices and cultural trends then, we seem to be moving in an unpleasant direction. Communities are formed ad hoc, around specific shared individual interests. This wouldn't be bad, of course, except that those communities seem to exist only within the constraints of those shared interests, and don't develop into close and meaningful relationships. The transient and specific nature of many of our relationships today can keep us socially busy without building the lasting relationships and communities that we want.

So what do we do about it if we want to change things? Harvard University's School of Government put together 150 ways to increase what they call "social capital" (the value of our social networks). Among their suggestions are: support local merchants; audition for community theater or volunteer to usher; participate in political campaigns; start or join a carpool; eat breakfast at a local gathering spot on Saturdays; and stop and make sure the person on the side of the highway is OK.

4. According to the author, which of the following was true in 2004:

a. The average American had three confidants and 9% of people depended totally on their spouse for discussion of important matters

b. The average American had two confidants, and 80% of people discussed important matters only with their spouses

c. The average American had two confidants, and 9% of people discussed important matters only with family members

d. The average American had two confidants, and 80% of people discussed important matters only with family members

e. The average American had three confidants, and 80% of people discussed important matters only with family members

5. The author argues that the transient nature of many of today's relationships is problematic because:

a. we don't share specific interests

b. we don't know many people

c. it prevents us building lasting relationships and communities

d. we have too much social capital

e. we talk to too many people about private matters

6. Which of the following are some of the causes to which the author attributes problems in American communities?

a. too much homework and devotion to television

b. devotion to television and decline of sports team membership

c. long work hours and too much homework

d. urban sprawl and decline of sports team membership

e. urban sprawl and long work hours

7. Which of the following is not something the author states was suggested by Harvard University as a way to increase social capital:

a. eat breakfast at a local gathering spot

b. join a bowling team

c. support local merchants

d. join a carpool

e. audition for community theater

Questions 8 – 11 pertain to the following passage:

George Washington Carver was always interested in plants. When he was a child, he was known as the "plant doctor." He had a secret garden where he grew all kinds of plants. People would ask him for advice when they had sick plants. Sometimes he'd take their plants to his garden and nurse them back to health.

Later, when he was teaching at Tuskegee Institute, he put his plant skills to good use. Many people in the South had been growing only cotton on their land. Cotton plants use most of the nutrients in the soil. (Nutrients provide nourishment to plants.) So the soil becomes "worn out" after a few years. Eventually, cotton will no longer grow on this land.

This was especially bad for poor African American farmers, who relied on selling cotton to support themselves. Carver was dedicated to helping those farmers, so he came up with a plan.

Carver knew that certain plants put nutrients back into the soil. One of those plants is the peanut! Peanuts are also a source of protein.

Carver thought that if those farmers planted peanuts, the plants would help restore their soil, provide food for their animals, and provide protein for their families--quite a plant! In 1896 peanuts were not even recognized as a crop in the United States, but Carver would help change that.

Carver told farmers to rotate their crops: plant cotton one year, then the next year plant peanuts and other soil-restoring plants, like peas and sweet potatoes. It worked! The peanut plants grew and produced lots of peanuts. The plants added enough nutrients to the soil so cotton grew the next year.

8. Why was George Washington Carver known as the "plant doctor"?

a. He studied medicine in college
b. He grew peanuts on sick soil
c. He was a plant pathologist
d. He could nurse sick plants back to health
e. He knew plants could put nutrients back into the soil

9. How is this passage structured?

a. cause and effect
b. problem and solution
c. chronological order
d. compare and contrast
e. proposition and support

10. According to the passage, what problem were cotton farmers facing?

a. They needed food for their animals
b. Peanuts were not recognized as a crop in the United States
c. They were growing too much cotton
d. Tuskegee Institute needed more teachers
e. The cotton had stripped the land of its nutrients

11. This passage is mainly about?

a. how George Washington Carver invented the cotton gin
b. how George Washington Carver became a teacher at the Tuskegee Institute
c. how George Washington Carver helped farmers improve their crop production
d. why George Washington Carver studied plants
e. how George Washington Carver made peanuts a recognized crop in the United States

Questions 12 and 13 pertain to the following passage:

From 1892 to 1954, over twelve million immigrants entered the United States through the portal of Ellis Island, a small island in New York Harbor. Ellis Island is located in the upper bay just off the New Jersey coast, within the shadow of the Statue of Liberty. Through the years, this gateway to the new world was enlarged

- 167 -

from its original 3.3 acres to 27.5 acres by landfill supposedly obtained from the ballast of ships, excess earth from the construction of the New York City subway system and elsewhere.

Before being designated as the site of one of the first Federal immigration station by President Benjamin Harrison in 1890, Ellis Island had a varied history. The local Indian tribes had called it "Kioshk" or Gull Island. Due to its rich and abundant oyster beds and plentiful and profitable shad runs, it was known as Oyster Island for many generations during the Dutch and English colonial periods. By the time Samuel Ellis became the island's private owner in the 1770's, the island had been called Kioshk, Oyster, Dyre, Bucking and Anderson's Island. In this way, Ellis Island developed from a sandy island that barely rose above the high tide mark, into a hanging site for pirates, a harbor fort, ammunition and ordinance depot named Fort Gibson, and finally into an immigration station.

12. Which of the following is true about Ellis Island?

    I. It houses the Statue of Liberty
    II. The local Indian tribes called it Oyster Island
    III. It was expanded using dirt from the construction of the subway system

  a. I only
  b. I and II only
  c. II and III only
  d. III only
  e. I, II, and III

13. The style of this passage is most like that found in a(n)

  a. immigrant's diary
  b. business letter
  c. history textbook
  d. persuasive essay
  e. short story

Questions 14 -16 pertain to the following passage:

Peanut allergy is the most prevalent food allergy in the United States, affecting around one and a half million people, and it is potentially on the rise in children in the United States. While thought to be the most common cause of food-related death, deaths from food allergies are very rare. The allergy typically begins at a very young age and remains present for life for most people. Approximately one-fifth to one-quarter of children with a peanut allergy, however, outgrow it. Treatment involves careful avoidance of peanuts or any food that may contain peanut pieces or oils. For some sufferers, exposure to even the smallest amount of peanut product can trigger a serious reaction.

Symptoms of peanut allergy can include skin reactions, itching around the mouth, digestive problems, shortness of breath, and runny or stuffy nose. The most severe peanut allergies can result in anaphylaxis, which requires immediate treatment with epinephrine. Up to one-third of people with peanut allergies have severe reactions. Without treatment, anaphylactic shock can result in death due to obstruction of the airway, or heart failure. Signs of anaphylaxis include constriction of airways and difficulty breathing, shock, a rapid pulse, and dizziness or lightheadedness.

As of yet, there is no treatment to prevent or cure allergic reactions to peanuts. In May of 2008, however, Duke University Medical Center food allergy experts announced that they expect to offer a treatment for peanut allergies within five years.

Scientists do not know for sure why peanut proteins induce allergic reactions, nor do they know why some people develop peanut allergies while others do not. There is a strong genetic component to allergies: if one of a child's parents has an allergy, the child has an almost 50% chance of developing an allergy. If both parents have an allergy, the odds increase to about 70%.

Someone suffering from a peanut allergy needs to be cautious about the foods he or she eats and the products he or she puts on his or her skin. Common foods that should be checked for peanut content are ground nuts, cereals, granola, grain breads, energy bars, and salad dressings. Store prepared cookies, pastries, and frozen desserts like ice cream can also contain peanuts. Additionally, many cuisines use peanuts in cooking – watch for peanut content in African, Chinese, Indonesian, Mexican, Thai, and Vietnamese dishes.

Parents of children with peanut allergies should notify key people (child care providers, school personnel, etc.) that their child has a peanut allergy, explain peanut allergy symptoms to them, make sure that the child's epinephrine auto injector is always available, write an action plan of care for their child when he or she has an allergic reaction to peanuts, have their child wear a medical alert bracelet or necklace, and discourage their child from sharing foods.

14. Which allergy does the article state is thought to be the most common cause of food-related death?
   a. Peanut
   b. Tree nut
   c. Bee sting
   d. Poison oak
   e. Shellfish

15. It can be inferred from the passage that children with peanut allergies should be discouraged from sharing food because:
   a. Peanut allergies can be contagious
   b. People suffering from peanut allergies are more susceptible to bad hygiene
   c. Many foods contain peanut content and it is important to be very careful when you don't know what you're eating
   d. Scientists don't know why some people develop peanut allergies
   e. There is no treatment yet to prevent peanut allergies

16. Which of the following does the passage not state is a sign of anaphylaxis?
    a. constriction of airways
    b. shock
    c. a rapid pulse
    d. dizziness
    e. running or stuffy nose

Questions 17 – 19 pertain to the following passage:

Daylight Saving Time (DST) is the practice of changing clocks so that afternoons have more daylight and mornings have less. Clocks are adjusted forward one hour in the spring and one hour backward in the fall. The main purpose of the change is to make better use of daylight.

DST began with the goal of conservation. Benjamin Franklin suggested it as a method of saving on candles. It was used during both World Wars to save energy for military needs. Although DST's potential to save energy was a primary reason behind its implementation, research into its effects on energy conservation are contradictory and unclear.

Beneficiaries of DST include all activities that can benefit from more sunlight after working hours, such as shopping and sports. A 1984 issue of *Fortune* magazine estimated that a seven-week extension of DST would yield an additional $30 million for 7-Eleven stores. Public safety may be increased by the use of DST: some research suggests that traffic fatalities may be reduced when there is additional afternoon sunlight.

On the other hand, DST complicates timekeeping and some computer systems. Tools with built-in time-keeping functions such as medical devices can be affected negatively. Agricultural and evening entertainment interests have historically opposed DST.

DST can affect health, both positively and negatively. It provides more afternoon sunlight in which to get exercise. It also impacts sunlight exposure; this is good for getting vitamin D, but bad in that it can increase skin cancer risk. DST may also disrupt sleep.

Today, daylight saving time has been adopted by more than one billion people in about 70 countries. DST is generally not observed in countries near the equator because sunrise times do not vary much there. Asia and Africa do not generally observe it. Some countries, such as Brazil, observe it only in some regions.

DST can lead to peculiar situations. One of these occurred in November, 2007 when a woman in North Carolina gave birth to one twin at 1:32 a.m. and, 34 minutes later, to the second twin. Because of DST and the time change at 2:00 a.m., the second twin was officially born at 1:06, 26 minutes earlier than her brother.

17. According to the passage, what is the main purpose of DST?

    a. To increase public safety

    b. To benefit retail businesses

    c. To make better use of daylight

    d. To promote good health

    e. To save on candles

18. Which of the following is not mentioned in the passage as a negative effect of DST?

    a. Energy conservation

    b. Complications with time keeping

    c. Complications with computer systems

    d. Increased skin cancer risk

    e. Sleep disruption

19. The article states that DST involves:

    a. Adjusting clocks forward one hour in the spring and the fall

    b. Adjusting clocks backward one hour in the spring and the fall

    c. Adjusting clocks forward in the fall and backward in the spring

    d. Adjusting clocks forward in the spring and backward in the fall

    e. None of the above

Questions 20 – 22 pertain to the following passage:

Judicial review, the power of courts to determine the legality of governmental acts, usually refers to the authority of judges to decide a law's constitutionality. Although state courts exercised judicial review prior to the ratification of the Constitution, the doctrine is most often traced to the landmark U.S. Supreme Court decision *Marbury v. Madison* (1803), which struck down an act of Congress as unconstitutional. In a now classic opinion, Chief Justice John Marshall found the power of judicial review implied in the Constitution's status as "the supreme Law of the Land" prevailing over ordinary laws.

Both federal and state courts have exercised judicial review. Federal courts review federal and state acts to ensure their conformity to the Constitution and the supremacy of federal over state law; state courts review laws to ensure their conformity to the U.S. Constitution and their own state constitutions. The power of judicial review can be exercised by any court in which a constitutional issue arises.

Judicial review gained added importance in the late nineteenth and early twentieth century's, as courts passed judgment on laws regulating corporate behavior and working conditions. In these years, the Supreme Court repeatedly struck down laws regulating wages, hours of labor, and safety standards. This is often called the *Lochner* Era, after *Lochner* v. *New York*, a 1905 decision ruling a New York maximum-hours law unconstitutional on the grounds that it violated the Fourteenth Amendment. During this period, the Supreme Court invalidated no fewer than 228 state laws.

Justice Oliver Wendell Holmes Jr., dissenting from many of these decisions, urged judges to defer to legislatures. In the later 1930's, the Supreme Court adopted the Holmes approach-partly in response to the threat of President Franklin Delano Roosevelt's "court packing" plan of 1937. Deferring to legislative judgment, the

Supreme Court thereafter upheld virtually all laws regulating business and property rights, including laws similar to those invalidated during the *Lochner* Era.

Under the chief justiceship of Earl Warren (1953-1969) and beyond, however, the Court moved toward striking down law restricting personal rights and liberties guaranteed by the Bill of Rights, particularly measures limiting freedom of expression, freedom or religion, the right of criminal defendants, equal treatment of the sexes, and the rights of minorities to equal protection of the law. In another extension of judicial review, the Court read new rights into the Constitution, notably the right of privacy (including abortion rights) and invalidated laws restricting those rights. Many other countries including Germany, Italy, France, and Japan, adopted the principle of judicial review after World War II, making constitutional law one the more important recent American exports.

20. Which of the following statements about judicial review does the passage best support?
    a. States should defer to the Federal Government when interpreting the Constitution
    b. Judicial Review was started due to the Lochner Era
    c. The Constitution overrides state law in some cases
    d. The Courts do not have the power to regulate business
    e. Judicial Review was founded by Earl Warren Chief Justice of the Supreme Court

21. From the passage, it can be inferred ordinary laws created by lawmakers must be within the framework of the Constitution. Which of the following sentences supports this claim the best?
    a. Although state courts exercised....
    b. Both federal and state courts....
    c. Judicial review gained added importance...
    d. During this period, the Supreme...
    e. Deferring to legislature judgment....

22. Which of the following words best characterizes the content of the passage?
    a. historical
    b. transcription
    c. prospective
    d. figurative
    e. demonstrative

Questions 23 – 26 pertain to the following passage:

Theodore Roosevelt first implied the term "muckrakers" to a group of journalists and writers who had exposed corruption in business and government in the early twentieth century. Roosevelt intended the term, borrowed from John Bunyan's *Pilgrim's Progress*, to be somewhat pejorative, but the muckrakers were very influential for a time and provided strong impetus to the ongoing Progressive Era reform movement.

Around 1902, a number of prominent magazines including *McClure's, Collier's, Cosmopolitan, Everybody's* and the *Arena*, began featuring crusading exposes or "muckraking" articles. Some of these pieces were later expanded into full length books. Among the best-known were Ida Tarbell's *History of the Standard Oil Company* (1902); Lincoln Steffen's *The Shame of the Cities* (1904), documenting corruption in municipal government; Samuel Hopkins Adams's *The Great American*

Fraud (1906), lambasting the patent-medicine industry; and Ray Stannard Baker's *Following the Color Line* (1908), a pioneering expose of American racism.

A few muckrakers made their case in works of fiction. Upton Sinclair's *The Jungle* (1906), a fictionalized account of the Chicago meatpacking industry, was the best known of the genre, but David Graham Phillips was perhaps the most prolific of the muckraking novelists. Among his numerous works were *Lightfingered Gentry* (1907), on the insurance industry; *Susan Lenox; Her Fall and Rise* (1908) published in 1917), on prostitution; and many others.

The muckraking spirit also influenced some of the major novelists of the time, although usually in less tractarian form. Frank *Norris's The Octopus* (1901) and *The Pit* (1903); Theodore Dreiser's *The Financier* (1912) and *The Titan* (1914); and Jack London's *Iron Heel* (1908) all address the social consequences of unregulated capitalist expansion.

After about 1912, the muckraking movement abated. The public tired of the exposes, some of which seem sensationalized and overly sordid. But muckraking already had exerted a major impact on the reform movement and would influence the policies of President Woodrow Wilson. Indeed, Ray Standard Baker became an aide to Wilson and later edited a six-volume collection of Wilson's public papers (1926-1927). Assuming many different forms, the muckraking impulse continued to influence American journalism as the twentieth century wore on.

23. Which of the following statements about Muckrakers does the passage best support?
   a. Muckrakers were viewed as criminologists during the early 1900s
   b. Muckrakers were exposing corruption during the Progressive Era
   c. Muckrakers were used by politicians during the 1900s to downplay social reforms
   d. The Muckrakers continued to have success following 1912
   e. Muckrakers had a background in detective operations and a passion for exposing the truth

24. From the passage, it can be inferred the muckrakers fueled the Progressive Era. Which of the following sentences supports this claim the best?
   a. After about 1912…
   b. A few muckrakers made…
   c. The muckraking spirit…
   d. Roosevelt intended the…
   e. Around 1902, a number…

25. Which of the following words best characterizes the content of the passage?
   a. cooperative
   b. degrading
   c. revealing
   d. conventional
   e. operational

26. Which of the following did not contribute to the rise of the mudrackers?

a. The Octopus
b. Journalists
c. The Jungle
d. The Pit
e. Pilgrim's Progress

Sentence Correction

These questions present a sentence, all or part of which is underlined. Beneath each sentence you will find five ways of phrasing the underlined part. The first of these repeats the original; the other four are different. If you think the original is best, choose the first answer; otherwise, choose one of the other answers.

These questions test correctness and effectiveness of expression. In choosing your answer, follow the requirements of standard written English; that is, pay attention to grammar, choice of words, and sentence construction. Choose the answer that produces the most effective sentence; this answer should be clear and exact, without awkwardness, ambiguity, redundancy, or grammatical error.

27. If he stops to consider the ramifications of this decision, it is probable that he will rethink his original decision a while longer.

    a. it is probable that he will rethink his original decision.
    b. he will rethink his original decision over again.
    c. he probably will rethink his original decision.
    d. he will most likely rethink his original decision for a bit.
    e. he probably will rethink his decision a while longer.

28. "When you get older," she said "you will no doubt understand what I mean."

    a. older," she said "you will no doubt
    b. older" she said "you will no doubt
    c. older," she said, "you will no doubt
    d. older," she said "you will not
    e. older", she said, "you will no doubt

29. Dr. Anderson strolled past the nurses, examining a bottle of pills.

    a. Dr. Anderson strolled past the nurses, examining a bottle of pills.
    b. Dr. Anderson strolled past the nurses examining a bottle of pills.
    c. Dr. Anderson strolled past, the nurses examining a bottle of pills.
    d. Examining a bottle of pills Dr. Anderson strolled past the nurses.
    e. Examining a bottle of pills, Dr. Anderson strolled past the nurses.

30. Karl and Henry raced to the reservoir, climbed the ladder, and then they dove into the cool water.

    a. raced to the reservoir, climbed the ladder, and then they dove into
    b. first raced to the reservoir, climbed the ladder, and then they dove into
    c. raced to the reservoir, they climbed the ladder, and then they dove into
    d. raced to the reservoir; climbed the ladder; and then they dove into
    e. raced to the reservoir, climbed the ladder, and dove into

31. Did either Tracy or Vanessa realize that her decision would be so momentous?

    a. Tracy or Vanessa realize that her decision would be
    b. Tracy or Vanessa realize that each of their decision was
    c. Tracy or Vanessa realize that her or her decision would be
    d. Tracy or Vanessa realize that their decision would be
    e. Tracy or Vanessa realize that their decision was

32. Despite their lucky escape, Jason and his brother could not hardly enjoy themselves.

    a. Jason and his brother could not hardly enjoy themselves
    b. Jason and his brother could not enjoy themselves
    c. Jason and Jason's brother could not hardly enjoy themselves
    d. Jason and his brother could not enjoy them
    e. Jason and his brother could hardly enjoy them

33. Stew recipes call for rosemary, parsley, thyme, and these sort of herbs.

    a. for rosemary, parsley, thyme, and these sort of herbs.
    b. for: rosemary; parsley; thyme; and these sort of herbs.
    c. for rosemary, parsley, thyme, and these sorts of herbs.
    d. for rosemary, parsley, thyme, and this sorts of herbs.
    e. for rosemary, parsley, thyme, and these sorts of herb.

34. Mr. King, an individual of considerable influence, created a personal fortune and gave back to the community.

    a. an individual of considerable influence, created a personal fortune and gave back
    b. an individual of considerable influence, he created a personal fortune and gave back
    c. an individual of considerable influence created a personal fortune and gave back
    d. an individual of considerable influence, created a personal fortune and gave it back
    e. an individual of considerable influence, created a personal fortune and then he gave it back

35. She is the person whose opinion matters the most.

    a. She is the person whose opinion matters the most.
    b. She is the person to whom opinion matters the most.
    c. She is the person who matters the most, in my opinion.
    d. She is the person for whom opinion matters the most.
    e. She is the person which has her opinion matter the most.

36. When are the Federal government, the State and the city going to realize <u>that they cannot raise its rates and taxes</u> year after year?

    a. that they cannot raise its rates and taxes
    b. that they cannot raise it's rates and taxes
    c. that they can not raise its rates and taxes
    d. that rates and taxes can not be raised by them
    e. that they cannot raise their rates and taxes

37. Since she moved into her own place, Janet <u>has been doing</u> her own cooking.

    a. has been doing
    b. does
    c. did
    d. is doing
    e. will do

38. To help install the software, instructions provided by the manufacturer.

    a. instruction provided by the manufacturer.
    b. instruction manuals provided by the manufacturer.
    c. manufacturer-provided instructions.
    d. instructions were provided by the manufacturer.
    e. instructions was provided by the manufacturer.

39. A daily routine of physical exercise is not only good for one's health, <u>and also improves one's mental outlook.</u>

    a. and also improves one's mental outlook.
    b. but also improves one's mental outlook.
    c. as it also improves one's mental outlook.
    d. and improves one's mental outlook, too.
    e. and would foster an improved mental outlook, as well.

40. King Lear is one of Shakespeare's greatest plays it explores the nature of human suffering and kinship.

    a. plays it explores the nature of human suffering and kinship.
    b. plays as it explores the nature of human suffering and kinship.
    c. plays who explores the nature of human suffering and kinship.
    d. plays; it explores the nature of human suffering and kinship.
    e. plays when it explores the nature of human suffering and kinship.

41. Given the price of going to a movie, <u>a ticket usually costs</u> around $10, more and more people are renting films to watch at home.

    a. a ticket usually costs
    b. which is usually
    c. which usually costs
    d. which can be usually
    e. a ticket costs

42. Composers of modern popular music can feature syncopated rhythms, multiple-part harmonies, <u>and used electronic instrument orchestration.</u>

    a. and used electronic instrument orchestration.
    b. and they use electronic instrument orchestration.
    c. and orchestration using electronic instruments.
    d. as well as using electronic instrument orchestration.
    e. with electronic instrument orchestration.

43. As the price of gasoline increased during the past ten years, American car manufacturers should have realized that a drop in the demand for gas-guzzling vehicles <u>was likely and would probably happen.</u>

    a. was likely and would probably happen.
    b. was likely and would probably happen in the future.
    c. would be likely and would probably happen soon.
    d. was a likely thing.
    e. was likely.

44. As more and more of the younger generation moves to Tokyo to find work, <u>the remaining population of Japan's rural towns gets older and older.</u>

    a. the remaining population of Japan's rural towns gets older and older.
    b. the average population of Japan's rural towns gets older and older.
    c. the population of Japan's rural towns continues to get older.
    d. the population remaining in Japan's rural towns gets older and older.
    e. the remaining population of Japan's rural towns gets older.

45. When the team got off the plane, they were met by a throng of adoring fans.

    a. they were met by a throng of adoring fans.
    b. they were met by many adoring fans,
    c. it was met by a throng of adoring fans.
    d. they encountered a throng of adoring fans.
    e. it meets a throng of adoring fans.

46. One of Shakespeare's favorite forms was the sonnet, <u>it is a fourteen line poem</u> written in iambic pentameter.

    a. it is a fourteen line poem
    b. a fourteen-line poem
    c. it is a fourteen-line poem
    d. these were fourteen-line poems
    e. it was a fourteen line poem

47. Home music production equipment has become so <u>sophisticated, and</u> amateur musicians can produce recordings that are competitive with the output of professional studios.

    a. sophisticated, and
    b. sophisticated, also
    c. sophisticated that
    d. sophisticated consequently
    e. sophisticated wherefore

48. Since people who drive while intoxicated are responsible for many injuries and deaths, <u>severely punished</u> is what they deserve.

    a. severely punished
    b. severe punishment
    c. severely punishment
    d. severeness of punishment
    e. severity in punishment

49. Tobacco use is still very high in China, where public health officials are urging the public to stop <u>smoking which has been linked to lung cancer</u>.

    a. smoking which has been linked to lung cancer.
    b. smoking because it has been linked to lung cancer.
    c. smoking on account of its being linked to lung cancer.
    d. smoking, which has been linked to lung cancer.
    e. smoking when it has been linked to lung cancer.

50. Even professional chefs disagree <u>about what is the best way to</u> cook a steak.

    a. about what is the best way to
    b. about, what is the best way to
    c. about how to
    d. about what the best way is to
    e. about the best way to

51. Across the country there are hundreds of thousands, if not millions, <u>of potentially affected families</u> by the distress of this industry.

    a. of potentially affected families
    b. of potential families affected
    c. of families potentially affected
    d. of families affected potentially
    e. of affected families

52. A ski holiday can be ruined either because of warm weather, <u>but also because</u> someone is injured in a fall.

    a. but also because
    b. but also owing to
    c. or the cause is
    d. or because of
    e. but possible because

53. Drug therapies are replacing a lot of <u>medicines as we used to know it.</u>

    a. medicines as we used to know it.
    b. medicine as we used to know it.
    c. medicines as we used to know.
    d. therapies as we used to know it.
    e. other therapies as we used to know it.

54. If you teach a child to read, <u>he or her will</u> be able to pass a literacy test.

    a. he or her will
    b. they will
    c. it will
    d. he will
    e. he or she will

Critical Reasoning

55. The latest movie by a certain director gets bad reviews before it opens in theatres. Consequently, very few people go to the movie and the director is given much less money to make his next movie, which is also unsuccessful. *What can be inferred from this scenario?*

    a. This director makes terrible movies
    b. The general public does not pay attention to movie reviews
    c. The movie reviewers were right about the first movie
    d. Movie reviewers exert influence on the movie quality
    e. The director will not make another movie

56. The most important determinant of success in life is education. Even children from broken or dysfunctional homes tend to establish themselves as solid citizens so long as they obtain a high school education. On the other hand, children who fail to earn a high school diploma are much less likely to avoid prison, welfare, or divorce. *Which of the following statements most effectively strengthens the above argument?*

    a. A recent study demonstrated a link between education and lifetime earnings
    b. Most federal prisoners receive a high school diploma while incarcerated
    c. Research indicates that college graduates from abusive homes are more likely to be arrested
    d. Individuals with heart problems are more likely to have postgraduate education
    e. Children from functional homes are more likely to attend preschool

57.   (1) All *A* are *B*.
        (2) Some *B* are *C*.

Which of the following is true?

    a. All A are *C*
    b. No *A* are *C*
    c. Some *A* are *C*
    d. No *C* are *A*
    e. None of the above

58. Shakespeare is the greatest writer of all time. This is because he wrote the greatest plays, and the greatest writer is the one who composes the greatest works. *Which of the following statements most effectively challenges the reasoning above?*

    a. This argument disproves its own premise
    b. This argument uses ambiguous language
    c. This argument assumes what it claims to prove
    d. This argument introduces irrelevant evidence
    e. This argument fails to make a clear claim

59. In the 2000 local election, only 28% of individuals between the ages of 18 and 25 voted. In the 2004 local election, however, candidates made more of an effort to appeal to these younger voters, so turnout was slightly higher at 39%. *Which of the following pieces of information weakens the above argument?*

    a. The candidates for city council were ages 55, 72, and 64
    b. The turnout among voters between the ages of 35 and 44 was 42% in 2004
    c. Turnout among African-Americans between 18 and 25 decreased from 2000 to 2004
    d. The polls stayed open later on Election Day in 2000
    e. In 2004, a referendum on lowering the legal age for purchasing alcohol to 18 was on the ballot

60. Members of Congress should not be paid. After all, members of the school board receive no payment, and are therefore not beholden to any particular group. *Which of the following facts most significantly weakens the above argument?*

    a. Members of Congress can also serve on the school board
    b. Being in Congress is a full-time job, while school board members have time to pursue other occupations
    c. Congress only is in session during part of the year
    d. Members of Congress typically have been successful in their prior professional lives
    e. Members of Congress are not allowed to show favoritism to any particular group

61. All German cars are safe. Dale drives a German car, so his car is safe. Which of the following arguments contains logic that closely resembles that of the preceding argument?

a. The newest cars often get better gas mileage. Helen has a new car, which must get better gas mileage

b. A few of the candidates for governor are women. Dr. Lopez is a woman

c. No brands of natural peanut butter contain preservatives. The peanut butter in Dave's cabinet contains preservatives

d. Every shark has a tailfin. The hammerhead is a kind of shark and therefore has a tailfin

e. Some days of the week are Saturdays and Sundays. Today is neither Saturday nor Sunday

62. The Tigers football team usually loses when they score fewer than 30 points. In their game against the Wildcats, they scored 24 points.

Which of the following statements would logically complete the argument with the above premises?

a. The Tigers lost to the Wildcats.

b. The Wildcats are the best football team in the league.

c. The Wildcats probably lost to the Tigers.

d. The Tigers are not a very good football team.

e. The Tigers probably lost to the Wildcats.

63. Dr. Jacobson stood up at the recent town hall meeting and declared that building a new shopping center at the corner of George and Vidalia Streets would be a bad move. He cited transportation department statistics indicating that the intersection would become overloaded with traffic, and would be very dangerous for motorists and pedestrians alike. The mayor dismissed Dr. Jacobson's opinion, on the grounds that the proposed shopping center is within a block of Dr. Jacobson's practice. *Why is the mayor's argument weak?*

a. He does not challenge Dr. Jacobson's argument, but merely challenges him personally

b. He does not acknowledge the location of his own office

c. He fails to recognize that Dr. Jacobson would probably welcome a new shopping center near his practice

d. He does not support his view with statistics from the transportation department

e. He doesn't realize that Dr. Jacobson is about to retire

64. Islam spread to Europe during the medieval period, bringing scientific and technological insights. The Muslim emphasis on knowledge and learning can be traced to an emphasis on both in the Qur'an [Koran], the holy book of Islam. Because of this emphasis, scholars preserved some of the Greek and Roman texts that were lost to the rest of Europe. The writings of Aristotle, among others, were saved by Muslim translators. Islam scholars modified a Hindu number system. Their modification became the more commonly used Arabic system, which replaced Roman numerals. They also developed algebra. Muslim contributions also include inventing the astrolabe, a device for telling time that also helped sailors to navigate. In medicine, Muslim doctors cleaned wounds with antiseptics. They closed the wounds with gut and silk sutures. They also used sedatives. *Based on the information above, which of the following conclusions is likely true?*

a. People of Muslim faith were braver than others when facing surgery

b. Fewer Muslim patients died of wound infections than did their European counterparts

c. The silk market expanded because of the Muslim use of silk sutures

d. Math classes would be easier without Muslim influence

e. No one would read Aristotle today had the Muslims not saved the translations

65. Mother Jones, who was a labor activist, wrote the following about children working in cotton mills in Alabama: "Little girls and boys, barefooted, walked up and down between the endless rows of spindles, reaching thin little hands into the machinery to repair snapped threads. They crawled under machinery to oil it. They replaced spindles all day long; all night through…six-year-olds with faces of sixty did an eight-hour shift for ten cents a day; the machines, built in the North, were built low for the hands of little children." *Which of the following do you predict occurred after this was published?*

    a. More children signed up to work in the factories
    b. Cotton factories in the South closed
    c. Laws were passed to prevent child labor
    d. The pay scale for these children was increased
    e. Night shift work ended

66. In 1781, a county court in Massachusetts heard the case Brom & Bett v. Ashley. What was unusual about the case was that the plaintiffs were both enslaved by John Ashley's family. They had walked out and appealed to a lawyer for help after Mrs. Ashley tried to hit Mum Bett's sister. Mum Bett, whose real name was Elizabeth Freeman, claimed that if all people were free and equal, as she had heard while serving at the Ashley table, slaves too were equal. The court agreed, basing their decision on the Massachusetts constitution of the previous year. The decision, affirmed in subsequent cases, led to the abolishing of slavery in that state. *Which of the following statements is most accurate?*

    a. Mrs. Ashley was probably just having a bad day when she tried to strike another person
    b. Elizabeth Freeman's actions helped to gain women the right to vote
    c. White people in Southern states applauded the court's decision
    d. The ideals of the American Revolution reached farther than the founders may have intended
    e. All slaveholders in Massachusetts rushed to free their servants

67. When the euro was introduced in January 2002, a single euro was valued at 88 cents in United States currency. In the summer of 2008, at one point it required $1.60 U.S. to buy 1 euro. In late October 2008, the euro fell to its lowest level against the dollar in two years. *Which of the following statements represents an accurate conclusion?*

    a. The world in 2008 was headed for another Great Depression
    b. The dollar regained strength after significant devaluing against the euro
    c. The euro remains the world's strongest currency
    d. Investors need to keep buying stocks
    e. Globalization is a very bad idea

68. Radio listener: Van Morrison and Nick Lowe started their music careers only a few years apart, but while both men have released numerous albums, their levels of fame and renown are wildly different. Morrison has had a long career in the popular eye, and has made many millions of dollars, as well as having had critical acclaim. Lowe has also made money, but substantially less than Morrison. Lowe is a respected songwriter, but hasn't had more than a couple of popular hits. Because of their differing levels of fame, Morrison is clearly the better musician. *This argument assumes which of the following?*

    a. There are only two relevant performers that can be compared
    b. Popular music covers country and classical arrangements
    c. Readers are familiar with a wide range of popular performers
    d. Quality of musicianship and popular appeal are directly related
    e. That a professional musical education is not relevant to future success

69. No one in the trauma unit that Dr. James belongs to can work more than one shift in the emergency room per any given work week. For the next week, all the shifts available to work are non-emergency room shifts. Thus, it is untrue that Dr. James can work any emergency room shift in the next week. *Which one of the following conditions, if true, most directly weakens the argument concerning Dr. James working in the emergency room?*

    a. The shifts are scheduled and set only a few days in advance
    b. The shifts still available were overtime shifts, and have no relation to regularly scheduled shifts
    c. Dr. James has privileges at a different nearby hospital
    d. The trauma unit is affiliated with a mobile medical clinic
    e. The scheduled shifts are randomly assigned

70. Infidelity can have a number of psychological effects on the partner committing the infidelity. Aside from the various factors that led to the act, one of the more common side effects has to do with the perception of trust. Often, the effort of keeping an illicit relationship from the other partner is extremely stressful, with the straying party having to resort to more and more elaborate tactics to keep the infidelity secret. As the pressure mounts, and the unfaithful party reflects on their own behavior, the cheating party will often reinterpret the other partner's behavior through the prism of the cheater's own duplicity, leading to _____. *Which of the following phrases most logically completes the argument?*

    a. increasing distrust and, ironically, suspicion that the other party is cheating
    b. a desire to lay down strict rules regarding communication
    c. isolating the other party through silence and rejection of affection
    d. erratic behavior and occasional fits of excessive attention or affection
    e. a desire to let go of strict rules regarding communication

71. The ability of an organism to adapt to environmental change is strictly controlled by how well it fits into the environment prior to the change, which is directly related to time spent in that ecology. If an environment is stable over long periods of time, as was seen during the lengthy period between the Triassic and Cretaceous eras, the lifeforms that appear and flourish in that environment are so specialized to the climate and ecological system that any sudden change, even if relatively insignificant, can result in species extinction. The rise of mammals after the Cretaceous-Tertiary extinction event and the subsequent fall of dinosaurs is simply the best-known example. *What assumption is made in the argument as stated that, if incorrect, could weaken the argument's logic?*

    a. The extinction event was a geological phenomenon
    b. Mammals developed some time after dinosaurs appeared
    c. The earth's climate stabilized into a subtropical system
    d. Dinosaurs first appeared in the pre-Triassic era
    e. The earth's climate stabilized into a polar system

72. An engineering manager reports that the latest revision of the company's product, a rotational ring used as part of the spindle assembly for high-revolution hard drives, is ready for production, barely within the stated deadline for ramping up production. Test results show that the ring performs above the 99% operational function standard within the narrow range of temperature and revolution laid out in the official product specifications. However, further analysis shows the failure rate rose dramatically when tested outside that well-defined range in temperatures and revolution rates that are common for those devices, falling to a 92% operational function standard. The manager states that because the product functions within stated tolerances inside the specified ranges, the product is ready to manufacture, and that modifications can wait for future revisions. *The reasoning in the manager's argument is flawed because the argument:*

    a. Bases a liability analysis on time factors only
    b. Follows a narrowly defined interpretation of the warranty
    c. Assumes that this rotational ring will be approved for a patent
    d. Is predicated on a timeframe that may not occur
    e. Assumes customers will primarily use the product in optimal conditions

73. In virtually all species of cockroach, the nervous and respiratory systems are heavily decentralized. Laboratory experiments have repeatedly demonstrated that cockroaches can be decapitated completely, yet continue to survive for up to several weeks before dying of lack of food or water. This demonstrates the relative superiority of cockroaches over virtually all other insect species, since hardly any other species has demonstrated such ability to survive after being introduced to extreme damage or environmental conditions. *Which of the following statements, if true, most seriously weakens the cockroach argument?*

    a. Cockroaches are found in the widest environmental ranges of any insect species
    b. The estimated cockroach population has increased dramatically since modern cities appeared
    c. More bird species prey on cockroaches than any other insect species
    d. The lethal dose for common household chemicals is far lower for cockroaches than most other insect species
    e. The estimated cockroach population has increased slightly since modern cities appeared

74. A poll of employees at Widgets, Inc. concluded that employee satisfaction levels were among the five highest-ranked companies in the United States. Poll data was gathered by representatives from human resources quizzing employees in private meetings about their satisfaction levels with their jobs, and the company as a whole, and then computing the results based on a predetermined index. A recruiter with a national staffing firm has argued with the results, claiming that the percentages listed do not match with surveys of former and present employees placed with the company. *The recruiter can most properly criticize the reasoning by which the poll reached its result on what basis?*

    a. The index used to measure satisfaction was not compiled to the same objectives and specifications as other companies
    b. The poll was not conducted by an objective party, and may have skewed the results
    c. Former employees were not included in the polling sample
    d. Polling was not conducted electronically, making tampering more likely
    e. Employees were not guaranteed anonymity with their answers

75. Teenage couch potato: My folks are always telling me to sit back from the TV set; they say my eyes will go bad if I sit too close to the screen. Our TV is a an older set with one of those tubes, and I read that the refresh rate on older TVs is the part that eyes have trouble focusing on, which is why computer screens on TV are always so hard to see. Flat-panel plasma TVs don't have that problem, since they have much higher resolution and refresh much faster, so instead of always sitting back so far, buying a flat-panel plasma TV will take care of any focus issues my eyes might have. *Which of the following best states the flaw in this argument's reasoning?*

    a. Refresh rates do not have an effect on the ability to read an image
    b. Simply moving back from the TV is a simpler and less expensive solution
    c. Flat-panel plasma TVs have a similar effect on the eyes, despite their higher performance standards
    d. The teenager does not have any vision issues
    e. The damage to the teenager's eyes after being close to the old TV may be negligible

76. All college students who play video games develop increased hand-eye coordination. All college students who major in the biological sciences make excellent doctors and surgeons. Everyone in Riley's study group, including Riley, is majoring in the biological sciences, and all of them except Riley play video games. Therefore, everyone in Riley's study group will make excellent surgeons. *What assumption is made in the above argument that is not explicitly supported in the argument's text?*

    a. Riley and her study group peers intend to be surgeons
    b. Riley and her study group peers started as biological science majors
    c. Riley and her study group peers are college students
    d. Riley and her study group peers are good at video games
    e. The use of video games translates to an improvement in study habits

77. Librarian: Every year, there are a handful of challenges from parents angry that Harper Lee's *To Kill A Mockingbird* is available for children to check out. For the last several years, the challenges have always been over the racially charged material and the "liberal" nature of Atticus Finch; although the library board has consistently ruled in favor of the book, the challenges keep coming every year. However, the movie version, which is also available for children to check out, has never been challenged once, despite the fidelity of the adaptation to the novel. *The reasoning in the librarian's argument is flawed because:*

    a. It assumes that parents are aware that the movie is also available for children to check out
    b. It fails to note whether other novels with similar thematic elements are also being challenged.
    c. It ignores the possibility that challenges are being issued for non-textual issues
    d. It assumes that the text and movie versions are being checked out at similar rates
    e. It fails to note whether teachers support the idea of the film being faithful to the book

78. The latest report from The Tabletop Stock Report indicates that Widgets, Inc. remains a sound long-term investment and is a good buy for casual investors, despite some mixed profit reports. However, the publisher of The Tabletop Stock Report is a minority owner of a small investment firm, which owns several hundred thousand shares of Widgets, Inc. Thus, since there is clearly reason to doubt the conclusions drawn, Widgets, Inc. is obviously a poor candidate for investment. *The reasoning in this argument is most vulnerable to criticism on what grounds?*

    a. The argument does not consider the previous advice from the Stock Report on Widgets, Inc.
    b. The argument draws a conclusion based solely on a statistically insignificant sample of the Tabletop Stock Report's articles
    c. The argument fails to take into account the possibility that the publisher may have just as much financial motivation to create negative publicity for Widgets
    d. The argument fails to provide evidence that Widgets, Inc. stock is not a good buy
    e. The argument equates an apparent bias as evidence that the Tabletop Stock Report's claims are false

79. All teenagers who play Dungeons and Dragons are excellent students. All teenagers who play World of Warcraft are indifferent students. Everyone in Mark's circle of teenage friends play both Dungeons and Dragons and World of Warcraft. Therefore, all of Mark's friends are students with performance scores in the mid-range. *Which of the following arguments most exemplifies the flawed reasoning used in the argument above?*

    a. All Grand Theft Auto players who practice rigorously score well in the game. But some players who do not practice rigorously also do well in the game. Jim practices moderately; therefore, Jim's scores are in the mid-range
    b. Every programmer knows Java. Every system analyst learns Visio. Susanne started working at Widgets as a programmer, and then was promoted to systems analyst. Therefore, Susanne knows Java and Visio
    c. All green Amazonian banana spiders are poisonous to humans. All blue Amazonian tree spiders are non-poisonous to humans. A new species of Amazonian spider was discovered that is a hybrid of the green Amazonian banana spider and the blue Amazonian tree spider. Thus, the new species is moderately poisonous to humans
    d. Every worker at Widgets lives in Pennsylvania. Every worker at Doodads lives in New Jersey. Alex has relatives that work at Widgets and relatives that work at Doodads. Thus, Alex has relatives in Pennsylvania and New Jersey
    e. All students who read several comic books are great artists. Some adults who do not read several comic books are great artists. Blake reads a few comic books; therefore, Blake is an average artist.

80. When a relationship ends, it is often emotionally similar to losing a loved one. The abrupt end of a relationship can create strong sensations of loss and depression among partners who were not aware of the impending end. Just as people who have lost someone to death may go through the common five-stage process of grieving, people whose relationship has abruptly ended may _____. *Which of the following phrases most logically completes the argument?*

    a. experience a fear of their own suitability as a romantic partner
    b. go through a grieving period for their relationship
    c. focus on the positive aspects of the past relationship
    d. withdraw from romantic pursuits completely
    e. realize their need to focus on friendships over romantic relationships

Answer Key and Explanations

Reading Comprehension

1. B: The author asserts both that earning money is increasingly easy and that managing money is difficult.

2. D: The author seems to believe that there are plenty of lucrative jobs for everyone.

3. E: The author insists that many people who have no trouble earning money waste it through lavish spending.

4. D: This information is all given in the second paragraph.

5. C: In the fourth paragraph, the author states that the transient nature of relationships based solely on shared interests is keeping us "socially busy without building the lasting relationships and communities that we want."

6. E: The author lists urban sprawl, long work hours, and devotion to television and the internet as causes of problems for American communities.

7. B: This is the only one of the answer choices that is not listed in the fourth paragraph as suggestions put forth by the Harvard University study.

8. D: The first paragraph gives the information to correctly answer this question

9. B: This passage in arranged by problem and solution. The author states a problem that the cotton farmers were having: "Eventually, cotton will no longer grow on this land." The author then presents a solution: "Carver told farmers to rotate their crops: plant cotton one year, then the next year plant peanuts and other soil-restoring plants, like peas and sweet potatoes. It worked! The peanut plants grew and produced lots of peanuts."

10. E: The second paragraph discusses the problem the cotton farmers were facing. The cotton crops had depleted the nutrients from the soil.

11. C: Answer choice (C) best summarizes what this passage is mainly about. Choices (A), (B), and (C) are not even discussed in this passage. Paragraph 5 does discuss choice (E), but it is not the main focus of the passage.

12. D: The only true statement about Ellis Island is statement III: The island was expanded using dirt excavated from the construction of the New York City subway system. Statement I is false. According to Paragraph 1, Ellis Island is "within the shadow" of the Statue of Liberty. This means that it is close to the Statue of Liberty, but does not house the Statue of Liberty. Statement II is also false. Paragraph 2 states that the local Indian tribes had called it "Kioshk" or Gull Island, not Oyster Island.

13. C: The author's style is giving facts and details, much like the style used in a history textbook. An immigrant's diary would be written in first-person and most likely give thoughts and feelings about the experience at Ellis Island. A business letter would have a date, salutation, and closing. A persuasive essay would use persuasive techniques to persuade the reader to adopt a particular argument or position, and a short story would be written to entertain, not inform.

14. A: The second sentence of the first paragraph states that peanut allergy is the most common cause of food-related death.

15. C: The passage implies that it is not always easy to know which foods have traces of peanuts in them and that it's important to make sure you know what you're eating. This is hard or impossible if you share someone else's food.

16. E: Paragraph two gives examples of symptoms of peanut allergies and, more specifically, examples of symptoms of anaphylaxis. A running or stuffy nose is given as a symptom of the former, but not of the latter.

17. C: The first paragraph states that the main purpose of DST it to make better use of daylight.

18. A: Energy conservation is discussed as a possible benefit of DST, not a negative effect of it.

19. D: The first paragraph states that DST involves setting clocks forward one hour in the spring and one hour backward in the fall.

20. C: This is discussed in second paragraph. None of the other statements are supported by the passage.

21. A: This sentence discusses an instance where a federal law was struck down because it was deemed to be unconstitutional.

22. A: The passage would be best described as historical. It gives an account of the history of judicial review in America.

23. B: The first paragraph talks about the muckrakers operating during the Progressive Era, and the rest of the passage discusses the specific corruption and societal ills that they brought to light.

24. D: This sentence states that the muckrakers "provided strong impetus to the ongoing Progressive Era reform movement."

25. C: The passage would be best characterized by the word "revealing." The theme of the muckrakers was to reveal things to the public that were previously kept hidden behind closed doors.

26. E: Pilgrim's Progress was the book from which the term "muckraker" was taken, but the book itself did not contribute to the success of the muckrakers.

Sentence Correction

27. C: The original sentence is redundant and wordy.

28. C: The syntax of the original sentence is fine, but a comma after *said* but before the open-quotation mark is required.

29. E: In the original sentence, the modifier is placed too far away from the word it modifies.

30. E: The verb structure should be consistent in a sentence with parallel structures.

31. A: The singular pronoun *her* is appropriate since the antecedents are joined by *or*. Also, the subjunctive verb form is required to indicate something indefinite.

32. B: The combination of *hardly* and *not* constitutes a double negative.

33. C: The plural demonstrative adjective *these* should be used with the plural noun *sorts*.

34. A: This sentence contains a number of parallel structures that must be treated consistently.

35. A: In this sentence, *whose* is the appropriate possessive pronoun to modify *opinion*.

36. E: The subject of the sentence comprises three items (the federal government, the state and the city) and is therefore plural. The sentence discusses raising the rates and taxes of all three.

37. A: The past progressive form indicates that Janet began doing something in the past, and continues to do so today.

38. D: The original lacks a verb, as do choices B and C. Choice E mismatches a plural subject and singular verb.

39. B: The expression "not only...but also" is used to compare two conditions that are mutually reinforcing.

40. D: The original is a run-on sentence. Choice D correctly separates two related independent clauses with a semi-colon. Choices B and E change the meaning, and choice C incorrectly uses the pronoun "who" for the inanimate "play."

41. B: The pronoun "which" refers to the price. The original and choice E are run-on sentences. In choice C, "cost" is redundant with "price," and choice D is awkwardly phrased.

42. C: This answer establishes a list separated by series commas. The original changes the verb tense in mid-sentence, choices B and D are awkwardly phrased, and choice E changes the meaning slightly and is not appropriate following a comma.

43. E: The original is redundant, since "likely" and "would probably happen" mean the same thing. The same holds for choices B and C. Choice D is awkward and less succinct than the preferred choice E.

44. B: This answer specifies that it is the average population age that is increasing. All of the other choices simply indicate that the people in these towns are getting older, not that the average age is changing.

45. C: The pronoun "it" matches the word "team" for which it stands, and which is singular, not plural.

46. B: This answer simply defines the word "sonnet" in a dependent clause.

47. C: The dependent clause shows a consequence of the condition described in the first clause, and is not separated by a comma when introduced by a correlative conjunction ("so...that").

48. B: The noun "punishment" is modified by the adjective "severe."

49. D: The absence of the comma in the original version suggests that only some smoking has been linked to lung cancer, and that it is only that smoking which nutritionists are urging the public to stop. The comma makes it clear that all smoking is linked to cancer. Choice E is similar to the original. Choice B requires a comma to separate the independent clause. Choice C is awkwardly phrased.

50. E: This answer is far more succinct than choice D. The original version is slang usage. Choice C does not explicitly state that the disagreement is about the best practice.

51. C: This answer links the verb "affected" to the cause of the effect, i.e., the distress of the industry, for maximum clarity.

52. D: This answer makes use of the correlative conjunction "either...or" to link two equivalent portions of a sentence. Note that "either...also", "either...owing to", and "either...but" do not make sense.

53. B: The pronoun "it" used at the end of the sentence must refer to a singular noun. The word "medicine" in Choice B refers to the practice of medicine, and is singular. Note that there are many other ways to fix this sentence by replacing "it" with "them", for example, but they are not offered as choices.

54. E: Note that "he" and "she" are both subjects of the verb "to be able", and so must be in the subjective case. The objective "her" is suited to be the object of a verb.

Critical Reasoning

55. D: The negative reviews led to the poor quality of the second movie.

56. A: This evidence would support the assertions of the given argument.

57. E: There is no way of determining whether any, some, or none of A are C.

58. C: This is an example of circular reasoning, in which the proof depends on assumptions which themselves have not been proven.

59. E: It seems likely that this referendum could influence many young people to vote.

60. B: Drawing an analogy between being a member of Congress and serving on the school board is highly dubious.

61. D: The logic of this argument can be expressed as follows: All A are B. C is A, therefore C is B.

62. E: There is no way to be certain that the Tigers lost, though it seems likely.

63. A: The mayor is essentially using an *ad hominem* argument, in which the character of the opponent rather than the merits of his reasoning is attacked.

64. B: By using antiseptics, Muslim doctors prevented the infection that often led to loss of limbs or life among Europeans. Antiseptics kept infections down. The other responses are opinion or not supported by the paragraph. We have no way of comparing the bravery of Muslim people with those of other faiths when facing surgery, so number 1 can be eliminated. Likewise, number 3 is incorrect; there would not be sufficient rise in silk use for sutures to account for an expanded silk market. Number 4 is an opinion, not a fact. It is not clear that the Muslims were the only people to have translations of the works of Aristotle, nor does the passage suggest such.

65. C: Mother Jones was agitating for laws protecting child workers, and legislators finally responded to her appeal and that of others. None of the other statements would logically follow. The words would not have been an inducement to children to work in factories, so response 1 is incorrect. Answer 2 is also not right; the South continued to be a major textile region. Increasing

pay for child labor was not the solution to the problem; thus the fourth response is incorrect. The final answer is also not true; running mills at night when it was cooler was profitable.

66. D: Many of the founders were also slaveholders, even though they believed the practice was wrong. Response 1 is an assumption that cannot be supported. The second answer is false; Freeman's actions had no effect on women's suffrage though it did have an impact on slavery. White Southerners, the majority of whom were sympathetic to slavery, were unlikely to applaud the decision of the court; the third answer is incorrect. Response 5 suggests a broader response to the ruling than actually can be determined from the passage.

67. B: Although the nation faced recession, the U.S. dollar made a comeback in world currency during the fall of 2008. Response 1 cannot be concluded from the information given, which focuses solely on the dollar and euro rather than on the entire world. Response 3 is incorrect as well; the euro fell in 2008 against the dollar. The wisdom of buying stocks cannot be concluded from the information given; therefore, option 4 is not viable. The final option is a statement of opinion having nothing to do with the strength or weakness of the dollar.

68. D: The assumptions of the argument are implicit in the statements used, so those statements must be examined in order to extract its assumptions. Although there are only two performers cited, the comparison being made is explicitly made only between the two listed; since there is no basis to assume the argument was constructed to apply to any other performers, Statement A can be rejected. There is no discussion of musical types in the argument, so no assumptions can be made about what genres are considered popular, which disqualifies Statement B. As the argument is constructed, it applies only to the two cited directly in the statements, and requires no prior knowledge of music or these musicians; thus, Statement C is irrelevant. Again, you do not have to be familiar with the background of these musicians, and the argument does not focus or raise their education as a point to the argument. So, Statement E is irrelevant as well. Only Statement D, which is indirectly stated in the conclusion and implied throughout, is relevant here; thus, D is correct.

69. B: In order for the argument to be weakened or refuted, there must be a condition or qualification that contradicts the conclusion without altering the statements given. With this in mind, Statement A and E are irrelevant, because the scheduling of the shifts does not affect who is assigned to which ones or the rules governing them. Since one specific emergency room is being discussed in the argument, the shifts Dr. James could work at a different emergency room have no bearing on the shifts being discussed, so Statement C is invalid. For identical reasons, Statement D is also invalid, as the mobile clinic is outside the scope of the argument. Only Statement B, which opens the possibility that the shifts discussed are separate from regularly scheduled shifts and thus Dr. James could already be scheduled for an emergency room shift, addresses the question, making B correct.

70. A: Since the argument is based on the perception of trust within a relationship, the completing phrase should reference the linchpin of the argument directly. Although issues of communication are implied to be a factor, there is no direct citing of this, nor is there any inferred reference, so Statement B and E are not suitable here. Both Statements C and D do not address the issue of trust perception, only potential side effects of this, which fails to logically complete the argument or support the main assertion; thus, both statements can be rejected. Only Statement A refers back to the central pillar of the argument and follows logically with the conclusion's first half; thus, A is the correct answer.

71. B: Since the thesis of the argument is that a direct relationship can be drawn between adaptability and time spent in an ecosystem, any assumption that would address time and/or

adaptability could greatly affect the argument if wrong. Statement A can be discarded immediately, because it addresses the possible cause of the extinction event; all that matters here is that there was an extinction event, not its cause. Similarly, Statement C and E can be rejected, as they only concern climate, not adaptability or time. While a weak connection is made with the idea of time in Statement D, it is irrelevant because the extinction event, not time itself, was the agent of change; thus, Statement D can be rejected. Only Statement B addresses the unspoken assumption that mammals came along later and thus were less finely tuned to the environment, making them more adaptable; thus, B is correct.

72. E: Although there are several real-world factors that must be considered in a business environment, the manager's argument is based on a small subset of these factors, which must be considered in the context of the larger issues. Statement A, while initially weakly implied, is invalid because the manager has not explicitly weighed liability factors, choosing to focus solely on deadline issues. Since warranty issues are generated by customer usage, and the product has not been manufactured yet, Statement B is invalid. There seems to be no issue with the manager applying or receiving a patent for the ring as that concern is not addressed in the argument and is not relevant to the customer's use of the product. So, Statement C is not correct. Time is the primary issue to the manager, which creates a connection to Statement D, but since the manager is deciding based on a defined deadline, the inference is too weak to use in this context. Only Statement E, which presupposes a practical limitation in product usage that the original conditions contradict, adequately answers the question, making E correct.

73. D: Since the point of the cockroach argument is to demonstrate their superiority through hardiness, the statement that best weakens that argument would downplay or disprove that quality. Statement A, since it argues for the adaptability of cockroaches, would support the cockroach argument, so it is invalid in this context. Similarly, Statement B and E would imply biological success, which supports the original argument. As a result, Statement B and E are also invalid in this context. Statement C is invalid because it refers to the larger role of cockroaches in the ecosystem, specifically the predator/prey relationship, and has no bearing on the relationship to other insects and the relative hardiness therein. Only Statement D, which would indicate a greater weakness in human habitation than other insect species, would contradict the cockroach argument's main conclusion if true, making D correct.

74. B: Since an analysis of the poll's veracity can only be based on the information given, any issues must be identifiable from that information. Since it is only known that a predetermined index was used, and not what that index measured or how, there is no way to properly analyze that index's utility in this context, so Statement A is invalid here. The company poll was intended to measure employee satisfaction, so former employees would not be a valid sample population in any case, making Statement C also inapplicable. Finally, there is no mention of how the poll answers were recorded, so any speculation on that aspect is irrelevant to the argument, thereby eliminating Statement D. While the employees were quizzed by human resources, we do not know if they were guaranteed anonymity with their responses. So, Statement E is not the best answer choice. Only Statement B, which rightfully questions the objectivity of a company-administered poll, is relevant grounds for criticism, making B correct.

75. B: Statement A can be discarded out of hand, since the rate of refresh has a definite and noticeable effect on how an image is perceived (as cited in the argument); thus, A is patently false and is irrelevant to the argument. Statement C can also be rejected for similar reasons; due to differing mechanisms and higher technology, the capabilities of flat-panel plasma TVs are much different than older technology, and as cited in the argument, the statement in C is contradicted by the supporting statements. While Statement D is arguably true, since the argument is designed to

help stave off such issues, it has no bearing on the argument's reasoning, and so can be rejected. Although the teenager relays the concern of his parents, Statement E can be rejected because one does not need to know the facts or details about damage from close exposure to older television to counter the conclusion. Moreover, the statement does not address the teenager's conclusion of purchasing a new TV. Statement B is the best answer choice because it directly contradicts the conclusion by pointing out a reasonable and simpler alternative, so in this context, B is the correct answer.

76. C: The argument as written is intended to argue that the students mentioned will make excellent surgeons, but not that they must, or even intend to pursue that path. Additionally, the argument states that such students make excellent doctors and surgeons, which thus opens the possibility of not being a surgeon; thus, Statement A can be rejected. Statement B is invalid, because the argument states only that they are biological science majors, which has no bearing on their initial majors. Since the argument explicitly states that Riley does not play video games, the question of whether or not she is good is unanswerable, which makes Statement D inapplicable. Statement E cannot be known from the arguments above because we do not know the results of playing video games and its improvement in study habits or grades. So, Statement E can be rejected. While the first supporting statements reference college students, the argument does not explicitly state that Riley and her peers themselves are college students. Other educational institutions allow one to study, focus, or major in a subject before they attend a college or university. Thus, C is correct.

77. A: As the argument states, the challenges are over the fact that the novel is available to check out by children, so the other statements in the argument must be evaluated in that light. Since the challenges are specifically against one novel, the similarity to other novels that are available, if such novels exist, are irrelevant in this case, so Statement B can be rejected. The argument gives specific reasons for the general challenges to the novel, so any other possibility for the challenges is also irrelevant, which invalidates Statement C. Since the challenges are directed toward the novel's availability with no reference to its actual circulation among children, Statement D has no bearing on the argument. While having the faculty's support would be appreciated by the librarian, Statement E is not relevant because we do not need to consider the faculty's opinion on the consistencies between the novel and film. The better concern is raised with Statement A, which refers to a possible and reasonable reason behind the lack of challenges to the film version, is relevant in this context, making A correct.

78. E: There is an implied conflict of interest criticism inherent in the argument and also an implication that the report's conclusions are false. We are told that this is the "latest report," and their advice on Widgets, Inc. continues to highlight the company as "a sound long-term investment." However, Option A is not a valid answer because it does not address the concern for a bias on the part of the "Tabletop Stock Report." Option B is not a valid answer, because it refers to statistical evidence which does not exist in the argument. There is no "statistically insignificant sample" submitted in the argument, so this assertion cannot be evaluated. Option C is not valid for much the same reason; the argument may not be valid for any number of reasons, but it can only be criticized for elements which are present. While the statement expressed in Option C is true, the speculations are not addressed in the presentation of the argument. Nor is there a discussion of implied motivation. Option D is not valid, because the existence of evidence is not in question, only the validity of the argument. Only Option E addresses the argument as presented, and thus, only Option E is valid.

79. C: The flawed argument of the original statement makes two statements about two separate groups of individuals, and draws an unsupported conclusion about both of the groups. Options A

and E are not good choices because they do not follow the logical sequence of the original statement. In addition, neither choice's conclusion is consistent with the original paragraph's conclusion. Options B and D are also ruled out based on the argument structure. Option B is ruled out because it has a logical argument structure with a correct conclusion, unlike the original paragraph, where the conclusion is flawed or erroneous. Option D is ruled out for the same reason; enough information is given in the statement to make a correct conclusion. Only Option C follows the original structure of the argument, and in so doing, duplicates the flawed logic therein. Thus, Option C is correct.

80. B: The argument outlined in the paragraph explicitly draws a parallel between losing a relationship and losing a loved one. Therefore, logic would demand a conclusion in line with the argument's terms. While each of the options listed can be seen as reasonable consequences of the end of a romantic relationship, only Option B points to the parallels between the end of a relationship and the death of a loved one. The five-stage grieving process is compared to the sense of loss felt in grieving for an abruptly ended relationship. The other options focus on individual reactions to a situation, which are outside the scope and intent of the argument. There is no metaphorical linkage. Thus, only Option B is correct.

How to Overcome Test Anxiety

Just the thought of taking a test is enough to make most people a little nervous. A test is an important event that can have a long-term impact on your future, so it's important to take it seriously and it's natural to feel anxious about performing well. But just because anxiety is normal, that doesn't mean that it's helpful in test taking, or that you should simply accept it as part of your life. Anxiety can have a variety of effects. These effects can be mild, like making you feel slightly nervous, or severe, like blocking your ability to focus or remember even a simple detail.

If you experience test anxiety—whether severe or mild—it's important to know how to beat it. To discover this, first you need to understand what causes test anxiety.

Causes of Test Anxiety

While we often think of anxiety as an uncontrollable emotional state, it can actually be caused by simple, practical things. One of the most common causes of test anxiety is that a person does not feel adequately prepared for their test. This feeling can be the result of many different issues such as poor study habits or lack of organization, but the most common culprit is time management. Starting to study too late, failing to organize your study time to cover all of the material, or being distracted while you study will mean that you're not well prepared for the test. This may lead to cramming the night before, which will cause you to be physically and mentally exhausted for the test. Poor time management also contributes to feelings of stress, fear, and hopelessness as you realize you are not well prepared but don't know what to do about it.

Other times, test anxiety is not related to your preparation for the test but comes from unresolved fear. This may be a past failure on a test, or poor performance on tests in general. It may come from comparing yourself to others who seem to be performing better or from the stress of living up to expectations. Anxiety may be driven by fears of the future—how failure on this test would affect your educational and career goals. These fears are often completely irrational, but they can still negatively impact your test performance.

> **Review Video:** <u>3 Reasons You Have Test Anxiety</u>
> Visit mometrix.com/academy and enter code: 428468

Elements of Test Anxiety

As mentioned earlier, test anxiety is considered to be an emotional state, but it has physical and mental components as well. Sometimes you may not even realize that you are suffering from test anxiety until you notice the physical symptoms. These can include trembling hands, rapid heartbeat, sweating, nausea, and tense muscles. Extreme anxiety may lead to fainting or vomiting. Obviously, any of these symptoms can have a negative impact on testing. It is important to recognize them as soon as they begin to occur so that you can address the problem before it damages your performance.

> **Review Video: 3 Ways to Tell You Have Test Anxiety**
> Visit mometrix.com/academy and enter code: 927847

The mental components of test anxiety include trouble focusing and inability to remember learned information. During a test, your mind is on high alert, which can help you recall information and stay focused for an extended period of time. However, anxiety interferes with your mind's natural processes, causing you to blank out, even on the questions you know well. The strain of testing during anxiety makes it difficult to stay focused, especially on a test that may take several hours. Extreme anxiety can take a huge mental toll, making it difficult not only to recall test information but even to understand the test questions or pull your thoughts together.

> **Review Video: How Test Anxiety Affects Memory**
> Visit mometrix.com/academy and enter code: 609003

Effects of Test Anxiety

Test anxiety is like a disease—if left untreated, it will get progressively worse. Anxiety leads to poor performance, and this reinforces the feelings of fear and failure, which in turn lead to poor performances on subsequent tests. It can grow from a mild nervousness to a crippling condition. If allowed to progress, test anxiety can have a big impact on your schooling, and consequently on your future.

Test anxiety can spread to other parts of your life. Anxiety on tests can become anxiety in any stressful situation, and blanking on a test can turn into panicking in a job situation. But fortunately, you don't have to let anxiety rule your testing and determine your grades. There are a number of relatively simple steps you can take to move past anxiety and function normally on a test and in the rest of life.

> **Review Video: How Test Anxiety Impacts Your Grades**
> Visit mometrix.com/academy and enter code: 939819

Physical Steps for Beating Test Anxiety

While test anxiety is a serious problem, the good news is that it can be overcome. It doesn't have to control your ability to think and remember information. While it may take time, you can begin taking steps today to beat anxiety.

Just as your first hint that you may be struggling with anxiety comes from the physical symptoms, the first step to treating it is also physical. Rest is crucial for having a clear, strong mind. If you are tired, it is much easier to give in to anxiety. But if you establish good sleep habits, your body and mind will be ready to perform optimally, without the strain of exhaustion. Additionally, sleeping well helps you to retain information better, so you're more likely to recall the answers when you see the test questions.

Getting good sleep means more than going to bed on time. It's important to allow your brain time to relax. Take study breaks from time to time so it doesn't get overworked, and don't study right before bed. Take time to rest your mind before trying to rest your body, or you may find it difficult to fall asleep.

> **Review Video: The Importance of Sleep for Your Brain**
> Visit mometrix.com/academy and enter code: 319338

Along with sleep, other aspects of physical health are important in preparing for a test. Good nutrition is vital for good brain function. Sugary foods and drinks may give a burst of energy but this burst is followed by a crash, both physically and emotionally. Instead, fuel your body with protein and vitamin-rich foods.

Also, drink plenty of water. Dehydration can lead to headaches and exhaustion, especially if your brain is already under stress from the rigors of the test. Particularly if your test is a long one, drink water during the breaks. And if possible, take an energy-boosting snack to eat between sections.

> **Review Video: How Diet Can Affect your Mood**
> Visit mometrix.com/academy and enter code: 624317

Along with sleep and diet, a third important part of physical health is exercise. Maintaining a steady workout schedule is helpful, but even taking 5-minute study breaks to walk can help get your blood pumping faster and clear your head. Exercise also releases endorphins, which contribute to a positive feeling and can help combat test anxiety.

When you nurture your physical health, you are also contributing to your mental health. If your body is healthy, your mind is much more likely to be healthy as well. So take time to rest, nourish your body with healthy food and water, and get moving as much as possible. Taking these physical steps will make you stronger and more able to take the mental steps necessary to overcome test anxiety.

> **Review Video: How to Stay Healthy and Prevent Test Anxiety**
> Visit mometrix.com/academy and enter code: 877894

Mental Steps for Beating Test Anxiety

Working on the mental side of test anxiety can be more challenging, but as with the physical side, there are clear steps you can take to overcome it. As mentioned earlier, test anxiety often stems from lack of preparation, so the obvious solution is to prepare for the test. Effective studying may be the most important weapon you have for beating test anxiety, but you can and should employ several other mental tools to combat fear.

First, boost your confidence by reminding yourself of past success—tests or projects that you aced. If you're putting as much effort into preparing for this test as you did for those, there's no reason you should expect to fail here. Work hard to prepare; then trust your preparation.

Second, surround yourself with encouraging people. It can be helpful to find a study group, but be sure that the people you're around will encourage a positive attitude. If you spend time with others who are anxious or cynical, this will only contribute to your own anxiety. Look for others who are motivated to study hard from a desire to succeed, not from a fear of failure.

Third, reward yourself. A test is physically and mentally tiring, even without anxiety, and it can be helpful to have something to look forward to. Plan an activity following the test, regardless of the outcome, such as going to a movie or getting ice cream.

When you are taking the test, if you find yourself beginning to feel anxious, remind yourself that you know the material. Visualize successfully completing the test. Then take a few deep, relaxing breaths and return to it. Work through the questions carefully but with confidence, knowing that you are capable of succeeding.

Developing a healthy mental approach to test taking will also aid in other areas of life. Test anxiety affects more than just the actual test—it can be damaging to your mental health and even contribute to depression. It's important to beat test anxiety before it becomes a problem for more than testing.

Review Video: Test Anxiety and Depression
Visit mometrix.com/academy and enter code: 904704

Study Strategy

Being prepared for the test is necessary to combat anxiety, but what does being prepared look like? You may study for hours on end and still not feel prepared. What you need is a strategy for test prep. The next few pages outline our recommended steps to help you plan out and conquer the challenge of preparation.

Step 1: Scope Out the Test

Learn everything you can about the format (multiple choice, essay, etc.) and what will be on the test. Gather any study materials, course outlines, or sample exams that may be available. Not only will this help you to prepare, but knowing what to expect can help to alleviate test anxiety.

Step 2: Map Out the Material

Look through the textbook or study guide and make note of how many chapters or sections it has. Then divide these over the time you have. For example, if a book has 15 chapters and you have five days to study, you need to cover three chapters each day. Even better, if you have the time, leave an extra day at the end for overall review after you have gone through the material in depth.

If time is limited, you may need to prioritize the material. Look through it and make note of which sections you think you already have a good grasp on, and which need review. While you are studying, skim quickly through the familiar sections and take more time on the challenging parts. Write out your plan so you don't get lost as you go. Having a written plan also helps you feel more in control of the study, so anxiety is less likely to arise from feeling overwhelmed at the amount to cover. A sample plan may look like this:

- Day 1: Skim chapters 1–4, study chapter 5 (especially pages 31–33)
- Day 2: Study chapters 6–7, skim chapters 8–9
- Day 3: Skim chapter 10, study chapters 11–12 (especially pages 87–90)
- Day 4: Study chapters 13–15
- Day 5: Overall review (focus most on chapters 5, 6, and 12), take practice test

Step 3: Gather Your Tools

Decide what study method works best for you. Do you prefer to highlight in the book as you study and then go back over the highlighted portions? Or do you type out notes of the important information? Or is it helpful to make flashcards that you can carry with you? Assemble the pens, index cards, highlighters, post-it notes, and any other materials you may need so you won't be distracted by getting up to find things while you study.

If you're having a hard time retaining the information or organizing your notes, experiment with different methods. For example, try color-coding by subject with colored pens, highlighters, or post-it notes. If you learn better by hearing, try recording yourself reading your notes so you can listen while in the car, working out, or simply sitting at your desk. Ask a friend to quiz you from your flashcards, or try teaching someone the material to solidify it in your mind.

Step 4: Create Your Environment

It's important to avoid distractions while you study. This includes both the obvious distractions like visitors and the subtle distractions like an uncomfortable chair (or a too-comfortable couch that makes you want to fall asleep). Set up the best study environment possible: good lighting and a comfortable work area. If background music helps you focus, you may want to turn it on, but otherwise keep the room quiet. If you are using a computer to take notes, be sure you don't have any other windows open, especially applications like social media, games, or anything else that could distract you. Silence your phone and turn off notifications. Be sure to keep water close by so you stay hydrated while you study (but avoid unhealthy drinks and snacks).

Also, take into account the best time of day to study. Are you freshest first thing in the morning? Try to set aside some time then to work through the material. Is your mind clearer in the afternoon or evening? Schedule your study session then. Another method is to study at the same time of day that you will take the test, so that your brain gets used to working on the material at that time and will be ready to focus at test time.

Step 5: Study!

Once you have done all the study preparation, it's time to settle into the actual studying. Sit down, take a few moments to settle your mind so you can focus, and begin to follow your study plan. Don't give in to distractions or let yourself procrastinate. This is your time to prepare so you'll be ready to fearlessly approach the test. Make the most of the time and stay focused.

Of course, you don't want to burn out. If you study too long you may find that you're not retaining the information very well. Take regular study breaks. For example, taking five minutes out of every hour to walk briskly, breathing deeply and swinging your arms, can help your mind stay fresh.

As you get to the end of each chapter or section, it's a good idea to do a quick review. Remind yourself of what you learned and work on any difficult parts. When you feel that you've mastered the material, move on to the next part. At the end of your study session, briefly skim through your notes again.

But while review is helpful, cramming last minute is NOT. If at all possible, work ahead so that you won't need to fit all your study into the last day. Cramming overloads your brain with more information than it can process and retain, and your tired mind may struggle to recall even previously learned information when it is overwhelmed with last-minute study. Also, the urgent nature of cramming and the stress placed on your brain contribute to anxiety. You'll be more likely to go to the test feeling unprepared and having trouble thinking clearly.

So don't cram, and don't stay up late before the test, even just to review your notes at a leisurely pace. Your brain needs rest more than it needs to go over the information again. In fact, plan to finish your studies by noon or early afternoon the day before the test. Give your brain the rest of the day to relax or focus on other things, and get a good night's sleep. Then you will be fresh for the test and better able to recall what you've studied.

Step 6: Take a practice test

Many courses offer sample tests, either online or in the study materials. This is an excellent resource to check whether you have mastered the material, as well as to prepare for the test format and environment.

Check the test format ahead of time: the number of questions, the type (multiple choice, free response, etc.), and the time limit. Then create a plan for working through them. For example, if you have 30 minutes to take a 60-question test, your limit is 30 seconds per question. Spend less time on the questions you know well so that you can take more time on the difficult ones.

If you have time to take several practice tests, take the first one open book, with no time limit. Work through the questions at your own pace and make sure you fully understand them. Gradually work up to taking a test under test conditions: sit at a desk with all study materials put away and set a timer. Pace yourself to make sure you finish the test with time to spare and go back to check your answers if you have time.

After each test, check your answers. On the questions you missed, be sure you understand why you missed them. Did you misread the question (tests can use tricky wording)? Did you forget the information? Or was it something you hadn't learned? Go back and study any shaky areas that the practice tests reveal.

Taking these tests not only helps with your grade, but also aids in combating test anxiety. If you're already used to the test conditions, you're less likely to worry about it, and working through tests until you're scoring well gives you a confidence boost. Go through the practice tests until you feel comfortable, and then you can go into the test knowing that you're ready for it.

Test Tips

On test day, you should be confident, knowing that you've prepared well and are ready to answer the questions. But aside from preparation, there are several test day strategies you can employ to maximize your performance.

First, as stated before, get a good night's sleep the night before the test (and for several nights before that, if possible). Go into the test with a fresh, alert mind rather than staying up late to study.

Try not to change too much about your normal routine on the day of the test. It's important to eat a nutritious breakfast, but if you normally don't eat breakfast at all, consider eating just a protein bar. If you're a coffee drinker, go ahead and have your normal coffee. Just make sure you time it so that the caffeine doesn't wear off right in the middle of your test. Avoid sugary beverages, and drink enough water to stay hydrated but not so much that you need a restroom break 10 minutes into the test. If your test isn't first thing in the morning, consider going for a walk or doing a light workout before the test to get your blood flowing.

Allow yourself enough time to get ready, and leave for the test with plenty of time to spare so you won't have the anxiety of scrambling to arrive in time. Another reason to be early is to select a good seat. It's helpful to sit away from doors and windows, which can be distracting. Find a good seat, get out your supplies, and settle your mind before the test begins.

When the test begins, start by going over the instructions carefully, even if you already know what to expect. Make sure you avoid any careless mistakes by following the directions.

Then begin working through the questions, pacing yourself as you've practiced. If you're not sure on an answer, don't spend too much time on it, and don't let it shake your confidence. Either skip it and come back later, or eliminate as many wrong answers as possible and guess among the remaining ones. Don't dwell on these questions as you continue—put them out of your mind and focus on what lies ahead.

Be sure to read all of the answer choices, even if you're sure the first one is the right answer. Sometimes you'll find a better one if you keep reading. But don't second-guess yourself if you do immediately know the answer. Your gut instinct is usually right. Don't let test anxiety rob you of the information you know.

If you have time at the end of the test (and if the test format allows), go back and review your answers. Be cautious about changing any, since your first instinct tends to be correct, but make sure you didn't misread any of the questions or accidentally mark the wrong answer choice. Look over any you skipped and make an educated guess.

At the end, leave the test feeling confident. You've done your best, so don't waste time worrying about your performance or wishing you could change anything. Instead, celebrate the successful completion of this test. And finally, use this test to learn how to deal with anxiety even better next time.

> **Review Video:** 5 Tips to Beat Test Anxiety
> Visit mometrix.com/academy and enter code: 570656

Important Qualification

Not all anxiety is created equal. If your test anxiety is causing major issues in your life beyond the classroom or testing center, or if you are experiencing troubling physical symptoms related to your anxiety, it may be a sign of a serious physiological or psychological condition. If this sounds like your situation, we strongly encourage you to seek professional help.

How to Overcome Your Fear of Math

The word *math* is enough to strike fear into most hearts. How many of us have memories of sitting through confusing lectures, wrestling over mind-numbing homework, or taking tests that still seem incomprehensible even after hours of study? Years after graduation, many still shudder at these memories.

The fact is, math is not just a classroom subject. It has real-world implications that you face every day, whether you realize it or not. This may be balancing your monthly budget, deciding how many supplies to buy for a project, or simply splitting a meal check with friends. The idea of daily confrontations with math can be so paralyzing that some develop a condition known as *math anxiety*.

But you do NOT need to be paralyzed by this anxiety! In fact, while you may have thought all your life that you're not good at math, or that your brain isn't wired to understand it, the truth is that you may have been conditioned to think this way. From your earliest school days, the way you were taught affected the way you viewed different subjects. And the way math has been taught has changed.

Several decades ago, there was a shift in American math classrooms. The focus changed from traditional problem-solving to a conceptual view of topics, de-emphasizing the importance of learning the basics and building on them. The solid foundation necessary for math progression and confidence was undermined. Math became more of a vague concept than a concrete idea. Today, it is common to think of math, not as a straightforward system, but as a mysterious, complicated method that can't be fully understood unless you're a genius.

This is why you may still have nightmares about being called on to answer a difficult problem in front of the class. Math anxiety is a very real, though unnecessary, fear.

Math anxiety may begin with a single class period. Let's say you missed a day in 6th grade math and never quite understood the concept that was taught while you were gone. Since math is cumulative, with each new concept building on past ones, this could very well affect the rest of your math career. Without that one day's knowledge, it will be difficult to understand any other concepts that link to it. Rather than realizing that you're just missing one key piece, you may begin to believe that you're simply not capable of understanding math.

This belief can change the way you approach other classes, career options, and everyday life experiences, if you become anxious at the thought that math might be required. A student who loves science may choose a different path of study upon realizing that multiple math classes will be required for a degree. An aspiring medical student may hesitate at the thought of going through the necessary math classes. For some this anxiety escalates into a more extreme state known as *math phobia*.

Math anxiety is challenging to address because it is rooted deeply and may come from a variety of causes: an embarrassing moment in class, a teacher who did not explain concepts well and contributed to a shaky foundation, or a failed test that contributed to the belief of math failure.

These causes add up over time, encouraged by society's popular view that math is hard and unpleasant. Eventually a person comes to firmly believe that he or she is simply bad at math. This belief makes it difficult to grasp new concepts or even remember old ones. Homework and test grades begin to slip, which only confirms the belief. The poor performance is not due to lack of ability but is caused by math anxiety.

Math anxiety is an emotional issue, not a lack of intelligence. But when it becomes deeply rooted, it can become more than just an emotional problem. Physical symptoms appear. Blood pressure may rise and heartbeat may quicken at the sight of a math problem – or even the thought of math! This fear leads to a mental block. When someone with math anxiety is asked to perform a calculation, even a basic problem can seem overwhelming and impossible. The emotional and physical response to the thought of math prevents the brain from working through it logically.

The more this happens, the more a person's confidence drops, and the more math anxiety is generated. This vicious cycle must be broken!

The first step in breaking the cycle is to go back to very beginning and make sure you really understand the basics of how math works and why it works. It is not enough to memorize rules for multiplication and division. If you don't know WHY these rules work, your foundation will be shaky and you will be at risk of developing a phobia. Understanding mathematical concepts not only promotes confidence and security, but allows you to build on this understanding for new concepts. Additionally, you can solve unfamiliar problems using familiar concepts and processes.

Why is it that students in other countries regularly outperform American students in math? The answer likely boils down to a couple of things: the foundation of mathematical conceptual understanding and societal perception. While students in the US are not expected to *like* or *get* math, in many other nations, students are expected not only to understand math but also to excel at it.

Changing the American view of math that leads to math anxiety is a monumental task. It requires changing the training of teachers nationwide, from kindergarten through high school, so that they learn to teach the *why* behind math and to combat the wrong math views that students may develop. It also involves changing the stigma associated with math, so that it is no longer viewed as unpleasant and incomprehensible. While these are necessary changes, they are challenging and will take time. But in the meantime, math anxiety is not irreversible—it can be faced and defeated, one person at a time.

False Beliefs

One reason math anxiety has taken such hold is that several false beliefs have been created and shared until they became widely accepted. Some of these unhelpful beliefs include the following:

There is only one way to solve a math problem. In the same way that you can choose from different driving routes and still arrive at the same house, you can solve a math problem using different methods and still find the correct answer. A person who understands the reasoning behind math calculations may be able to look at an unfamiliar concept and find the right answer, just by applying logic to the knowledge they already have. This approach may be different than what is taught in the classroom, but it is still valid. Unfortunately, even many teachers view math as a subject where the best course of action is to memorize the rule or process for each problem rather than as a place for students to exercise logic and creativity in finding a solution.

Many people don't have a mind for math. A person who has struggled due to poor teaching or math anxiety may falsely believe that he or she doesn't have the mental capacity to grasp mathematical concepts. Most of the time, this is false. Many people find that when they are relieved of their math anxiety, they have more than enough brainpower to understand math.

Men are naturally better at math than women. Even though research has shown this to be false, many young women still avoid math careers and classes because of their belief that their math abilities are inferior. Many girls have come to believe that math is a male skill and have given up trying to understand or enjoy it.

Counting aids are bad. Something like counting on your fingers or drawing out a problem to visualize it may be frowned on as childish or a crutch, but these devices can help you get a tangible understanding of a problem or a concept.

Sadly, many students buy into these ideologies at an early age. A young girl who enjoys math class may be conditioned to think that she doesn't actually have the brain for it because math is for boys, and may turn her energies to other pursuits, permanently closing the door on a wide range of opportunities. A child who finds the right answer but doesn't follow the teacher's method may believe that he is doing it wrong and isn't good at math. A student who never had a problem with math before may have a poor teacher and become confused, yet believe that the problem is because she doesn't have a mathematical mind.

Students who have bought into these erroneous beliefs quickly begin to add their own anxieties, adapting them to their own personal situations:

I'll never use this in real life. A huge number of people wrongly believe that math is irrelevant outside the classroom. By adopting this mindset, they are handicapping themselves for a life in a mathematical world, as well as limiting their career choices. When they are inevitably faced with real-world math, they are conditioning themselves to respond with anxiety.

I'm not quick enough. While timed tests and quizzes, or even simply comparing yourself with other students in the class, can lead to this belief, speed is not an indicator of skill level. A person can work very slowly yet understand at a deep level.

If I can understand it, it's too easy. People with a low view of their own abilities tend to think that if they are able to grasp a concept, it must be simple. They cannot accept the idea that they are capable of understanding math. This belief will make it harder to learn, no matter how intelligent they are.

I just can't learn this. An overwhelming number of people think this, from young children to adults, and much of the time it is simply not true. But this mindset can turn into a self-fulfilling prophecy that keeps you from exercising and growing your math ability.

The good news is, each of these myths can be debunked. For most people, they are based on emotion and psychology, NOT on actual ability! It will take time, effort, and the desire to change, but change is possible. Even if you have spent years thinking that you don't have the capability to understand math, it is not too late to uncover your true ability and find relief from the anxiety that surrounds math.

Math Strategies

It is important to have a plan of attack to combat math anxiety. There are many useful strategies for pinpointing the fears or myths and eradicating them:

Go back to the basics. For most people, math anxiety stems from a poor foundation. You may think that you have a complete understanding of addition and subtraction, or even decimals and percentages, but make absolutely sure. Learning math is different from learning other subjects. For example, when you learn history, you study various time periods and places and events. It may be important to memorize dates or find out about the lives of famous people. When you move from US history to world history, there will be some overlap, but a large amount of the information will be new. Mathematical concepts, on the other hand, are very closely linked and highly dependent on each other. It's like climbing a ladder – if a rung is missing from your understanding, it may be difficult or impossible for you to climb any higher, no matter how hard you try. So go back and make sure your math foundation is strong. This may mean taking a remedial math course, going to a tutor to work through the shaky concepts, or just going through your old homework to make sure you really understand it.

Speak the language. Math has a large vocabulary of terms and phrases unique to working problems. Sometimes these are completely new terms, and sometimes they are common words, but are used differently in a math setting. If you can't speak the language, it will be very difficult to get a thorough understanding of the concepts. It's common for students to think that they don't understand math when they simply don't understand the vocabulary. The good news is that this is fairly easy to fix. Brushing up on any terms you aren't quite sure of can help bring the rest of the concepts into focus.

Check your anxiety level. When you think about math, do you feel nervous or uncomfortable? Do you struggle with feelings of inadequacy, even on concepts that you know you've already learned? It's important to understand your specific math anxieties, and what triggers them. When you catch yourself falling back on a false belief, mentally replace it with the truth. Don't let yourself believe that you can't learn, or that struggling with a concept means you'll never understand it. Instead, remind yourself of how much you've already learned and dwell on that past success. Visualize grasping the new concept, linking it to your old knowledge, and moving on to the next challenge. Also, learn how to manage anxiety when it arises. There are many techniques for coping with the irrational fears that rise to the surface when you enter the math classroom. This may include controlled breathing, replacing negative thoughts with positive ones, or visualizing success. Anxiety interferes with your ability to concentrate and absorb information, which in turn contributes to greater anxiety. If you can learn how to regain control of your thinking, you will be better able to pay attention, make progress, and succeed!

Don't go it alone. Like any deeply ingrained belief, math anxiety is not easy to eradicate. And there is no need for you to wrestle through it on your own. It will take time, and many people find that speaking with a counselor or psychiatrist helps. They can help you develop strategies for responding to anxiety and overcoming old ideas. Additionally, it can be very helpful to take a short course or seek out a math tutor to help you find and fix the missing rungs on your ladder and make sure that you're ready to progress to the next level. You can also find a number of math aids online: courses that will teach you mental devices for figuring out problems, how to get the most out of your math classes, etc.

Check your math attitude. No matter how much you want to learn and overcome your anxiety, you'll have trouble if you still have a negative attitude toward math. If you think it's too hard, or just have general feelings of dread about math, it will be hard to learn and to break through the anxiety. Work on cultivating a positive math attitude. Remind yourself that math is not just a hurdle to be cleared, but a valuable asset. When you view math with a positive attitude, you'll be much more likely to understand and even enjoy it. This is something you must do for yourself. You may find it helpful to visit with a counselor. Your tutor, friends, and family may cheer you on in your endeavors. But your greatest asset is yourself. You are inside your own mind – tell yourself what you need to hear. Relive past victories. Remind yourself that you are capable of understanding math. Root out any false beliefs that linger and replace them with positive truths. Even if it doesn't feel true at first, it will begin to affect your thinking and pave the way for a positive, anxiety-free mindset.

Aside from these general strategies, there are a number of specific practical things you can do to begin your journey toward overcoming math anxiety. Something as simple as learning a new note-taking strategy can change the way you approach math and give you more confidence and understanding. New study techniques can also make a huge difference.

Math anxiety leads to bad habits. If it causes you to be afraid of answering a question in class, you may gravitate toward the back row. You may be embarrassed to ask for help. And you may procrastinate on assignments, which leads to rushing through them at the last moment when it's too late to get a better understanding. It's important to identify your negative behaviors and replace them with positive ones:

Prepare ahead of time. Read the lesson before you go to class. Being exposed to the topics that will be covered in class ahead of time, even if you don't understand them perfectly, is extremely helpful in increasing what you retain from the lecture. Do your homework and, if you're still shaky, go over some extra problems. The key to a solid understanding of math is practice.

Sit front and center. When you can easily see and hear, you'll understand more, and you'll avoid the distractions of other students if no one is in front of you. Plus, you're more likely to be sitting with students who are positive and engaged, rather than others with math anxiety. Let their positive math attitude rub off on you.

Ask questions in class and out. If you don't understand something, just ask. If you need a more in-depth explanation, the teacher may need to work with you outside of class, but often it's a simple concept you don't quite understand, and a single question may clear it up. If you wait, you may not be able to follow the rest of the day's lesson. For extra help, most professors have office hours outside of class when you can go over concepts one-on-one to clear up any uncertainties. Additionally, there may be a *math lab* or study session you can attend for homework help. Take advantage of this.

Review. Even if you feel that you've fully mastered a concept, review it periodically to reinforce it. Going over an old lesson has several benefits: solidifying your understanding, giving you a confidence boost, and even giving some new insights into material that you're currently learning! Don't let yourself get rusty. That can lead to problems with learning later concepts.

Teaching Tips

While the math student's mindset is the most crucial to overcoming math anxiety, it is also important for others to adjust their math attitudes. Teachers and parents have an enormous influence on how students relate to math. They can either contribute to math confidence or math anxiety.

As a parent or teacher, it is very important to convey a positive math attitude. Retelling horror stories of your own bad experience with math will contribute to a new generation of math anxiety. Even if you don't share your experiences, others will be able to sense your fears and may begin to believe them.

Even a careless comment can have a big impact, so watch for phrases like *He's not good at math* or *I never liked math*. You are a crucial role model, and your children or students will unconsciously adopt your mindset. Give them a positive example to follow. Rather than teaching them to fear the math world before they even know it, teach them about all its potential and excitement.

Work to present math as an integral, beautiful, and understandable part of life. Encourage creativity in solving problems. Watch for false beliefs and dispel them. Cross the lines between subjects: integrate history, English, and music with math. Show students how math is used every day, and how the entire world is based on mathematical principles, from the pull of gravity to the shape of seashells. Instead of letting students see math as a necessary evil, direct them to view it as an imaginative, beautiful art form – an art form that they are capable of mastering and using.

Don't give too narrow a view of math. It is more than just numbers. Yes, working problems and learning formulas is a large part of classroom math. But don't let the teaching stop there. Teach students about the everyday implications of math. Show them how nature works according to the laws of mathematics, and take them outside to make discoveries of their own. Expose them to math-related careers by inviting visiting speakers, asking students to do research and presentations, and learning students' interests and aptitudes on a personal level.

Demonstrate the importance of math. Many people see math as nothing more than a required stepping stone to their degree, a nuisance with no real usefulness. Teach students that algebra is used every day in managing their bank accounts, in following recipes, and in scheduling the day's events. Show them how learning to do geometric proofs helps them to develop logical thinking, an invaluable life skill. Let them see that math surrounds them and is integrally linked to their daily lives: that weather predictions are based on math, that math was used to design cars and other machines, etc. Most of all, give them the tools to use math to enrich their lives.

Make math as tangible as possible. Use visual aids and objects that can be touched. It is much easier to grasp a concept when you can hold it in your hands and manipulate it, rather than just listening to the lecture. Encourage math outside of the classroom. The real world is full of measuring, counting, and calculating, so let students participate in this. Keep your eyes open for numbers and patterns to discuss. Talk about how scores are calculated in sports games and how far apart plants are placed in a garden row for maximum growth. Build the mindset that math is a normal and interesting part of daily life.

Finally, find math resources that help to build a positive math attitude. There are a number of books that show math as fascinating and exciting while teaching important concepts, for example: *The Math Curse; A Wrinkle in Time; The Phantom Tollbooth;* and *Fractals, Googols and Other Mathematical Tales*. You can also find a number of online resources: math puzzles and games, videos that show math in nature, and communities of math enthusiasts. On a local level, students can compete in a variety of math competitions with other schools or join a math club.

The student who experiences math as exciting and interesting is unlikely to suffer from math anxiety. Going through life without this handicap is an immense advantage and opens many doors that others have closed through their fear.

Self-Check

Whether you suffer from math anxiety or not, chances are that you have been exposed to some of the false beliefs mentioned above. Now is the time to check yourself for any errors you may have accepted. Do you think you're not wired for math? Or that you don't need to understand it since you're not planning on a math career? Do you think math is just too difficult for the average person?

Find the errors you've taken to heart and replace them with positive thinking. Are you capable of learning math? Yes! Can you control your anxiety? Yes! These errors will resurface from time to time, so be watchful. Don't let others with math anxiety influence you or sway your confidence. If you're having trouble with a concept, find help. Don't let it discourage you!

Create a plan of attack for defeating math anxiety and sharpening your skills. Do some research and decide if it would help you to take a class, get a tutor, or find some online resources to fine-tune your knowledge. Make the effort to get good nutrition, hydration, and sleep so that you are operating at full capacity. Remind yourself daily that you are skilled and that anxiety does not control you. Your mind is capable of so much more than you know. Give it the tools it needs to grow and thrive.

Thank You

We at Mometrix would like to extend our heartfelt thanks to you, our friend and patron, for allowing us to play a part in your journey. It is a privilege to serve people from all walks of life who are unified in their commitment to building the best future they can for themselves.

The preparation you devote to these important testing milestones may be the most valuable educational opportunity you have for making a real difference in your life. We encourage you to put your heart into it—that feeling of succeeding, overcoming, and yes, conquering will be well worth the hours you've invested.

We want to hear your story, your struggles and your successes, and if you see any opportunities for us to improve our materials so we can help others even more effectively in the future, please share that with us as well. **The team at Mometrix would be absolutely thrilled to hear from you!** So please, send us an email (support@mometrix.com) and let's stay in touch.

If you'd like some additional help, check out these other resources we offer for your exam:

http://MometrixFlashcards.com/GMAT

Additional Bonus Material

Due to our efforts to try to keep this book to a manageable length, we've created a link that will give you access to all of your additional bonus material.

Please visit https://www.mometrix.com/bonus948/gmat to access the information.